HOW TO FINANCE
A GROWING BUSINESS
Revised Edition

HOW TO FINANCE
A GROWING BUSINESS

By
Royce Diener

Revised Edition

Frederick Fell Publishers, Inc.   New York

For information address:

Frederick Fell Publishers, Inc.
386 Park Avenue South
New York, N. Y. 10016

Library of Congress Catalog Card No. 73-80451

Published simultaneously in Canada by
George J. McLeod, Limited, Toronto 2B, Ontario

Manufactured in the United States of America

International Standard Book Number 0-8119-0223-4

Dedication

During the last decade the emergence of the Euro-currency financing pool has created an exciting new development in international cooperation. In a rapidly shrinking world, this viable pool of capital may be the financial community's major contribution to global unity and equal economic opportunity for all people on the planet Earth.

It is to the participants in this development, the new breed of international financiers who conduct themselves under a self-imposed code of integrity, putting aside old chauvinistic attitudes—and always with a sensitivity and sense of humor that transcends national or racial boundaries—that I dedicate this book.

Royce Diener

Acknowledgments
for the Second Edition

Between the publication dates of the first and second editions, the formats and statutory laws concerning various types of secured financing changed drastically. The change—and it was a good one—created consistency, logic and equal standards in all states under the Uniform Commercial Code. Robert Diener, Esq., (who happens to be my son) has made a detailed study of this subject and I gratefully acknowledge his rewriting most of Chapters 5 and 6, which deal with secured loans.

My interest in Eurocurrency financing was originally stimulated by a 1966 meeting with Sir Siegmund Warburg in the coffee shop of the Frankfurter Hof in Frankfurt, Germany. In subsequent years I gained most of my knowledge of this subject from information supplied by, and experience working with, Mr. Peter Darling, Count Gian Luca Salina, Mr. Michael Bentley and their colleagues of S. G. Warburg and Company, London, England.

Publisher's Preface

I published the first edition of *How To Finance A Growing Business* to satisfy a need I had recognized for several years.

All of us who wish to make our mark in the business world find that we must come to grips with the need for establishing credit in order to achieve our goals. Despite the prevalence of this need, I could not find a financial specialist who could write a book covering the field of business finance in a comprehensive yet easily understood fashion.

Royce Diener and his manuscript provided what I had been seeking. In the pages which follow are described some of the most advanced techniques in modern financing; yet the author also spells out even the most elementary credit arrangements in terms which the layman can grasp. Previous books on this subject had been lender-oriented. This text is written from the viewpoint of the businessman-borrower.

Since the publication of the first edition Royce Diener has continued to implement the expertise described in this book—with remarkable results. As a financial consultant and corporate director he has arranged programs ranging from single bank loans to public and private financings, domestic and international, totaling as much as $50 million per year. More recently he has become President of a company listed on the New York and London Stock Exchanges. Over the period from 1969 to 1973 he was instrumental in building the capital of that company from less than $3 million to more than $100 million.

Accomplished projects of various types, whether large or small, domestic or international, provide the actual excerpts used in the text, plus the authoritative background from which the author's information has been drawn.

For this revised edition I am happy to see included strong, well-planned chapters on both Eurodollar Financing and Evaluation of Potential Acquisitions. Royce Diener has made a truly comprehensive book out of this new edition by the inclusion of this material.

I am confident that every reader will find in the following pages a multitude of facts which can be potentially profitable to him.

Frederick Fell

Contents

Charts

Editor's Note
to the Second Edition

The two new chapters added to the second edition represent some of the most viable and advanced forms of modern corporate finance. Because the subjects treated are so advanced, some of the terminology used will be more technical. However, consistent with the publisher's request to the author for an easily understandable book, all technical terms in the latter chapters are explained in earlier portions of the book and these explanations can be found by referring to the index.

Introduction to the
Second Edition

Seven years ago, when the first edition of this book was published, the initial chapter included the following two statements:

—Every business needs money in order to grow.
—The availability of capital keeps pace with greater and more varied business growth needs.

Looking at the scene today, I see no reason to change the above two statements. Corporate growth continues to be the most important measurement of business success. Capital requirements for individual businesses—and for the world economy as a whole—are today greater than ever.

At the end of the decade of the sixties, we saw the demonstration of another reason for increasing business capital: namely, the severe money crunch of 1970-71. As the old saying goes, that was the period when the men were separated from the boys. Sophisticated financial planners saw the money tightness beginning to develop in 1969 and took defensive steps. They arranged for adequate financing to carry them through the tight money period and—as the typical cyclical reaction appeared in 1971 and 1972—more corporations went to the well of finance than during any other period in our history. As a result, the second half of the economic shake-out created what is now recognized as one of the greatest periods of increasing corporate liquidity we have ever witnessed.

During the past five years, I have been involved in arranging an average of more than 50 million dollars per year financing for my corporate clients. Actually, the somewhat drastic change in money markets did not tend to stifle innovative financing—in fact, new funding markets were created, and techniques were refined.

The emergence of one such new market and set of techniques—the Eurocurrency market—probably has the greatest significance, particularly as it extends into the future. For this reason, in the second edition we are adding a special new chapter, *Eurodollar Financing*.

Domestic financing techniques have also been refined and simplified; therefore, the sections dealing with secured financing have been updated to reflect the effects of the new Uniform Commercial Code. Additional material has been added to reflect the increasing importance and the sophistication of the growing *venture capital* market, as well as the present increased tendency for use of equity securities in private placements with institutions.

During the decade of the sixties we saw the meteoric rise of acquisition and merger activity, along with the financing which was necessary to accomplish these business combinations. Growth for the sake of growth was the word of the day, but the real justification for this activity —increased return on investment—was frequently overlooked. It took several years for the true effects of these dealings to surface, but when they did, many corporate darlings of the go-go mutual funds became the doormats of the Stock Exchange. Once again, however, some constructive lessons were learned, and this second edition addresses itself to them.

A new chapter, *Evaluation of Potential Acquisitions*, presents many new ideas relative to this sophisticated and exciting subject. These techniques are not purely theoretical; they have, in fact, proved themselves over a period of time sufficient to demonstrate their effectiveness. To my knowledge this will be the first time that these acquisition evaluation principles will have been presented in a printed format. I hope that the reader will be as stimulated by the exposition on this subject as I was when, following the empirical process of having been involved in more than twenty acquisitions in the past five years, the intrinsically valid principles revealed themselves to me.

Royce Diener

HOW TO FINANCE
A GROWING BUSINESS
Revised Edition

CHAPTER 1

The Paradox
of Business Finance

This book is based on a very simple fact: that every business needs money in order to grow.

No businessman can continually limit his activities to being solely a manufacturer, distributor, or retailer— he must also become a seeker of capital.

Paradoxically, although there are numerous capital sources, the means of tapping them are not generally known. This is because, to many individuals, the field of finance is an area of mystery; and it is easy to understand why.

Banks and other financial institutions have not in the past provided clear explanations of the basis on which they make capital available. To those seeking funds, the operations conducted in these temples of finance seem esoteric. The picture is clouded by ivory-tower double-talk and insider jargon. As a result, a businessman whose knowledge of his own industry is far advanced, compared with that of a predecessor a decade ago, may have no more financial know-how than his earlier counterpart.

Meanwhile, the need for proper financing for growth business has become increasingly acute. As costs have risen, sales dollar volume figures have increased, markets have broadened, and more working capital to sustain these higher levels has become necessary. Taxes take a much greater portion of earnings, decreasing the availability of funds arising from company profits which could otherwise be used in financing growth.

Capital planning has therefore inevitably become— far more than it used to be—a factor which requires almost continuous attention during the development of any business. Fortunately, the availability of capital has kept pace with today's greater and more varied needs. In this book I hope to bridge the gap between the need and the availability. I will explain simply the details of most financeable business situations, lay out the indicated financial application, and describe *specifically* the actual procedures which should be followed in order to obtain such financing. Here are some of the subjects covered:

How to compute your working capital and how to determine your working capital needs.

How to approach a bank for a business loan.

The difference between secured and unsecured loans, and when each is more desirable.

How to mix long-term, short-term and revolving loans.

What are the incentives for a lending officer to sponsor your loan? The unstated reasons why some loan applications are turned down.

How you can get your accountant's statement to reflect your business in the best possible light.

How to analyze your statement from a financier's point of view, and what steps you can take to enhance this picture.

How to utilize the services of a commercial finance company.

How to obtain financing far in excess of the net worth of your company.

Purchase leasebacks, chattel loan financing and time sale purchases.

Import and export financing—foreign letters of credit.

How to set up the financial structure of a new business using the form of proprietorship, partnership, corporation or "sub-chapter S."

Using investor loans, debentures, or other classes of stock to obtain additional capital without giving away a proportionate share of profits.

How to determine cash flow—why this is necessary in obtaining certain types of financing.

The use of private placements from institutions, the Small Business Administration, Small Business Investment Companies, venture capital companies, and subordinated private lenders.

How to create a captive finance company for greater profits and increased leverage on your own capital.

Time sales financing for your customers as a means to increase volume and profits.

How to finance acquisitions.

When and how to have a public issue of your company's stock underwritten by an investment banker.

Sophisticated acquisition and merger procedures; evaluation of acquisition candidates.

Eurodollars—the new world-wide currency financing market.

The above list is generalized, yet it does reflect most aspects of finance which today's businessman should consider. As we go into these subjects, I am confident you will be surprised to see how many are applicable to your own particular business situation.

The early parts of the first chapters of this book

may appear elementary to some readers, but this is because a basic approach has been taken to make sure that all the ground is covered for those less experienced in financial management. Also in the same sections, terms and definitions are established—and familiarity with these is required if the reader is to understand the more advanced financing techniques which follow.

CHAPTER 2

The Different Types
of Capital

During the past quarter century substantial progressive changes have occurred in the methods of business finance. This evolution, in both domestic and international spheres of trade, derived its basic momentum from the steady growth of our economy. Further impetus came from activation of new government programs, and—you may be surprised to learn—from the development of keen competition among lending institutions to devise new financing applications in an effort to put more of their money to work. The result has been the creation of a broad spectrum of business finance, whose analysis is a prerequisite for every seeker of capital.

In financial circles, capital is usually categorized by referring to its *source* and *function.* In its simplest form, the analysis stems from two questions: Where is the money to come from? What is it to be used for?

Here, then—with these questions before us—is our starting point; and we should begin by differentiating among the three generic *souces* of capital: "public," "institutional," and "private" financing.

Public financing is obtained by the issuance of securities to more than a very small group of investors and requires registration with the Securities and Exchange Commission (with the exception of intrastate issues). Public financing almost always involves the services of stock brokerage firms (who refer to this function as "investment banking") and—since it is usually applicable to experienced businesses which have already traveled the other routes of financing—we will defer discussion of public issues to the latter part of this book.

Institutional financing encompasses the greatest range of borrowing variations which business firms utilize. These are the types of institutions which may serve as sources:

Commercial banks

Insurance companies

Commercial finance companies

Pension and welfare funds

SBIC companies (Small Business Investment Companies)

Factors

Venture capital companies

The Small Business Administration

Industrial loan banks

Investment bankers (for private placements)

The size of this list gives you some idea of the wide variety of funding available. However, you should recognize that all lending institutions stay on one side of a definite boundary line. This line is drawn somewhat short of what we might term "hundred per cent financing."

Many businessmen have the erroneous idea that financial institutions may occasionally provide, on a loan basis, *all* the money required to commence operations in a particular endeavor. This is not so, say the institutions properly, although we will see later that they may advance as much as 90% of the required capital. Of course, we are referring here only to the limitations of the *lending institutions*. There still remains the large amorphous group of *private financing* sources from which the other increment of capital may be obtained. This group ranges from relatives and friends, or a small group of hopeful investors, to substantial backers of new ideas and operations. Professional men in the larger cities—attorneys, accountants, and particularly financial consultants—are often helpful in providing access to private investors.

Financiers frequently refer to investments from such sources as "venture capital." This phrase describes money invested on a frank risk basis, with meager tangible security at the outset, in a gamble for future capital gain or substantial income return. Whereas institutions look primarily for more nominal interest income, taking little or no share of any large profits which might be realized in the future, venture investors are more interested in sharing in the future profits of a business and in the gain in the value of their participation. It is this type of venture financing which leads us into the first *functional* category of capital: "basic equity."

Equity is the foundation stone in the financial structure of any company. It is usually represented by the original investment in a beginning business plus later retained earnings. Technically, equity is that part of the balance sheet which reflects *ownership* of the company by the principals and other investors. It also represents the total value of the business, since all other financing (with the exception of publicly issued stock) amounts to some form of borrowing which must ultimately be repaid. When a lending officer asks, "What do you have in the business?"—and the question is frequently put exactly so—he is asking about your equity. As will be illustrated in later examples of financial statement analysis, equity is what we are discussing when we refer to the

book value "net worth" of a business. Even then, there
are shadings to this definition when it is applied to certain
financing arrangements. For example, funds obtained
through the issuance of subordinated debentures or notes
(to be described later) are usually also considered as
equity by lending institutions. As you will see, this viewpoint can be extremely helpful to any efforts you make
to *pyramid* the borrowing abilities of your business.

You will get a better understanding of equity capital
if we now make a clear distinction among these three
functionally different types of funding:

1. Equity capital
2. Working capital
3. Growth capital

The importance of this distinction is not academic.
Rather, it is needed to satisfy the practical requirement
that, in order to obtain adequate financing, you must first
know the exact nature of what you seek.

This last statement may seem a platitude, but the fact
is that most lending officers will not make these distinc-
tions for you. They will only consider the *exact* request
you make, and may reject your application simply because
your company does not qualify for the type of financing
you specified. Yet, you might qualify for the entire
amount you seek in a *different form* of funding. During
my years as chief financial executive of companies whose
capital structure I was attempting to build, I encountered
this situation on numerous occasions; rarely did a lending
officer make a meaningful countersuggestion if the type
of loan I sought did not qualify. Later, when I became a
lending officer, I tried to fill this void. If I could not
approve, for example, the long-term fixed asset loan my
client requested, I might frequently be able to give him
all the money he needed by arranging a revolving line
of secured credit on receivables or inventory which, although technically short-term, would be available for

the length of time the client envisaged in his original application.

Returning to the distinction between the basic types of funding, you will find that equity capital, as previously described, is not generally obtainable from institutions— at least not during the early stage of a venture. Working and growth capital, on the other hand, can be obtained in a number of ways. Both become necessary when equity capital has been used to the limit of its availability. They extend the effectiveness of equity by providing the *leverage on investment* present in the financial picture of every successful business.

Working capital needs arise from the generation of activity in a going business. For example, as sales increase, the amount of money owed to a firm by its customers (arising from the billings of sales) increases, and funds are required to carry these "accounts receivable." Concurrently, inventories enlarge and payroll costs mount— these, too, require additional money. It is to satisfy such needs that working capital is required; and, fortunately, it can usually be obtained on a steady, revolving basis. Although borrowed funds may be used for working capital over fairly long periods of time, the amount used *fluctuates*, depending on the cyclical aspects of a particular business. In fact, it is the varying use of greater or lesser amounts of money over a single year which most quickly identifies the funds used on such a fluctuating basis as "working capital."

In the giftware and toy manufacturing industries, for example, inventories must obviously be built up during the summer and early fall in order to meet the demands of heavy pre-Christmas purchasing by retailers. Even after orders are shipped, and the inventory decreases, money is tied up in accounts receivable due from the retailers. Therefore, working capital needs in these industries reach a peak each December. Immediately after the holidays, particularly about January 10 of the new year, customer payments reduce the accounts receivable, quickly creating a highly liquid cash position. At this point, loans are reduced and the use of borrowed working capital drops.

In contrast, the building trades industry reaches its peak requirement for working capital in the early summer, switching to its point of greatest liquidity in midwinter when construction is retarded by bad weather. The cycle of fluctuating borrowing is almost the opposite of the first example cited. Yet, in either case, the role of working capital is the same. It provides the money to carry a business through its annual period of greatest cash need.

Growth capital, although frequently grouped with working capital by many financiers, is different because it is not directly related to the cyclical aspects of a business. Instead, growth capital is usually involved with a planned program of expansion, or cost reduction, through purchase of better production or handling facilities. If, based on activating such a program, a projection of greater profits can reasonably be demonstrated, various types of financing can be arranged. Rather than looking toward seasonal liquidity for reducing this type of borrowing, institutions which make growth capital available will rely on the creation of increased profits to provide for orderly repayment of such loans over a longer period of time.

The need for the presence of *all three* types of capital (equity, working, and growth) continues in every growing business. No competent financier expects a single financing program, maintained for a short period of time, to eliminate every future need. The reason is very simple.

Take, for example, a small manufacturer who last year achieved an average sales volume of $40,000 per month and, on his annual volume of $480,000, made a healthy profit of $35,000 after taxes. He foresees a wider demand for his products and arranges for a growth capital loan to purchase additional production equipment. As a result, this year he jumps his sales to $80,000 per month, and profit doubles to $70,000 per year. Does this handsome earnings increase reduce his financing needs? Not at all.

When his monthly billings were $40,000, he was probably carrying accounts receivable totaling at least $55,000. As his sales doubled, he would require accounts receivable carrying ability of $110,000—an increase of $55,000—and this increase is *$20,000 more than his total additional profit* over the previous year. Actually, his retained profit also has to be used for other good causes, such as expansion of inventory-in-process, and making amortization payments on the growth capital loan used to purchase the equipment that helped to create his increase in volume. Although the manufacturer is obviously doing very well, his working capital needs continue to mount—a fact which the financial community will immediately recognize. It is hardly necessary to mention that he will easily get the additional required financing, as we shall later describe.

We have reached the point where we can use one-word descriptions in analyzing a need into the three functional types of capital:

1. Fluctuating (working capital)
2. Amortizing (growth capital)
3. Permanent (equity capital)

The differentiation which exists in the mind of a lending officer—between equity, growth, and working capital—should now be plain.

If you are asking for a *working capital* loan, you will be expected to demonstrate how the loan can be reduced during your firm's period of greatest liquidity in a cycle of one year.

If you are asking for a *growth capital* loan, you will be expected to demonstrate how the purchase of additional fixed assets, or an increase in funds spent for promotional activities, will yield a profit enabling you to repay the loan over several years.

If you are not clearly asking for either working or growth capital, a banker will say to you, "We would like to accommodate you, but we cannot *invest* in a business —that is the role of equity capital; we only make loans." Specifically, the banker will explain that the loans he can make are only temporary, and that the bank cannot be "locked in" with its money, as would be the case with a stockholder who invests in a private corporation for a dividend return and/or a future capital gain.

Actually, working capital loans can be arranged which, in practice, almost entirely serve equity capital functions and purposes—but we are getting ahead of our story. The greatest portion of this book will be devoted to exploring the various methods of obtaining growth and working capital. These are the types of funding primarily involved in financing a growing business. We cannot overlook, however, the logical prior requirement for equity in almost every situation. For this reason we will cover, in the next chapter, various arrangements of equity capital.

CHAPTER 3

Equity Capital

...How much to seek
...What to give in return
...Various forms and arrangements

Prior to the inception of any business, the structure of its equity capital must be determined. While it is true that most of the methods of business finance we shall cover are applicable to the successive stages after inception, it is also true that many equity problems encountered during later growth stages are the same as those which arise even before a new business has begun. You may be starting from scratch, with nothing but an idea—or you may be looking for a means to capitalize an already established entity which is ready to take its first giant step forward. In either case it is possible that you will have to make some of the same choices.

Equity planning cannot be accomplished from an egocentric position. Regardless of the arrangement you finally select as the one best suited for your purposes, your approach should have an objective orientation. In other words, when you seek to implement your financing plan, you must be sure that it contains certain basic appeals to your prospective sources of capital. These are:

1. Potential investors must have confidence in the management of the company. They must also be enthusiastic about the plans proposed by the active participant.

2. The offer of an equity interest (stock or partner share) must be attractive when compared to other investment possibilities.

When you have satisfied the above two requirements, you are qualified to prepare a program to seek equity capital from partners or backers. It should come as no surprise that, at this point, the most important prerequisite is an accurate and comprehensive presentation.

THE INITIAL PRESENTATION

In my role as a financial consultant, I have seen some amazing results produced by good presentations. In one case, a man with a jewelry-sales background came into my office. He had formulated the idea of distributing a tastefully designed line of costume jewelry which, although modestly priced, used new metal alloys to reproduce effects previously seen only in much more expensive pieces. Not only were the products unusual, but they had been cast in a cleverly oriented promitional program. Since the line was keyed to teen-agers and young women, my client had obtained the endorsement of the most publicized designer of junior dresses, who had agreed to use the costume jewelry in all of his fashion shows and fashion-magazine advertisements.

In our preliminary meeting I observed that the presentation included a series of display cards which showed artists' drawings of some proposed items, the proposed packaging, several merchandising schemes, and a few rough layouts of trade advertisements. In addition, my client had brought with him an actual sample, showing type of workmanship and finish. Other than working out a capital projection to determine the need—$50,000— and agreeing what should be given up in return for this, no further preparation was required.

Several days later, I arranged for the embryonic jewelry manufacturer to meet several private investors in my office. In exactly forty-five minutes he had a commitment for the equity capital he needed—almost solely as the result of a fine presentation!

Even if you go to friends for your money, you can expect the same reaction. It is simply a matter of salesmanship with good preparation. Some of the elements which should be included are the following:

1. Description of the products or services. Remember, a picture or a sample is worth a thousand words.

2. Estimated size of the market, projected annual sales volume for the next several years.

3. Cost breakdowns, pricing policies, and profit projections.

4. Past sales volume and earnings, in the case of a going business.

5. The nature of competition in the same field.

6. Information about management. Be sure to include general background as well as any experience which should contribute positively.

7. References—trade, banking, personal.

8. Sources of supply.

9. The specific financing which is being sought.

Several types of professional men, such as accountants, can assist you in the presentation of this information. However, the financial consultant is probably the specialist most familiar with all the aspects involved, particularly the actual financing arrangements. You will note that the last item on the above list is the most important single consideration: how much money you seek,

and how much you will give up for it. This is something
you must have firmly in your mind before making a
presentation.

HOW TO DETERMINE YOUR EQUITY NEED

How much money is to be sought should be answered
only after sufficient analysis has been made to enable
you to come up with a *specific* figure. "Ball park" figures
just won't do. The investor wants to know exactly how
you arrived at the total amount you feel is required.
He is just as concerned over the possibility of your asking
for *too little* as he would be if he thought you were asking
for too much.

Too little money can be as bad as none at all. If
you obtain insufficient capital to accomplish what you
propose, these funds may be lost through programs which
fail because they are only partially sustained. On the
other hand, to a sensible investor no one presents quite
such a ridiculous picture as a promoter who asks for a
ridiculously high sum. It is surprising how many seekers
of capital think that prestige is added to their presentations when they ask for large, rounded-off figures. Such
individuals usually have little idea of their specific needs.

Whenever I am approached with requests for many
times more capital than a proposition would normally
seem to require, I usually find there has been practically
no delineation of the need. I have received, for example,
requests for "half a million" (a nice round figure, indeed)
from misguided businessmen who, when pressed for
analysis, could detail the actual requirement for only
$70,000 or $80,000. This absence of realisic thinking
immediately proclaims a lack of experience with substantial sums of money, and raises serious doubt about the
qualifications of the applicant to handle them. In the face

of such requests, investor confidence melts like the spring snow.

Another practice which has no sound basis is the tendency to throw in a large extra cash increment as a stand-by or reserve, far in excess of a reasonable amount for this purpose. This type of thinking appears frequently in otherwise well-prepared presentations. I remember a proposal made by a former vice-president of a large air-craft manufacturing concern. He showed a well-delineated need for about $300,000, but was asking for $450,000. "You see," he explained, "I think the company should always keep about $150,000 in the bank, over and above its actual needs. I don't want to have to scurry around for more money *if* suddenly we should need it."

It was easy to correct this type of thinking in an otherwise seasoned executive whose employment in a large government-subsidized industry had insulated him from some of the realistic attitudes of sophisticated in-vestors. As is taught in the economics classrooms, there is an "opportunity cost" of money—the cost which consists of its not earning the return that it would yield if it were invested elsewhere; for example, in government bonds, listed securities, or real estate. Money sitting idly in a company bank account is certainly subject to opportunity cost, and its value is being wasted, in the eyes of an investor.

We come down, therefore, to an amount—neither too little nor too much—which is just right. In a later chapter we will go into a cash-need flow analysis, but this more detailed approach is not needed for elementary equity considerations. Your analysis should, however, consist of the following:

1. *Cost of physical plant assets.* In the case of a manufacturing business, this would include equipment and plant improvements, such as electric power installa-tion, gas lines, compressed air lines, etc. Tooling—dies,

jigs, molds—will be required if proprietary items are involved, whether you have your own plant or use subcontractors.

2. *Cost of ancillary physical equipment.* Distributors, manufacturers, retailers, and even sales organizations can have requirements for materials handling equipment, storage or display units, pickup and delivery trucks, packing and shipping equipment.

3. *Cost of office physical equipment.* This would include office furniture and machines, intercommunication, photocopy, mailing equipment, etc.

4. *Cost of supplies.* Included are production supplies; shipping, office and mailing supplies; office stationery and forms.

5. *Pre-opening deposits.* Although these will sometimes be carried as assets on the later balance sheets of the business, they require cash at the outset. Included are rent security deposits, telephone and power deposits, prepaid insurance and workmen's compensation for one year, sales and franchise tax deposits. You must also provide for business license fees and—in the case of corporations and the more complicated partnerships—you must pay for "organization expense," which covers attorney's charges and state and federal fees connected with the legal formation of these entities.

6. *Beginning capital to reach break-even position.* This category takes the most thought, and the next paragraphs will therefore be devoted to an explanation of the procedure for determining the amount required for this purpose.

The figure you finally project for beginning capital (whether it be for a new venture, or for a new direction to be taken by an established business) is arrived at by plotting two trends against each other—expense versus income—until they achieve equilibrium. By so doing, you are at the same time computing the *break-even point.*

Obviously, income develops from sales, including lease income, royalties, licensing or service fees. In order to make a meaningful projection, the expected growth of income must be predicted on a monthly basis, usually over a twelve- to twenty-four month period into the future.

Even if you are fortunate enough to possess purchase orders before starting a business, these sales do not create income until each order is completed by the shipment of, or transfer of title to, your products (which takes place even in over-the-counter sales), or by rendering the service which has been purchased. After inception, a business may take several months before it can deliver goods or services. Normally, sales thereafter gradually approach a first plateau over a series of monthly increases. Only the individual entrepreneur can make this projection, based on his own estimate of pricing and volume. For example, imagine that you wish to begin a business which we will call the Pot-Bellied Stove Corp. It would have a projection of income which would look simply like this:

Table "A"—Monthly Sales Projection

Month	Sales
1st	——
2nd	$ 3,000
3rd	5,000
4th	10,000
5th	16,000
6th	20,000
7th	23,000
8th	25,000
9th	25,000
10th	25,000
11th	25,000
12th	25,000

In the above example the fledgling business begins to create income at the end of the second month. Thereafter, income climbs at a fairly steady rate until it stabilizes between the eighth and ninth months. Most businesses arrive at such plateaus and, after sufficient time has been devoted to assuring efficiency at this achieved level, they are again ready to move forward by expanding product lines, sales efforts, and marketing areas.

Against the income trend must be plotted the monthly cash outflow. This will consist of a total of the expenses which, in an operation the size of the Pot-Bellied Stove Corp. whose sales trend is charted above, would include the following items (with theoretical amounts shown):

Table "B"—Fixed Monthly Expenses

Salaries	$3,000
Payroll taxes	150
Compensation & insurance	190
Rent	400
Maintenance	60
Telephone & telegraph	100
Utilities	40
Auto expense	65
Advertising	200
Legal & audit	100
Travel	200
Postage	25
Supplies	70
Total	$4,600 per month

There are other expenses which must be included later when the business is under way, such as depreciation, bad-debt reserves, and accrued income taxes. However, these are *non-cash* expenses and do not enter into this projection. More significant is a group of real cash expenses which, rather than consisting of *fixed* monthly amounts, like the items in the above table, are determined as *percentages* of sales. Usually this group consists of salesmen's commissions, cash discounts for prompt payment by customers, delivery expense, and cost of goods sold.

Cost of goods sold is actually what you pay for the products or services you sell. Later, when we go into advanced cash-need projections, we will develop this cost more professionally. In preparing to seek simple equity, however, it is usually only necessary that you compute the cost of the items you purchase either for resale or for converting into a product you manufacture and sell. Since we have included salaries and various overhead items in the listing of fixed monthly expense (Table "B") you need concern yourself solely with the actual cost of the outside purchases of raw materials, parts, sub-assemblies, or complete products or commodities. The relationship of such costs to the selling prices of your products is expressed as a *percentage* in stating the cost of goods sold.

If you intend to sell an item for $100, for example, and must expend $35 to purchase the parts and raw materials needed to produce this item, your cost of goods sold is 35%. You will note that this is the complement of your *gross profit margin* which, in the above example, would be 65%. In some businesses, such as retail and wholesale distributorships, there are patterns established that items are purchased for resale at a fixed discount off the established list prices, and this discount is obviously the gross profit margin. Therefore you can obtain cost of goods sold in such cases merely by deducting your purchasing discount from 100%. As you can see, if there is an established normal margin in the industry you enter, this will establish your cost of goods sold as the complementary percentage of that margin. In basic commodity distributorships, like lumber, for example, the gross profit margin may be as low as 15% (therefore cost of goods sold is 85%). Normal retailing margins average 40% (cost of goods sold, 60%); manufacturing operations can run from 25% to over 50%. Service industries, of course, can conceivably have 100% gross profit margins as they receive income for services they perform rather than for goods they have purchased to resell.

Returning to the income projection shown in Table "A," let us assume that the Pot-Bellied Stove Corp. has a 60% cost of goods sold (a fairly median figure for most manufacturing firms). In the fifth month, according to the table, sales income reaches $16,000; therefore, a 60% cost of goods sold would be $9,600. Now, to complete the example, let us postulate cash discounts of 2% to customers, sales commissions of 10%, delivery expenses of 1%. We will combine these with the fixed monthly expenses of $4,600 (shown in Table "B") to arrive at the following picture for the fifth month of operation:

Table "C"—Analysis of Monthly Income vs. Expense

Sales income for fifth month (Table "A")		$16,000
Cost of goods sold (60%)	$9,600	
Sales commissions (10%)	1,600	
Customer cash discounts (2%)	320	
Delivery expense (1%)	160	
Fixed monthly expense (Table "B")	4,600	
Total monthly cash costs		$16,280
Cash under (need) for month		$280

As you will see from the above analysis, the fifth month of operation is just about the time at which the Pot-Bellied Stove Corp. will *break even;* the break-even sales volume requirement is therefore established at slightly more than $16,000 per month. By applying the same schedule of costs and percentages (as shown in

Table "C") to each of the preceding month's sales income projections (from Table "A") we arrive at the following net monthly cash need figures:

Month	Projected Income	Cash under (need)
1st	——	$ 4,600
2nd	$ 3,000	3,700
3rd	5,000	3,200
4th	10,000	1,900
5th	16,000	280
	Total cash under	$13,680

Thus, $13,680 is the beginning capital requirement, the money that will have to be expended merely on operations before the break-even point is reached.

Finally, to complete our basic list, there are two additional categories of cash need which can only be postulated after you have computed the beginning capital requirement. These are:

7. *Money required to carry inventory.* This depends on the turnover, which we can anticipate in most cases to run about sixty days. In other words, you must have an inventory on hand equivalent to about two months' sales at break-even level. If the turnover in your particular industry is slower or faster than this, you can adjust accordingly. In the case of the Pot-Bellied Stove Corp., the cost of goods sold in the fifth month when break-even is achieved is $9,600. Therefore you would have to purchase at least twice this amount—$19,200— to obtain a two-month inventory. However, you will not have to pay out this entire amount immediately if you obtain normal thirty-day terms from your suppliers. Therefore you need to plan on an inventory cost of only half the total purchased for the two months, or $9,600. Incidentally, this introduces a point which will become much more significant as your business grows; namely,

that *accounts payable constitute a part of the working capital of every company.*

8. *Money required to carry accounts receivable.* This need takes into consideration—even though you may sell on ten- to thirty-day terms—that not all your customers will pay on or before the due date. So you must allow at least a forty-five-day average outstanding time for your accounts receivable. In our example, where break-even was reached at a level of $16,000 sales per month, you would have to allow for at least one and one-half months' sales, or an accounts receivable outstanding total of $24,000.

What happens, you may ask, when my sales continue to climb? How do I carry the increasingly larger inventories and accounts receivable? The answer is simple. This is the point at which working capital will be available to you; no further equity is required for these purposes after you have passed the break-even point and are beginning to show a profit. Later chapters will cover this situation in detail.

Now, let us recapitulate. The business we have used for illustration—the Pot-Bellied Stove Corp.—is projected to reach break-even point after the fifth month of operation. Assume that we are speaking of a manufacturing business which will lease a small plant. Here is our presentation of the amount of equity capital being sought:

1.	Cost of plant physical assets	$25,000
2.	Cost of ancillary physical equipment	6,000
3.	Cost of office physical equipment	3,500
4.	Cost of supplies (original requirements, replenishment cost included in Table "B")	800
5.	Pre-opening deposits	1,600
6.	Beginning capital to break-even	13,680
7.	Cash to carry inventory	9,600
8.	Cash to carry accounts receivable	24,000
9.	Contingencies (nice if you can get it) 10%	8,500
	Total equity capital requirement	$92,680

As you can see, a projected business venture such as the Pot-Bellied Stove Corp., by the above analysis, would require nearly $100,000 equity capital. However, if the cost-versus-income projection is carried through the eighth month, at which point a $25,000 monthly sales income is achieved, the cash-need analysis will indicate that the business will begin to create a monthly cash surplus of $2,150. This means that the company will be producing a net positive cash flow at the annual rate of over $25,000 before the end of the first year—a projection which should certainly create the appeal needed to induce a prospective investor to feel that the proposition is attractive compared to other investment opportunities he might have.

WHAT TO GIVE FOR EQUITY CAPITAL

After the needed amount of equity capital has been determined, the other side of the coin turns up—how much should one give in return for this investment? Although there are no absolutely precise answers to this question, there are many ground rules established by precedent.

First, it is important to remember one distinction. When you seek equity investment, you are not selling out your position. You are asking investors to *join* with you in an effort to achieve a goal of mutual benefit. When you sell out, it is normal that you try to obtain the best price, to make the best bargain. When you take in partners or investors, however, the attitude should be that all parties fare equitably, that there be as fair as possible an equity received in return for each contribution. Neither the promoter nor the investor should seek to profit at the other's expense by the mere act of concluding the equity arrangements between them; rather, both sides should look to profit mutually from future progress of the business *after* these arrangements are made.

You will note that in the previous paragraph I refer to the "promotor." This is a term which will reappear in this book, and—since it is a frequently misunderstood word—I would like to define it in the context of our subject. To the financial world, there is nothing derogatory about being called the "promotor" of a project. The promotor is the founder, the organizer, the man with vision and unique ideas. Without him, no new business takes shape. He innovates, plans, and inspires. From the impetus he provides, lines on a drawing board, and even inchoate aspirations are transformed into tangible products or actual services. The promotor, therefore, as a fountainhead of business activity, deserves our full respect.

Returning to our analysis of compensation for equity capital, let us look at one of the simplest, yet most frequently used arrangements—the joining of a promotor with inactive partners or investors. In many such cases the promotor has little or no money of his own to put into the venture; his contribution will consist of the basic idea (products, services, or marketing programs he has conceived), his special knowledge of, or experience in, the proposed field of endeavor, and his willingness to be active in the daily operation of the business. As a rule of thumb in this simple arrangement, the promotor will receive 50% of the equity, and the investors 50%. Should the promotor also have capital to contribute, he will be given the same proportion of equity for his additional cash capital that the investors receive for theirs. Note that *additional* cash is referred to in the foregoing sentence, as money spent *prior* to the presentation of the deal to investors is usually included in the promotor's basic contribution. Also, even if the promotor does have additional money to place alongside the funds coming in from the investors, it is common practice that he takes a deferred position on his own cash equity as a demonstration of good faith to the inactive backers.

A good example would be the case cited earlier in this chapter concerning the manufacturer of costume jewelry. In return for 50% of the equity, the promotor agreed to make the following contributions: (a) The *de facto* arrangement of a promotional marketing tie-in with a leading fashion designer; (b) a group of product designs; (c) his experience as a salesman in the jewelry field; and (d) his willingness to work full time as chief executive of the proposed operation. It was further agreed that, in return for their providing $50,000 cash needed, the investors would receive 50% of the company.

Now, here is an important point concerning the evaluation of a venture. If, as in the case we are discussing, 50% ownership of the company was to be given in return for $50,000 cash equity, the total company—100% —must obviously be worth $100,00 in the minds of the investors. Therefore, the contributions of the promotor, other than his cash, were evaluated at $50,000. The promotor also had $10,000 of his own cash to put up along with the other investors, which justifiably was included in the total $50,000 cash investment. For this $10,000 he received proportionally the same equity as the other investors; namely, one-fifth of 50%, or 10%. Therefore the promotor wound up with a 60% equity; 10% for his additional cash investment, plus 50% for his other contributions. In this particular case, to show good faith, he put his cash investment in a position subordinate to the inactive investors and gave them voting rights on all stock he held over 50%.

From the above example it is obvious that, except in the simplest 50-50 promotor-investor deal, somewhat specific evaluation of the promotor's contribution must be made. It should be emphasized that, where existing businesses are involved, the applicable principles vary considerably from those which apply to entirely new ventures.

In new business ventures the general 50-50 split be-

tween the promotor and the investors is fairly prevalent
—up to a point. This point is reached when more than
a nominal amount of money is required. In today's financing market, from $10,000 to about $150,000 is the usual
range of nominal outside equity investment in a new
venture. However, the 50-50 approach may still hold when
greater amounts, even in the $250,000 range, are obtained
if the promotor is extremely valuable to the venture because of the specialized experience, contacts, or know-how
he may possess. Beyond this level, if the promotor has no
cash to invest it is ordinarily not possible for him to obtain
50% of the deal unless he contributes something of great
value, such as a patent, an advantageous option, or an
exclusive contract.

Occasionally the promotor and the investors cannot
agree on the equity worth of some of these intangible
contributions. Take, for example, a very promising but
unmarketed patent, the worth of which is in dispute. To
resolve such a disagreement, the promotor, instead of
contributing the patent to the new venture, can merely
contribute the *right to use* the patent in return for a
mutually acceptable amount of equity. The venture may
then also agree to pay a modest royalty to the promotor,
based on profits or gross income. Therefore, if the patent
is as good as the promotor claims, he will receive increased benefits in the form of royalties, beyond the equity
he accepted for the right to use the patent. To satisfy
the investors, the agreement might further give the venture the right to purchase the patent in the future, at
a higher price when a greater value has been proven,
thereby terminating the royalty arrangement.

When a going business is involved, the promotor-
principal of the business can include normal business
assets in the evaluation of equity. If he is merely presenting an opportunity for invested equity to participate in the
regular growth of his business, he will get credit for the

book value of his company, or for what is known as an *earnings multiple*. Bear in mind that you cannot get credit for *both* book value and multiple; therefore the higher method of evaluation is usually selected. Normally, a small company is lucky to be evaluated at five times its earnings (always computed *after* taxes) in connection with obtaining private equity capital. Larger private companies, with longer records of successful operation, may obtain multiples as great as six to eight times earnings. When we discuss public issues in a later chapter you will see that multiples can go even higher. In any case, it is important to stress that after-tax earnings must be computed on a *pro-forma* basis; that is, using the tax and capital structure which will be present after the new equity is brought in.

Take, for example, a case of equity capital being sought for a company having $50,000 net worth and earning $18,000 after taxes. Using an earnings multiple of five, the evaluation of the company would be $90,000, to be credited to the promotor-principal. On the other hand, if the earnings were the same, but the net worth was $110,000, this higher evaluation figure might be used, as the liquidation value of the business would be higher.

If a promotor is seeking equity capital to add to his existing business a new phase which will greatly enhance its profit potential, then he should receive credit for the value attributable to the contemplated new phase. This is particularly true if the promotor's present business is such that it can provide unique opportunities for growth and/or cost savings to the projected new operation which is to be added to the picture.

For example, an established importer-distributor of housewares might be offered a very promising distributorship of German cutlery. To obtain the franchise, however, the importer is required to stock a large inventory for which he must seek some equity capital. In this case the importer can offer unique advantages to his investors. Not only has he been able to secure an offer of this valuable franchise, but he already has an established distribution in the applicable field. The cost of setting up a sales organization would virtually be eliminated as his established clientele would provide a ready market. Profits should be realized far more quickly than would be the case with a distributorship of the same cutlery which attempted to start from scratch. Therefore it is conceivable that the promotor could be given credit for 50% of the new phase of his venture—plus the value of his present business.

Let us assume that (a) the existing distributorship makes a normal profit and has a net worth of $50,000; and (b) $25,000 is required as outside equity for the new cutlery franchise. If the promotor's contribution to the new franchise is considered to be worth 50% of the new equity, this is therefore also evaluated at $25,000. The total evaluation would appear like this:

Net worth value of existing distributorship	$ 50,000
Value of promotor's contribution to new franchise	25,000
Cash equity capital from investors	25,000
Total value of resultant entity	$100,000

Obviously the promotor will own 75% of the resultant package which, considering that he is contributing the new franchise *plus* his own going business, is reasonable.

Occasionally investors feel that the money they are providing, although in an amount required for proper financing, is more than they should contribute for the percentage of equity the promotor is willing to offer. To break these stalemates, part of the money can be advanced as equity and part as a loan. The amount of equity is limited to that percentage agreeable to the promotor. To balance the scales, a part of the investors' contribution is reflected as a loan which is superior to the equity, on which interest is earned, and which must be repaid before the equity holders can take any profits out of the business.

This is just one variation on the basic theme that there is a format to satisfy almost any type of equity requirement. An investor may decline a greater share in the future profits of a venture in favor of receiving a prior, safer position for his money. Another investor, or the promotor, may prefer that his funds occupy the riskier position in return for a higher percentage of the equity or future profits. Any combination of such desires can be blended satisfactorily by the selection of the proper equity structure.

FORMS OF EQUITY STRUCTURE

The simplest form of business venture—the irreducible element—is the individual proprietorship. In a sense, the day you decide to go into business for yourself you have begun a proprietorship. If initially you require no outside capital, and can hire any assistance you need, it may be wise to continue along this route for a while. It is certainly in some ways appealing to be able to make your own decisions without having anyone looking over your shoulder, and with no need to be concerned about the effect your acts may have on the investments of others. There are also early tax advantages—up to a certain limit—and the greatest amount of freedom from government regulation. Unfortunately, there are also some serious drawbacks.

It is not our purpose to go into detail about strictly legal aspects, such as the fact that all of your personal worth can be subject to business liabilities (as opposed

to the protection from same in the case of corporations).
More significant is the fact that the means by which a
sole proprietoreship can obtain equity capital are almost
nil. The only exception is the possibility of securing what
you might call a "stake" from a friend or relative. Even
then you would have to come up with some vague arrangement, which could later lead to misunderstandings
(and lost friends). Although the basic concept of equity
is money which does not have to be repaid, just about
the only way a sole proprietor can obtain equity money
from a friend is to *borrow* it, usually with some loose
method of having the lender share in future profits. And,
let us face it, this amounts to nothing more than a personal
loan, with all the troublesome possibilities not usually
found in strictly business arrangements. Proprietorships
have long been basic in our economic history and many
of them have achieved enormous success. Along the line,
they have qualified for many types of financing—but—
their inability to attract equity has been a major short-
coming.

We move, therefore, to the *partnership;* and here
we discover an unusual fact. In many ways, from an
equity capital point of view, the forms of partnership
and corporation offer similar financing possibilities, and
rest on similar considerations. This is because, aside from
tax differences, some partnerships include facets found
in corporations, and some closely held corporations are
nothing more than partnerships cast into a superficial
corporate mold. In fact, you will frequently hear two
businessmen, each of whom holds 50% of the common
stock of a corporation, refer to each other as "my partner."

There are a few businesses which we might call "true
partnerships." In these cases, two or more individuals
join on an absolutely equal basis. The partners contribute
the same amount of capital, and all devote the same
amount of time to operation of the business. They take

the same partnership drawings (technically, there are no "salaries" for partners) for their efforts, and share equally in the accumulation of the net worth "partnership account." True partnerships are, however, the exception to the rule; most partnerships, like corporations, arise from the need for equity capital. To the individual proprietor who is seeking equity, there is sometimes little difference between "taking some partners into the business," and "obtaining investors for the business."

Equity capital can be obtained from one or more partners on any arrangement which is mutually acceptable. Here are some variations:

1. Fifty-fifty partnerships wherein the promotor is active and the equity investor is inactive (a "silent partner"). Usually the active partner is allowed to take a reasonable draw for the actual work he performs, then the remainder of profits is split equally.

2. Partnerships in which the assets are owned equally by all partners but where the operating partner receives no draw, yet does receive a greater share of the profits than do the inactive investors.

3. Partnerships in which part of the investor's contribution is considered a loan on which interest and principal payments must be paid before there is any sharing in the profits by the active partner.

In other words, varying arrangements can be made covering the way the profits are to be shared, and covering the priority of claims on assets by the investors and the promotor. All of this is covered by the *partnership agreement,* a document which it is advisable to have drawn up by an attorney.

The sharing of profits in a partnership is not necessarily in proportion to the money invested by the various principals. For example, the active partner may put up $10,000 while the inactive partner (or partners) may contribute $40,000. It may be agreed that the first $20,000 profit each year be used to repay the investors and that the remainder be split equally between the investors and the promotor. When the investors have been paid down to a position where they have only $10,000 still tied up in the business—an amount equal to the investment of the promotor—the profits will thereafter be split equally among all partners (50% to the active promotor and 50% to the inactive silent partners), with no further requirement to reduce the initial investors' equity. Several points are illustrated by this example. Such an arrangement gives the inactive partner a priority for his larger investment, and—to balance the scales—gives the promotor an ultimate position of receiving an equal share of the profits on his smaller investment. The priority position of the investor reduces his risk, while the promotor is willing to take a riskier position in return for a greater share of the profits in ratio to his initial investment.

More involved requirements for varying positions of risk versus profit sharing can be achieved through the *Limited and General Partnership.* In a normal partnership all partners are bound by the acts of any single partner and can be personally liable to the extent of their entire personal fortunes. In Limited and General Partnerships, however, only the General partners are fully liable, whereas the liability of the Limited partners is limited to their investment in the partnership. The Limited partners are almost always the investors and usually have some priority on assets and profits. The General partners are usually the promotors and they constitute the active management.

A very good example of this mixed type of partnership can be found in land promotion companies. Typically, the promotors are experienced land developers who put up little money of their own. They begin a deal by obtaining an option on a large parcel of land which can be divided into many salable lots. The promotors may take in, for example, fifteen partners who will invest almost all the money required for the project. The partnership agreement will list the promotors as General Partners and the investors as Limited Partners. Although the General Partners manage the operation, the agreement will call for the investment of the Limited Partners to be repaid in full before there is any split in the profits. Thereafter, the General Partners may receive an amount equal to the amount repaid to the investors, after which General and Limited Partners will share equally in the profits. In one such venture for which I arranged financing, the Limited Partners invested $1.5 million in a project which ultimately achieved $7 million in sales of lots. As the profits developed, they were first allocated to repaying the $1.5 million investment of the Limited Partners. Next, the General Partners received $1.5 million; and finally the remaining profits were split fifty-fifty between the Limited and General Partners. Expenses during the development and selling periods were about $1 million. Therefore, after the payments of $1.5 million to both the Limited and the General Partners, respectively, there was still $3 million to split. For the Limited Partners this meant that their investment was repaid in full *plus* an additional 100% profit of $1.5 million. The promotors, who had made no cash investment, received profits of $3 million. It is true that the promotors made a handsome profit; however, they had to wait until the Limited Partner investors were repaid in full before they could collect their first penny. Had the project fallen short of their expectations, the General Partners might have received nothing, and ownership of all the remaining assets would have gone to the investors.

Partnerships have the advantage of a relatively simple form, freedom from governmental regulation, and certain tax advantages, especially during the early stages of a venture. However, for complete flexibility in financing, the most useful form of company structure is unquestionably the corporation. You do not have to start out with a corporation, but it is almost inevitable that every successful proprietorship or partnership will ultimately incorporate. Not only are certain types of financing available only to corporations (such as public issues), but it is also true that the many types of corporate securities present the greatest number of variations capable of satisfying equity funding requirements. Through the use of various classes of common stock, preferred stock, debentures, notes, etc., every conceivable type of arrangement can be accomplished. There is a corporate security to fill every need.

HOW TO SELECT CORPORATE SECURITY ARRANGEMENTS FOR EQUITY FINANCING

So that we may analyze the utilization of corporate securities in obtaining satisfactory equity financing, we will first briefly examine the major classes of such securities. In the order of their priority of claim on assets, they are:

1. *Capital notes.* These are obligations of the corporation and must ultimately be repaid. However, they are called *capital* notes because they do not represent ordinary borrowings (like loans from a bank) and they are subordinate to them. In fact, such notes are often a part of the permanent capital of a business, since, for tax or equity balancing purposes, they may represent money invested by the principals. Another use of capital notes is the issuance of such instruments in return for long-term private placements from institutions. It is important to remember that, for equity purposes, they must be *subordinated* to current borrowings from banks and other financial institutions. As is the case with all other borrowings, these notes have definite terms for repayment,

and call for the payment of interest at regular intervals.

2. *Debentures.* Although these are also corporate obligations, as are the capital notes, they are cast more in the mold of a classic security. Debentures are usually evidenced by printed bonds with various indenture provisions included in the wording, along with descriptions of the other types of authorized securities of the company. Debentures must have definite stated terms of repayment and call for a fixed rate of interest which is normally paid semi-annually or quarterly. In addition, there are usually a number of protective provisions contained in a document called an *indenture,* relating to missed payments, maintenance of certain stated levels of earnings, net worth, liquidity, and debt limits.

3. *Preferred stock.* As the name implies, preferred stock has a prior claim on assets over any other form of stock (but subordinate to other types of securities, such as those described above). Preferred stock has no stated term of repayment because it is a true stock, not an obligation of the corporation. However, it may be "called" (that is, paid off for face value) at any time the retained earnings of the corporation will permit. Quarterly or semi-annual returns are usually paid on preferred stock, but these are *dividends,* not interest payments, and can therefore only be paid out of earnings. Normally, preferred stock has no voting right, but if two consecutive dividends are "passed" (not paid) because of failure to earn sufficient profits, the preferred stock may take over voting rights from the common stock.

4. *Common stock.* This is the basic ("bottom line") stock of every corporation and usually has the only voting rights. For this reason, control of the company is vested in the common shareholders except, as described above, in case of certain defaults. All increases in net worth accrue to the benefit of common stockholders, therefore this is the true "growth stock." On the other hand, no

dividends may be paid to common stockholders until all note and debenture interest is paid and prefered dividend requirements are satisfied.

In the above analysis, we have merely described in general terms the major categories of corporate securities and have not mentioned numerous variations. For example, debentures can be convertible into common stock; preferred stock can be convertible, cumulative or non-cumulative as to dividends—or even have voting rights. There can be two classes of common stock (class "A" and class 'B"). We will cover these more thoroughly in our chapter on Public Issues; from a practical viewpoint these subvarieties are not necessary to consider in seeking basic equity.

As you can see, the higher the priority of a security, the lower is its risk. Conversely, there is *potentially* a much greater return on the low-priority high-risk securities. Senior notes and debentures usually carry an interest return of 5% to 9% per annum. Preferred stocks can yield 7% or 8% dividends on face value. Common stock, which promises no set yield, can nevertheless earn the most handsomely if the corporation does well.

The simplest corporate form, of course, is that which utilizes only one class of common stock. Individual equities are determined as we have previously described and are reflected by the percentages of common stock holdings of the promotor and of the investors. In a typical fifty-fifty deal, the stock issued to the investors will be reflected at the dollar value of their investment under the "capital" section of the balance sheet, and the offsetting entry will be shown as cash under "current assets." The stock given to the promotor for his services will also be reflected under "capital;" however, the offsetting entry will be called "promotional stock" or "good will" and is listed under the "other assets" section of the balance sheet. Of course, any actual cash invested in the corporation by the promotor will be treated in exactly the same way as the cash put up by the investors.

While the use of promotional stock provides a simple solution to the requirement of compensating the promotor for his services, it is not always wholly acceptable to the investors. One objection frequently raised is that the promotor is immediately presented with ownership of a sizable portion of the cash investment—even before the new venture begins operation. This is because the stock he receives for promotional services has the same rights of ownership of assets as any other common stock and, therefore, the right of part ownership of the cash investment made in the corporation is attached to his promotional stock. For example, if the investors pay $100,000 for their stock, and the promotor receives 50% of the total common stock issued for his promotional efforts, the investors are immediately subject to a 50% dilution of their interest in the corporate cash account—the cash asset value of their stock has dropped $50,000 before operations have begun. The investors may not object to sharing in future profits with the promotor; however, many are not willing to give away as much as 50% of their cash investment simultaneously with their agreeing to subscribe to the stock of the corporation. By using more than one class of security, there are several ways to correct this situation.

Frequently a large part of the cash investment, sometimes as much as 80%, is represented by a senior security such as a capital note or debenture. The balance of the investment will then be represented by common stock. Using again the example of a $100,000 cash investment, the investors could receive corporate notes for $80,000, and they would further share fifty-fifty with the promotor in $20,000 of common stock. In this way, they would be subject to a dilution equal to only 10% of their cash investment (50% of 20%) and would receive repayment of

80% of their total investment before the promotor begins
to share in the profits.

Another approach involves the issuance of *voting* preferred stock to the investors for the greatest part of their
investment, plus a small amount of common stock for the
balance. This arrangement can give initial control to the
investors and at the same time provide a prior claim on
the corporate assets, including the cash they have paid
in. As profits are made, the preferred stock can be called
and paid for out of earned surplus, so that voting control
later shifts to the promotor, but only after the investors
have been paid off with the exception of the common
stock they continue to hold. Of course, this common stock
now becomes worth many times what was originally paid
for it.

There is still another method which entirely eliminates dilution at the time of investment; namely, the
unitized combination. This method utilizes a packaging
of two types of securities, usually debentures and common
stock. For example, it might be decided to raise $100,000
by the issuance of $90,000 in debentures and $10,000 in
common stock. The investors would be allowed to purchase $5,000 of the common stock packaged with the
$90,000 of debentures—in other words, a ratio of eighteen
to one. Let us say that the debentures were priced at
$100 per bond, and the common stock, at $1 per share.
Therefore the unitized package would consist of eighteen
bonds (at a cost $1,800) plus 100 shares of common
stock (at a cost of $100), for a total unit cost of $1,900.
The only person allowed to purchase common stock without buying the debenture bonds would be the promotor,
who would pay $5,000 in cash for his 5,000 shares. In this
way, although the promotor owns 50% of the common
stock, he has paid the same price for it as the investors;
however, he has no claim whatsoever on the debentures
which represent a great majority of the funds invested.

Despite the fact that we have arrived at a classic fifty-fifty split of control and future profits, there has been dilution neither of the debenture nor of the common stock investments.

The use of priority securities is also indicated when it is necessary to "plug" (or equalize) differences in contributions by the various parties to obtain a desired equity arrangement. One group I worked with, for example, joined forces with some qualified professionals to purchase an electronics firm. The final purchasing group consisted of several investors plus two experienced electronics engineers. Four hundred thousand dollars was required to make the purchase, of which the engineers were able to provide only $100,000. Yet the group opinion was unanimous that, since the engineers would constitute the active management, they should have 50% of the company to be purchased. Therefore, $200,000 of common stock was issued, the engineers receiving 50% of this stock for their $100,000. To plug the difference arising from the fact that the investors were putting up $300,000, capital notes for the additional $200,000 were issued to the investors.

From a financing viewpoint, there are varying reasons why one form of senior or preferred security should be used instead of another. Although debentures and notes are both corporate obligations, there are differences in the eyes of lending officers. Notes require more specialized attention, as to varying due dates and also to subordinations; and for this reason lenders prefer seeing debentures on a financial statement. These instruments must be subordinated to current borrowings of working capital. Therefore, almost all debentures are issued with a subordination provision, which is printed on the face of the bond. Lenders can readily satisfy themselves that, by the very nature of such a security, it is satisfactorily subordinated. Where there are capital notes, however, the lender must obtain a separate subordination agree-

ment from each investor, and, if this is required at a later
date, requesting it can sometimes cause second thoughts
on the part of an investor who, at an earlier time, had
willingly made the investment for which he received the
note. Also, debentures are usually issued in large groups
("series"), each group having a single common due date,
which is much easier for a lender to reckon with, as opposed to notes of varying terms and due dates from a
number of investors. It is true, however, that issuing
debentures is more costly and time-consuming. So, if you
are involved with only a handful of investors whose subordinations are easily obtained, the use of notes may
cause you no future financing problems when you seek
to arrange for additional current borrowings.

The decision between the use of notes or debentures,
as opposed to the use of preferred stock, rests on a different set of criteria. It should be remembered that preferred stock is not a corporate obligation. From a tax
point of view, the common stockholder frequently benefits by the use of a corporate obligation rather than the
use of preferred stock. This is because the obligations
bear *interest*, which is tax deductible; the mandatory
dividends on prefered stock are not deductible. If your
corporation is in the 54% tax bracket, it will therefore
take more than twice as much money to pay preferred
stock dividends as to pay debenture or note interest.
However, preferred stock *is* a permanent part of capital
and lenders therefore view it more favorably than debentures, since there is no fixed due date for repayment.
This same fact—the lack of a fixed requirement for repayment—removes what can be a sword of Damocles
hanging over management, particularly during early
growth stages when working capital is tight. While the
preferred dividend is somewhat more costly, as described
above, it can later be eliminated entirely if the corporation does well, because of the unrestricted right to call

preferred stock whenever there is sufficient earned surplus to do so.

Tax considerations can also influence your prospective equity investors and you must give consideration to their personal tax positions. Some investors are happy to find an opportunity to obtain better than bank interest in the form of ordinary income from interest or dividends. Many others, however, because they have money to invest, are obviously in a position of looking for tax shelter relative to ordinary income. In the past this has been one of the chief reasons for what are known as "thin corporations."

In the thin corporation, much of the capital is put into the company in return for notes which are reflected on the balance sheet as "Advances from Stockholders." Usually these bear little or no interest and have no set due date. Since an unspecified term on a note can be construed as a demand loan, it is very important once again to stress that the investors at the outset agree to subordinate such notes to borrowings from banks and other financial institutions.

The Internal Revenue Service seems to have allowed a ratio of about four or five to one—stockholder advances in ratio to stock. Following this rule, after equity percentages have been agreed upon by the investors and promotors of a company, about one-fifth of the cash investment can receive stock, and the balance can be evidenced by corporate notes. The first profits to be distributed are allocated to repayment of these notes, and therefore the investors can receive 80% of the cash they originally advanced as a tax-free return of investment.

If there are no profits, but ultimate losses, these may be tax deductible for the investor in several ways. Since January 1960, small corporations have been able to take advantage of the tax shelter provided by "Sub-chapter

S" of the Revenue Code. Under this section, a corporation with ten or fewer investors can elect to be taxed on
an *individual* basis. In other words, each individual investor can report his pro-rata share of corporate profit
or loss on his own personal income tax return. This is very
helpful in obtaining equity investments from individuals
in the higher tax brackets. Under the "thin corporation"
arrangements, losses could only be taken after a company
had failed so finally that there was no hope of repayment
of "stockholder advances." Even then, the loss could only
be taken as a short-term capital loss which is very limited
in tax benefit. In the case of a Sub-chapter S corporation,
an individual can take—as a loss against *ordinary* income
—his proportionate share of any corporate loss during the
year it takes place. This gives him the opportunity to
chance relatively tax-free dollars when the risk is greatest,
at the inception of a venture. Later, if the corporation
prospers, the high-income-bracket investor is still well
situated because the law then allows the corporation to
cease reporting under Sub-chapter S, electing instead to
report income as a true corporation with no tax liability
for the individual investor on undistributed profits. At
that point, with profits assured, the investor moves comfortably into an ideal capital gains tax position.

CHAPTER 4

Unsecured Borrowing
for Working Capital

WHAT IS UNSECURED BORROWING?

The simplest means of obtaining working capital financing is by borrowing on an unsecured basis. The mechanics are the least cumbersome; loan-handling requirements are minimal and therefore the cost is low. For this reason we find that commercial banks—the largest source of this type of financing—prefer to make unsecured loans to operating businesses (or even to qualified individuals) whenever they can. Unsecured loans have the following basic characteristics:

1. They have no lien on any assets of the borrower.
2. They are short term *but renewable*.
3. They fluctuate according to seasonal needs or follow a fixed schedule of reduction.
4. They call for periodic full payouts (resting the line).

5. They have no priority over any common creditor of the borrower.

6. They are granted primarily in ratio to the net current asset (working capital) position of the borrower.

7. They usually require that all indebtedness of the borrowing company to its principals be subordinated.

An understanding of the above criteria will enable you to determine whether the credit you seek fits the general unsecured borrowing pattern. If not, you can try some of the other methods of financing described in subsequent chapters, or you may find you can easily adjust your presentation to fit these criteria. Let us, therefore, study the qualifications in detail.

The first qualification—that the loan has *no lien* on any asset—is actually the fact which creates the definition of an *unsecured* credit. Putting it simply, the lender has no prior legal claim on any property of the borrower. The term "lien" has a very specific meaning in the financial field: it represents a priority claim on property *which has been created through a legal process* stipulated on the statute books of the state where the loan transaction is localized. Without a lien, a lender holds no priority over any other common creditor of the borrower. The unsecured lender does have a claim; but he enjoys no special position. The security behind a loan—in other words, the loan collateral—can only be isolated for the benefit of a lender by creating a lien,[1] which an unsecured lending arrangement does not include.

Why do banks prefer unsecured loans even though they do not include liens? Because they are so easy to handle and cost the least to administer. Since they do not enjoy a priority position among creditors, when the banks grant unsecured credit they must place more emphasis on general liquidity, over-all financial strength relative

1. For more complete discussion of the role of liens in financing, see Chapter 5.

to the size of the credit, and present indicated ability to repay. This does not mean that the possibility of obtaining small initial unsecured bank credit is precluded; quite the contrary, as we shall discover shortly.

USUAL TERMS OF UNSECURED WORKING CAPITAL LOANS

Unsecured loans are short term, at least in their superficial configurations. They do realistically contain short-term "outs." They may be amortizing or renewable, the latter being more typical. The term is usually one year or less and for this reason they are ideally suited for "spot" transactions. You may have a completely credit-worthy situation which would qualify you for a loan from almost any type of institution, but if your need is only for a few months, a bank may be your only source. This is because other institutions are generally geared to longer-term financing arrangements and their contracts and procedures are too complex and costly to apply to a spot situation which a bank is ideally equipped to handle on an unsecured basis. If, for a specific purpose, you have need, for example, of a two-month, five-month, or seven-month loan, the credit can be issued with that specific term—as long as it is for less than one year.

More frequently, however, the need is for a continuing credit over the cyclical growth pattern of a business. As we described in an earlier chapter, the usual function of working capital is to complement the role of equity in connection with fluctuating needs over a period of one year. For this reason most unsecured credits are established on a year's basis and set up on the bank records as such. Despite the fact that a one-year credit is established, the bank will still handle the transaction with a series of 90-day notes.

A bank will advise you of having established an "open line" of credit, up to a limit, say, of $30,000. This line is considered to be available to you—the funds are yours to use—for a period of one year. You may use as little or as much of this total credit at any time during the year. As a matter of general practice, some banks will send you a letter confirming your line; other banks will give you such a letter on request. Still others have a policy against written confirmation, but you can still count on the line if they have so advised you. I mention this latter point as reassurance in face of the fact that, despite the granting of a one-year line, you will probably be required to sign notes which have only 90-day maturities.

In connection with these short-term notes, there are a few technicalities to be understood. Although your credit has been granted, you cannot obtain the funds until you sign a note, at which time the money will be deposited in your checking account or given to you as a cashier's check. (It is more politic to have it placed in your checking account so that the bank will benefit, at least briefly, from the deposit; besides, it simplifies your own bookkeeping.)

Generally, you sign a note in the amount you actually borrow at the outset, not necessarily the maximum of your line if you do not immediately need it. However, there is no harm in signing a note for, say $20,000, even though at first you may only want $10,000 credited to your account. The bank can only hold you responsible for repayment of the actual funds they have advanced you and you may need the additional increment of your loan availability when you are out of town, or when it is otherwise not convenient for you to pick up a note and return it signed to the bank. Many businessmen keep a supply of blank unsigned bank notes in their offices for this reason.

The note will be dated and will stipulate that it be paid on or before 90 days after this date. Some banks prefer the phrase ". . . *on demand,* or on or before 90 days after date . . ."; however, this represents no practical difference in handling. The procedures of banks which use such wording parallel exactly the practices of other banks which do not include the "on demand" part of the phrase in their note preparation.

Theoretically, at 90-day intervals the bank reappraises the credit situation and can call the note, asking for payment in full. In actual practice, the bank feels it has screened the credit sufficiently carefully to review only once a year. Therefore the 90-day maturity date is only technical; however, you must handle it properly. This is done by paying it off in cash on or before due date, or, usually, "paying by renewal." The latter procedure is based on the fact that, as long as the one-year period of your line has not expired, you can merely sign and present a new note in substitution of the old note which is due and which is then returned to you, usually rubber-stamped "paid by renewal." Remember—this procedure is not taken lightly; the bank wants to see you handle the payment or substitution promptly, or it can call the loan and charge your account. Some banks do not even send maturity notices ahead of time, so you should flag your calendar for the due date. In recent years, however, many banks have provided a notice mailed about ten days prior to maturity so that it is only necessary to act promptly after receiving the notice.

Although the majority of unsecured loans falls into the category just described—the one-year line of credit consisting of a series of renewable 90-day notes—there is another frequently used variation. I am referring to an amortizing loan over a somewhat longer period. Whereas the one-year loan may remain at the same level for nearly a full year, the amortizing loan follows a fixed program of reduction, usually on a monthly or quarterly basis. If these stipulated reductions are met according to schedule, banks will agree to terms longer than one year because they feel that such performance indicates the ability of the borrower ultimately to repay the loan in full. Even then, in order to conform to the classic short-term façade of an unsecured loan, the whole program will still be structured with 90-day notes.

For example, you might borrow $10,000 unsecured with a verbal agreement (the banker will record these verbal agreements informally in your credit folder, and you should also make note of them, to be sure that your understandings coincide at renewal times) to reduce the total by $1,000 each quarter, the note to be fully paid in 18 months. You will sign a 90-day note for $10,000, then, at the end of the first quarter, repay $1,000 and sign a new 90-day note for $9,000. This will continue until the end of the sixth quarter, when your original 18-month term will have elapsed and the full remaining unpaid balance is due. Your payments made at the time of each of the five previous quarterly renewal times would have totaled $5,000; therefore, there would still remain $5,000 to be paid off at the end of the sixth quarter. Possibly you can then easily make the full and final payment. On the other hand, if this were hard for you to manage, you could arrange to make another $1,000 reduction and liquidate the balance over another four subsequent quarters in similar fashion. Having seen your ability to make steady reductions as promised, and now looking at a new loan arrangement which—from its new starting date—has only a year to run, the banker will undoubtedly accommodate you if your financial picture has not deteriorated.

The situation I have just described illustrates a very good principle of unsecured lending; namely, that a loan commitment can only be undertaken for a relatively short term, but that, after satisfactory performance during that term, the arrangement can be continued on the assumption that there is then established the beginning of a new loan and that the lender, now in possession of current information, is only required to project the validity of his credit appraisal to hold good over a short period in the future.

"RESTING THE LINE"

In both arrangements of unsecured working capital borrowing we see manifestation of the policy earlier mentioned in connection with this type of financing: the bank cannot be "locked in" with its funds, as would be the case with an equity investor. Therefore, these programs require demonstration of the borrower's ability to repay after a relatively short lapse of time. We have described how the amortizing arrangement can satisfy this requirement. However, in the case of the more frequently used one-year "open line" unsecured working capital programs, the requirement is met in another way, by what is known as "resting the line." Once a year the bank expects an unsecured borrower to pay off his open line entirely. Preferably, the borrower remains out of debt for at least 60 days; however, circumstances can frequently justify resting the line for only three or four weeks out of the year. The mere ability to pay off the line completely, even for a short period, is usually ample proof to the bank examiners that the borrower has not "locked in" the bank funds. The funds are being used for true working capital purposes, for seasonal increases in volume and in inventory.

The line is usually rested at the period of greatest liquidity during the year, when debt can be at its lowest level. This is normally the time immediately following the seasonal sales peak, when inventories have been shipped out, when accounts receivable have been largely paid off by the customers, and during the lull (though brief) before the beginning of the climb to next year's peak. Just as there are peaks at a particular time of the year for even the most stable, fairly nonseasonable businesses, so there are corresponding relatively slow periods at the opposite end of the pole. It is during these less active phases of your yearly business cycle that you should plan to rest your unsecured line, for then you will have the least need for funds to carry inventories and accounts receivable. It is also, as you will see below, the best time to set as the date of the fiscal year end of the business for financial statement purposes.

COMBINING VARYING TERMS

Frequently the condition of a business will justify a combination of both open-line and amortizing types of unsecured capital loans. As we have seen, there is almost always a need for open-line financing to handle seasonal peak cash needs. If just normal growth is experienced, this growth can be carried, even during the yearly slack period when the open line is rested, by utilizing the retained surplus from the previous year's profit. However, there are exceptions when merely this procedure will not do the job, usually because of the following reasons:

1. You are growing more rapidly to the extent that this year's period of least activity represents a considerable increase over the corresponding period of the previous year. In other words, you are growing faster than your retained profits can handle.

2. You are increasing your immediate short-term capital requirement because of some new program you are adding to your operation.

3. You have suffered a temporary operating loss

during your current year, but the trend has now been favorably reversed.

Such factors create a condition where a portion of your working capital need does not arise from the cyclical nature of your business. If, as for the first reason cited above, your rate of growth creates this need, you must try to arrange a *combination* of unsecured loans. This is because you will have a growth curve with superimposed seasonal fluctuations. For example, in a business with $300,000 annual sales volume you might have a $25,000 open line of credit to handle your peak in the fall and winter months. You plan on resting your line in January, your slowest month, when during the previous year your sales were only $8,000. However, during the past year your volume has increased steadily and in the current January, still your slowest month, your sales are now over $20,000. This increase requires you to tie up additional funds; $12,000 more for accounts receivable and $6,000 more for inventory, or a total of $18,000 compared to the previous January.

Now suppose you decide to invest some of the year's profit in equipment and the rest in a promotional campaign to sustain your growth. If it can be demonstrated to the bank that these decisions are sound, you should have no difficulty in obtaining a separate amortizing loan of $18,000 with an agreement to repay at the rate of $3,000 per quarter. Your increased profits will make repayment possible, provided you also again have the availability for the coming year of the $25,000 open line you have just paid off in January to rest the line. This is because, as you move into your peak season, you will be paying *down* on your amortizing line at a time when your capital needs are *increasing* because of your business cycle. Since this is in reverse of your need, your situation could be untenable if you were restricted solely to the amortizing line. The presence of *both* types of loans, however, gives you a combination geared to accommodate your growth as well as your seasonal fluctuation. The open line can be repaid during the next slow period, and your amortizing line will be liquidated gradually out of profits.

This is definitely a sound and realistic banking arrangement. You may not be able to obtain such a combination when you first qualify for unsecured borrowing; however, with a show of satisfactory performance, you will probably be able to secure it when the need occurs.

CREDIT CRITERIA OF UNSECURED LOANS

As was mentioned earlier, unsecured loans provide no prior claim or lien on assets for the benefit of the lender. Therefore, to qualify for this type of financing, a borrower must have a financial picture which gives certain assurances as to liquidity and general freedom from heavy debt and pressure from creditors. Credit acceptability is usually based on the following:

1.   Debt-to-worth ratio
2.   Net current asset position

The debt-to-worth ratio is a determination of whether there is an overbalanced condition with regard to the claims which can be made against the total equity capital of the borrower. The lender wants to feel that, since he has no specific assets reserved for his particular benefit, the possibility of a forced liquidation by creditors is slight, and also that there is sufficient over-all asset strength to look to. Since there are many assets which offset liabilities on a balance sheet, there can still be ample protection to an unsecured financing source if the debt is several times the worth. This is because the net worth is the remainder left after subtracting the liabilities from the assets. For example, let us analyze the following simplified statement:

Assets

Cash	$ 5,000	
Accounts receivable	35,000	
Inventory	45,000	
Total current assets		$ 85,000
Machinery & equipmt. (net)	$18,000	
Office equipmt. (net)	4,000	
Autos & truck (net)	9,000	
Total fixed assets		31,000
Prepaid items	$3,000	
Deposits	1,000	
Good will	4,000	
Total other assets		8,000
Total assets		$124,000

Liabilities

Accounts payable	$14,000	
Notes & acceptance payable	10,000	
Taxes	4,000	
Current contracts payable	15,000	
Total current liabilities		$ 43,000
Equipment contracts, long term	$12,000	
Notes due after 1 year	25,000	
Total noncurrent liabilities		37,000
Total liabilities		$ 80,000
Net worth		44,000
Total liabilities & capital		$124,000

As you can see from the above, although the net worth is only $44,000, there is a total of $124,000 assets in the company to which the creditors and lenders can look, with only $80,000 in claims (liabilities) against these assets. The debt-to-worth ratio is slightly under two to one ($80,000 liabilities to $44,000 net worth, a not unusual ratio. Debt-to-worth ratios of two to one or even three to one can be quite acceptable to banks. Beyond that limit, however, other financing techniques may have to be used.

The most specific yardstick used in analysis of eligibility for unsecured borrowing is the *net current asset* position. This is obtained by simply subtracting the total current liabilities from the total current assets; the remainder is the net current asset total, or, as it is more commonly known, *working capital*. In the sample balance sheet above, you obtain the working capital as follows:

Total current assets	$85,000
Subtract: total current liabilities	43,000
Net current assets (working capital)	$42,000

Banks normally limit their unsecured open lines to 40% or 50% of working capital, sometimes going a little higher to allow for seasonal peaks. Therefore, on the $42,-000 working capital shown in the above example, an open line of credit of between $20,000 and $25,000 should be obtained.

Another very common yardstick is the "current ratio." This is the ratio of current assets to current liabilities. It is obviously a rough index of liquidity. An acceptable current ratio is 1.5 to 1; for example, a financial statement which reflects $15,000 current assets to $10,000 current liabilities. A current ratio of 2 to 1 is excellent; 3 to 1 is outstanding, and rarely encountered in modern growth business. Any current ratio less than 1 to 1 (where the current assets are *less* than the current liabilities) is what is known as an "inverse ratio," and definitely will not qualify for unsecured borrowing.

From a realistic point of view, the current ratio is not as meaningful as the working capital position; yet, partially because of custom and partially because it is such an easy fact to determine, the current ratio is almost invariably the first element of the balance sheet to be checked by analysts and lending officers. Whereas selection of the fiscal year-end date has no effect whatever on the working capital and worth, it can definitely influence the current ratio and debt-to-worth ratio. Therefore, consideration should be given to selection of the optimum date as of which your statement is prepared. We have previously mentioned that this date—the fiscal year end you select—should coincide with the lull which follows the annual peak of your business. There can be a significant difference in your ratios as a result of your financial statement being prepared as of the date of greatest liquidity.

For example, let us look at two different statements which could legitimately be prepared for the same company. The first of these statements is hypothetically prepared at the height of the peak season and reflects the following:

Assets

Cash	$10,000	
Accounts receivable	50,000	
Inventory	60,000	
Total current assets		$120,000
Fixed assets		20,000
Total assets		$140,000

Liabilities

Accounts payable	$45,000	
Bank loan	20,000	
Accruals & taxes	15,000	
Total current liabilities		$ 80,000
Long-term liabilities		18,000
Total liabilities		$ 98,000
Net worth		42,000
Total liabilities & net worth		$140,000

Current ratio in the above statement is 1.5 to 1 ($120,000 current assets to $80,000 current liabilities). You will note that working capital (current assets minus current liabilities) is $40,000, which is certainly eligible for the $20,000 peak unsecured bank loan reflected. The net worth is $42,000. Debt-to-worth ratio is almost 2½ to 1.

In comparison, let us postulate a probable statement of the same company two months later, in the lull following the seasonal peak. It should look something like this:

Assets

Cash	$ 5,000	
Accounts receivable	25,000	
Inventory	50,000	
Total current assets		$ 80,000
Fixed assets		20,000
Total assets		$100,000

Liabilities

Accounts payable	$30,000	
Bank loan	——	
Accruals & taxes	10,000	
Total current liabilities		$ 40,000
Long-term liabilities		18,000
Total liabilities		$ 58,000
Net worth		42,000
Total liabilities & net worth		$100,000

Note that the fixed assets and long-term liabilities are unchanged. The net worth is still the same—$42,000. Yet during the 60-day interim some natural shifts have taken place. The peak receivables have dropped from $50,000 to $25,000; inventory has decreased $10,000, and —along with $5,000 cash—these changes have provided $40,000 in liquid funds. The funds have been used to pay off the bank loan and reduce the accounts payable and accruals. Working capital is still $40,000. Yet, with net worth and working capital remaining constant, the ratios have changed as follows:

    a. Current ratio—which was 1.5 to 1—is now 2 to 1.

    b. Debt to worth ratio—which was nearly 2½ to 1 —is now less than 1½ to 1.

Obviously, the business is being reflected in the best possible way in the statement prepared as of the date of greatest liquidity.

Unsecured lending credit criteria are somewhat more streamlined and flexible in the case of smaller loan applications from an individual or from the aspiring proprietor of a starting or young business. I am referring to loans of $2,000 to $10,000. Because the exposure in total dollars is nominal, and because banks recognize that these small accommodations are one of their best means of attracting potential growth customers and depositors, the loan officers are given some leeway to grant these credits on an informal, personal basis. Naturally, they will want to hold the loan down to a sensible percentage of the individual's net worth. Also, they still have to postulate the ability to repay within a year or more, based on sound indications that this is possible. Beyond that, the lending officer's personal impression of the ability and integrity of the applicant will probably tip the scales.

The practice of extending small unsecured loans, even to individuals, has become prevalent during the present economic era. Banks in big cities led the way; others have had to follow in order to compete for customers. I have known of a millionaire with an annual income exceeding $150,000, who was asked to pledge his life insurance to secure a $25,000 short-term loan. In another case, a surgeon with good net worth and income was asked to put up blue-chip stocks as security for a $16,000 loan. Both these individuals were well qualified for simple unsecured borrowing requiring no pledges of collateral;

however, they were dealing with old-fashioned, small town bankers. In each case both men were quickly offered unsecured accommodations by competitive bankers. Almost any professional man qualifies for nominal unsecured credit solely on his ability to earn and repay. An application for a small business loan is judged in part on the same basis, a little more emphasis being placed on the preparation of a statement of financial condition.

PREPARATION FOR SEEKING UNSECURED CREDIT

Since unsecured bank borrowing ranges from very small credits to multimillion-dollar lines, it is difficult to generalize on prerequisites. Actually, the amount of preparation increases roughly in proportion to the size of credit being sought. For loans of nominal size, up to about $10,000, it may only be necessary to fill in properly the one-page blank financial information form the bank will give you. In recent years, most banks have settled on the use of a fairly standard form with only minor differences to suit their particular concepts. If you are an individual functioning as a business, such as an attorney, doctor, sales agent or representative, real estate, or any kind of independent broker, the use of the form will usually suffice. Such activities generally involve only the simplest level of bookkeeping and it is not necessary to have an accountant prepare the bank form.

Most loans made to individuals are granted largely on the basis of personal information about, and faith in, the integrity and abilities of such individuals. In the case of a small business, however, since the accounting requirements are more complex, it is assumed that such operations use the services of an accountant as a tool for management. Under such circumstances the accountant should certainly be consulted about preparation of the bank form. Banks do very little detail auditing of a business in connection with unsecured lending; in fact, the audit is usually conducted by making comparisons between the submitted statement and the general books of the company on the premises. Therefore, if an accountant checks or closes these books, at least on a semi-annual or annual basis, you can be sure of consistency if he helps in the preparation of the bank information form.

Larger businesses, of course, must regularly use the services of an accountant, who not only audits and closes the books, but also prepares periodic detailed statements in a conventional format. In such cases, these statements are attached to the bank form; it is not then necessary to fill in those parts of the bank form which call for accounting information. However, bankers still want the form to be used because it contains certain background questions they wish answered; and also because they want the principals of the borrowing company to sign certain warranties and representations contained in the fine print above the signature lines. As was mentioned earlier, unsecured loans are based, not on liens, but primarily on the representations of the borrower; the warranties on the bank form are so worded that a misrepresentation of the facts constitutes a felony or fraud.

TYPES OF FINANCIAL STATEMENTS REQUIRED

As the size of the credit increases, the accounting requirements are stiffened. Actually, even for a small business, a *company-prepared* statement is not very satisfactory. The banks prefer a statement prepared by an *outside* accountant—and submitted on his stationery. There is also, sometimes unfairly, greater weight given to a statement prepared by a *certified* public accountant, as compared to a submission from a licensed public accountant. I have seen excellent work done by public accountants. If he is well known in his own locality, a public accountant's statements will be well received. However, banks realize that CPAs are more strictly licensed, conform to a more uniform and definite national code; and therefore the title "certified public accountant" after the name of the man who prepared the statement is somewhat like "sterling" stamped on silver. As the size of the business increases, management may find itself pondering the advisability of using one of the "prestige" CPA firms. There are about two dozen of these, all national (or even international) in scope, with offices in the major cities. You will note that their specialized services are used very frequently in public stock offerings. Also, where a business seeks to establish credit with banks in various parts of the country, these prestige CPA firms are very helpful because of their reputation. However, except for such special purposes, their use is not mandatory in obtaining credit (although they can usually be counted on to provide competent information to management for effective control of the business). Many local CPA firms are excellent, are well recognized by banks in the area, and can "affiliate" with a national prestige CPA firm if the specialized need arises.

Even in CPA statements there are qualitative differences. The terminology describing these differences is widely misunderstood. The word "certified," when applied to an inventory, usually means the accountant has personally supervised the taking of the inventory and verified the prices. Yet lenders will frequently refer to any statement prepared by a CPA as "certified," even if no verification procedures were undertaken. The important—and generally agreed upon—differences are as follows:

1. "Unaudited" statements
2. "Audited" statements with *qualifications*
3. "Unqualified" statements

Since the above terms are somewhat misleading, a detailed explanation is in order. The most widely used form —and quite acceptable in a great number of cases—is the "unaudited" statement. Actually, the accountant will perform auditing functions in the preparation of this type of statement. He will check the trial balance, possibly make postings to the general ledger, make the journal entries, and close the books. He will also probably check into any items which he does not understand or agree with, and satisfy himself as to their validity. He will prepare the financial statements from these figures on which he has worked. However—and here is the important difference—he does not verify the detailed accounts receivable by checking with each customer; he does not personally supervise the taking of inventories, and his general scope of going into the background of the facts behind the figures is limited. Therefore, he will refer to this as an "unaudited" statement, often using the phrase "taken from the books and records of the company," or "prepared from figures submitted by management."

The type of audit is generally described on a cover page of the statement, called the *transmittal*. The transmittal is typed on the letterhead of the accountant, addressed to the company, and signed by the name of the accounting firm, not by an individual. In fact—once again prescribed by custom—the signature of the firm is usually rubber-stamped.

Many accounting firms will issue the "unaudited" type of statement without a transmittal, merely typing or stamping the phrase "prepared without audit" on the bottom of the balance sheet and profit-and-loss analysis. I find this practice deplorable; it practically denies the fact of the work that went into the bookkeeping and preparation of the statement. It almost gives the impression of the accountant's saying "the less said, the better."

Such accountants should be requested to splurge on another piece of paper to provide the routine transmittal; the impression on the lender is worth it.

Banks and other lenders will accept "unaudited" statements in situations going up to fairly high levels of credit. It is felt that the presence of an outside accountant creates a further reassurance and that, even if he has not completed a total verification, he could probably uncover—and report on—any irregularities. The training of a CPA qualifies him in this regard, and he is sufficiently concerned about his license and reputation so that he would not issue even an "unaudited" transmittal if he felt there was some misrepresentation. In fact, the accountant would be willing to prepare an "audited" transmittal as well; but, since this entails more work and expense, he will do so only at the request of a client who finds he needs it to enhance his credit. An unaudited accountant's statement is usually required only once a year by lenders.

Most businesses which have arrived at what we might call the "middle level" of their growth—no longer in the beginning stage, but not yet truly big—require the audited statement with qualifications. Statements of this type usually represent a very competent and complete audit. They satisfy all requirements of management for information needed to run the business properly—a function that is at least as important as the preparation of these reports for credit purposes. Every realistically significant facet of the operation will be checked by the auditors. The statements will be sufficiently detailed, including notes appended, to provide understanding of the background and composition of the entries. Bank balances may be orally verified and spot tests made of the accounts receivable. However, since the audit will stop short of completing certain activities which are not realistically required, the transmittal will contain certain qualifications. Frequently the accountant will cover this fact by writing in the transmittal that there was not a "complete" audit, that the audit was "limited in scope," that he is therefore "unable to render an opinion." However, such wording does not do justice to the quality of such a statement and the audit behind it. Therefore, you should insist that the accountant prepare a transmittal for you which details the few exceptions which constitute the qualification. Financiers and lenders recognize the realistic immateriality of many of these qualifications and they will render to your statement the respect it deserves. They know, for example, that it is not necessary to check all receivables individually because they can get a good idea of their quality by postulating the turnover from the total receivables shown in the statement in comparison to sales volume. They also know that there are certain technical qualifications which may arise, such as is the case with an unaudited inventory of a year ago which your accountants cannot now check, although they have verified the current inventory figure.

Here is an example of a good qualified transmittal.

"We have examined the balance sheet of the ABC Company at December 31, 196–, and the related statement of income for the fiscal year then ended. Our examination was made in accordance with generally accepted auditing standards but it did not include all of the tests of the accounting records and other auditing procedures which we considered necessary, in that, under the terms of our engagement, we did not confirm the customers' accounts by direct correspondence, nor did we test the physical existence or the pricing of inventories.

"Because of the materiality of the investment in inventories and accounts receivable in relation to total assets, and as we did not apply generally accepted auditing procedures with respect to the examination thereof nor satisfy ourselves in regard thereto by other means, we are unable to express an independent accountant's opinion on the fairness of the over-all representations in the accompanying finacial statements."

—*Journal of Accountancy*
MARCH 1951

The "unqualified audit" is the ultimate in financial reporting form. It follows a rigid set of requirements. The taking of inventories must be supervised by the accountants. Every account receivable must be verified by mail, and the return reply must be made unopened to the accountant's office. Even non-accounting items such as correspondence, corporate minutes and legal files are reviewed to check the possibility of contingent liabilities or claims which could affect the worth of the company. *Full disclosure* is required.

If a lender or investor feels he has been misled by a statement and caused financial damages, he can sue the accountant for misrepresentation, failure to disclose, or incompetence. Therefore CPA firms are very careful about preparation of such statements which, when issued, contain an *absolutely standard* wording in their transmittal. Here is an example:

"We have examined the balance-sheet of X Company as of December 31, 196–, and the related statement (s) of income and surplus for the year then ended. Our examination was made in accordance with generally accepted auditing standards, and accordingly included such tests of the accounting records and such other auditing procedures as we considered necessary in the circumstances.

"In our opinion, the acommpanying balance-sheet and statement(s) of income and surplus *present fairly the financial position of X Company at December 31, 196–, and the results of its operation for the year then ended, in conformity with generally accepted accounting principles applied on a basis consistent with that of the preceding year.*"

—*Journal of Accountancy*
MARCH 1951

The above italicized words constitute the sole identification of the statement as being totally audited and without a single qualification. Such a statement will be accepted without question by any lender. It is absolutely mandatory in a public issue which is registered with the S.E.C. It may be required in merger or acquisition activities. Because it is costly, an unqualified audit is frequently not necessary. It does, however, present the highest quality engraved calling card to a potential financing source; therefore it is often used even though it may not be a strict prerequisite. If the cost of such an audit is not disproportionately high, relative to the size and other expenses of a business, it will be advantageous to use it. Your decision concerning its use should be made on the basis of whether or not you can expect to gain in return, to offset the annual higher cost of an unqualified audit.

Besides the financial statement you should present certain other information to the lender. This will fall into the following categories:

1. General activity description
2. Statistics
3. Forecasts

In seeking unsecured short-term financing, you will want to be eclectic about the material you submit. Choose what will best tell the story *briefly*. Do not clutter your presentation with items which can divert attention from your main objective. In other forms of financing you will find that much more information is required by the lender or investor. Unsecured lending, however, is characterized by its being based on fewer criteria and by its loan application procedure being as streamlined as possible. It will be beneficial to present a few pictures or catalogue pages if products are involved. Letters of interest from potential customers, or purchase orders, will help tell the story.

The statistical information required here may be merely a record of the last several years' operations; not necessarily previous years' complete financial statements, just a single spread-sheet of past sales volumes and earnings. If you are making a new business credit application, you should have a simple cost analysis, comparing your anticipated sales with expected costs, to predict profit. In all cases, with either new businesses or established ones, a simple forecast should be supplied to project future growth and earnings.

CHOOSING THE BANK

The choice of a bank will have a great deal to do with the possibilities of obtaining the credit you seek. Banks vary greatly, depending on policy, location, and staff lending officers. I should stress that we are here referring to full-service commercial banks; there are certain types of savings institutions which accept public deposits and carry the title "bank" in their names, but which specialize largely in making real estate mortgage loans. You are unlikely to receive unsecured credit from such banks. On the other hand, as was mentioned earlier, certain commercial banks have not yet joined the competitive ranks of unsecured lenders. In some cases this is because of unchanged custom; in other cases it may be a question of locality. Banks in towns somewhat removed from financial centers can fall into the latter category. Country banks, which are by far the best sources for crop and livestock loans, may have so little call for commercial unsecured borrowings that they do not think in these terms.

In most cities, particularly since the spread of branch banking, you will find a choice of eligible banks. If all other advantages are equal, you will probably want to deal with the bank nearest your office or business. This is not only because of the convenience, but also because your proximity may provide certain incentives to the lending officers as will be described below.

The size of a bank can be important for two reasons. A smaller bank is more susceptible to being "loaned up" during periodic tight-money times, a circumstance which can inhibit the increase of your credit line when you may need it, or which can make the lending officers temporarily less eager to grant loans to new applicants. On the other hand, small independent banks are frequently easier to work with because their officers have more autonomy. The more specific differentiation between banks of various sizes is the variance in their capital limitations. Banks lend money which primarily comes from deposits made by the public. However, banks also use some of their own money; namely their capital and surplus. The combination of these two items (usually lumped together in financial discussions as "capital") determines the limitation on the size of the maximum allowable loan a particular bank can make.

Generally, a bank may not make a loan to one customer in excess of 10% of the bank's capital. Since public deposits are usually many times bank capital, this limitation insures that there is no concentration of public money in any single risk. Determination of the bank's loan limit is obviously very simple. If a bank reports, for example, $600,000 capital and $400,000 surplus, the loan limit would be 10% of this "capital" combination, or $100,000. Incidentally, every bank keeps copies of its most current "Statement of Condition," usually in a handy pocket-size form, available in its lobby where anyone may obtain same.

You may very well select your bank on the basis of the presence of a particular officer. It is only natural, since these men vary greatly in their personalities, preferences, and authorities. Depending on their rank, bank officers are usually granted certain "automatic" or "personal" approval limits. This is the limit on the maximum size loan which an officer can grant individually without going to the loan committee. For example, an assistant

vice-president might have individual authority up to $10,-
000 loan limit; a vice-president, up to $25,000 loan limit;
a senior vice-president, up to $50,000 loan limit. This also
varies among banks, sometimes on the mere basis of size
of the bank, sometimes as a matter of policy. Of course,
the larger credits require loan committee approval, but
since the application is presented by the officer whom
you contact, preferably he is your enthusiastic protagonist.
This is where the personality of the officer enters into the
picture and why you may have to try more than one bank
in order to find an officer who seems receptive to your
activities and enthusiastic about your prospects.

Even though a loan officer may have authority to
grant a large-size request, he will frequently defer giving
you a final answer after he has all the facts. This is because many banks have a procedure which requires all
approvals to be officially recorded in the minutes of the
loan committee meetings, despite the fact that committee
action is not required. Since most bank loan committees
meet at least several times a week, such a procedure will
usually cause only a one- or two-day delay.

The officer's individual loan limits are not public
information; therefore, you can only make an educated
guess as to the authority of the man you contact, based
on his rank and the size of his bank. However, this does
not mean you should necessarily seek out the highest
ranking loan officer. He may be so busy that your situation will not receive the individualized attention it deserves, at least relative to its size. More important, in my
opinion, is that you find an officer with whom you can
establish good rapport. He can always go to the committee for approvals over his personal limit and—remember this—a good officer in a progressive bank can move
up in rank fairly quickly, sometimes concurrently with
your own business growth. Such a man, upon reaching a
more important position, will remember that, in effect,

he and you started out together—a fact that can only enhance your chances of matching your future growth with adequate working capital.

STATEMENT OF FINANCING AIMS

In your conversations with the banker, he is going to ask you what you are looking for. It is surprising how many seekers of credit become vague at this point. And it may further surprise you to learn how important it is to have a specific answer to this question. If the request is not specific, the banker may propose a program which is unsuitable. In any event, if you cannot present your loan need specifically, he will wonder at your ability to manage your financial affairs. Lenders respond far more positively to someone *who knows exactly what he wants.* Therefore, you should be prepared to supply answers to the following questions:

1. How much are you seeking? What is the maximum you will need at one time? Will you need it all at once? Or will you build up to peak borrowing?

2. What will the money be used for? The answer to this question demands good constructive purposes for the loan.

3. For how long a period do you need the money? What is to be the term of the loan?

4. How will you repay the loan; in other words, what method of repayment will you follow? A complete payment after a year? A monthly or quarterly amortization? A combination?

5. What is the *source* of repayment? Where will the money come from to liquidate the loan? From a seasonal drop in the requirement for funds? From projected earnings?

These are the definitive elements of the financing you

seek. Your ability to enumerate them specifically is vital to your chances of success.

WHAT IS THE BANK LOOKING FOR?

As in any normal business transaction, a financing agreement has the requirement that both parties benefit thereby. Otherwise, there is no deal. Naturally, you are well aware of your own desires; it is equally important that you present the banker with a picture which includes elements appealing to his bank. An examination of these elements will provide constructive guidelines for shaping your application for credit.

Let us face one hard financial fact of life: A bank needs no particular loan just to earn an interest charge. It is true that bank profits arise primarily from interest earnings; however, in normal times banks can easily obtain all the lending opportunities they can handle. Even during periods when this is not so, the banks have other avenues of fund employment. They can participate in loans to large national companies at "wholesale" interest rates, or they can invest in short-term government securities. The gross yield may not be as high, but these placements are preferable to making loans in greater risk situations where there are no compensating benefits. Bear in mind that banks are confronted with one vicious circle; they must lend money to obtain income, but they must also obtain deposits in order to make loans—and making loans is one of their best means of enticing future good depositors. The present or future possibility of deposits is therefore a prime incentive to lending officers.

Whereas a large increment of bank deposits is created by savings accounts of individuals, businesses cannot place their funds in such a dormant position. However, the business borrower is expected to establish at least a commercial checking account in a bank which extends credit to him. Checking accounts definitely create deposits for the bank, arising not only from the balances which the business maintains but also from the "float." Float is money which remains in the bank until the checks you have written against it clear through your own bank. For example, if you pay a bill to a supplier, you deduct the amount from your checkbook; however, four or five days may elapse by the time it reaches your supplier, is entered on his records and deposited in his bank, then cleared through correspondent banks or the Federal Reserve, finally to be collected against your own bank. If your supplier is located in a different city, a week or more may go by before your bank must make payment. Meanwhile your bank has enjoyed the use of the money at no cost because interest is not paid on checking accounts. If, for example, you paid $100,000 in bills each month, and the checks took an average of five days to clear (which is 1/6 of a month) your bank would benefit from float alone a possible 1/6 of $100,000 or over $16,000 in balances. (Some of the larger banks which engage heavily in unsecured business loans perform a special analysis of your average monthly balances in which they apply the weighting of a standard three-day float against the collection of the funds arising from checks received from customers which you deposit in your bank. In such cases, some of the plus benefits of your own float will be diminished, but they will still usually constitute a material factor.)

In connection with the above example, you might further be in a position to carry an average of $10,000 bank balance in your checkbook. This is because you accumulate funds until the tenth of the month when you pay bills and you might have over $20,000 at your most liquid part of the month to average against only $2,000 or $3,000 immediately after you pay your bills. Therefore, if you add this checkbook balance and the $16,000 float figured above, you could reasonably postulate having the bank statements reflect average balances during the month of over $25,000 despite the fact that—at the tightest period—you might have written checks to utilize practically all the money at your disposal.

Let us suppose you were seeking a $100,000 line of unsecured credit. You would make a point of advising the bank officer you felt you could average about $25,000 balances in your checking account. This would represent a definite side benefit to the bank. Balances of 20% or more are considered excellent for a growth company to which the bank is lending. In fact, the picture will be even better, as should be explained.

I have mentioned that an unsecured line should be rested one or two months each year. Assuming the average resting period to be approximately 10% of a year, the bank also assumes that your balances will be maintained during the resting period because of the nature of business in general, and because your money needs will be less during the slack period. This means the bank actually lends no money during 10% of the year and therefore its annual loan to you averages 10% less, or—in the example being used—$90,000. Since your balances average over $25,000 for the year, the bank is enjoying deposits equal to 28% of its loan to you. It can lend this money at interest to someone else; therefore, a loan with stated interest of 6% per annum could conceivably be earning over 7½%. Also, the presence of your balances provides funds which can be used to create another customer for the bank.

If you have employees, your local bank will see an incentive in granting you credit on the basis that you will issue payroll checks on the lending bank. The bank knows that your employees may come into the bank to cash their paychecks and it hopes that this may lead to the opening of more savings and checking accounts without the necessity of making additional loans to obtain these new depositors.

Finally, of course, a bank from which you obtain working capital is making the credit available because of faith in your ability to make profits and grow. Out of this progress they expect surplus eventually to be accumulated to the extent that you may indeed some day become a substantial depositor with relatively little need for the financing you required in your earlier days.

BUYING TIME DEPOSITS

There are some situations, and some industries, which require working capital loans, yet which cannot truly hold forth a claim that they will create deposit balances. The banks are aware of these. A good example is the construction industry to which banks customarily provide funds for interim financing purposes. Since construction loans are not made without a previously obtained takeout commitment from an institutional long-term lender, this type of loan is creditworthy. Moreover, because "points" are usually charged in addition to interest on interim construction loans, they are quite lucrative. When money is tight, however, this kind of financing loses favor, along with others which do not provide bank balances as do the normal operating businesses. Under such circumstances, one answer is to "buy a deposit."

Deposits can be purchased by utilizing a *time certificate of deposit,* commonly referred to as a "TCD." Institutions such as insurance companies and pension funds provide TCDs. They can be placed into almost any bank in the country, provided the capital of the bank is not too small relative to the size of the TCD. The supplier of the TCD receives bank savings account interest on its deposit plus a fee from the purchaser of the deposits. For example, you might find it necessary to provide a compensating balance of 50% to obtain a construction loan of $400,000. (Balance requirements as high as 100% are not uncommon when money is tight, or when your particular bank is relatively "loaned out.") Therefore you would buy a deposit from, say, a life insurance company in the amount of $200,000. You might have to pay the insurance company 3% or $6,000, in return for which a deposit would be made in a savings account in your bank, under the name of the insurance company. The depositor guarantees to keep the money in the bank for one year as the result of your having paid him your TCD purchase fee in advance (always a requirement with TCDs).

A point frequently misunderstood about the use of TCDs is that the depositor takes no risk. The deposit may help fund the loan, but it in no way guarantees the credit. Where there are ordinary balances created by a business borrower, such balances on deposit stand as a possible buffer against credit loss. This is because banks enjoy a legal "right of offset"; they can remove funds from your bank account to apply against your loan any time they feel the credit is in jeopardy. However, a bank obviously cannot offset a loan to one party against the deposit of another. Therefore, purchased TCDs are immune to offset. For this reason, the mere provision of a TCD does not change the *credit* criteria of the loan, merely the fund availability. The loan must still stand on its own credit merits.

Of course, there is additional cost involved with TCDs but this is usually justified. Taking the above example of a $400,000 loan at 6% with a $200,000 TCD costing 3%, we find total per annum cost of the arrangement to be $30,000. In other words, you will be paying interest of 7½% for the loan. To unsophisticated borrowers this might seem high for bank interest. And here, in answer to such an attitude, emerges a principle of finance based simply on realistic thinking: *Rate of interest on a loan is of secondary importance if you can determine that, after deducting the cost of the money you use, there results a profit which you could not have earned without the availability of this financing.*

Assuming there is the normal amount of equity in the construction project we have used for an example, it would be reasonable to postulate a profit of about $75,-000 after all costs including interest. Compared to the more usual 6% interest cost, a 7½% rate would mean an additional cost of $6,000. Does a profit of $75,000 justify a cost of $6,000? Of course it does. Yet I have seen certain businessmen assume the ridiculous position of taking a haughty stand on interest rates, sometimes letting their predisposition on this subject prevent them from realizing an excellent profit.

GUARANTEES AND SUBORDINATIONS

Many people confuse the requirement of a guarantee with the requirement of collateral for security. For this reason, they are sometimes surprised when they are asked to *personally* guarantee an unsecured loan. As a matter of fact, since unsecured financing involves no security of liens on collateral, the use of personal guarantees is almost mandatory for this type of financing where a corporation is involved. Loans to proprietorships or partnerships obviously include the personal liabilities of the borrowers. On the other hand, officers or principals of corporations are in no way automatically personally liable for loans made to the corporation. Therefore banks must ask for guarantees if they want to look to the personal worth of the principals. This is true of almost all financing extended to privately owned corporations except for very large firms with a long history of successful operation. Public corporations are usually not required to provide such guarantees. However, these are the only exceptions.

If, when establishing an initial line of credit, you object to signing a personal guarantee, the bank will say to you, "You are running the business. You are closer to it and know far more about it than we do. If you don't have enough faith in the business to back it with your guarantee, perhaps we should be reticent about lending our depositors' money to it."

Actually, most lenders want a business loan to stand on its own merits. Regardless of the personal worth of the guarantor, they do not want to finance an undertaking which does not appear economically feasible. Therefore, it is not correct to assume that loans are made because of the guarantees. Rather, there is the consideration that, in smaller corporations, the company and the principals are almost inseparable. This explains why, in some cases, an individual principal will be asked to guarantee a line of credit which is far higher than his own worth. Obviously, the strictly financial aspect of the guarantee is relatively meaningless. However, the lender has another purpose which is based on the confidence placed in the management abilities of this principal. If the principal leaves the corporation or sells out his interest, he will, of course, notify the bank of his desire to terminate his guarantee. By such a notice, the bank will be alerted to the change in management and will have the opportunity of calling its loan if the new management does not appear to have the necessary qualifications.

In financing corporations, there are also frequently requirements for subordinations. A subordination is an agreement on the part of a lender to place his loan in a position inferior to that of another lender. In privately held corporations this situation arises where the principals have fashioned their investments in the company to be reflected partly as common stock and partly as loans ("principals' advances to the corporation"). As explained in the previous chapter on equity arrangements, this procedure is primarily followed for tax purposes. However, these loans are just as much an obligation of the corporation as are bank loans and could occupy an equal priority in case of liquidation. In such a position, principals' advances reduce the net worth when, as a matter of fact, they were intended by the investors to be a part of capital. For example, look at the following liability section of a statement:

(Total Assets		$200,000)
Liabilities		
Accounts payable	$15,000	
Notes payable, bank	40,000	
Accruals	5,000	
Total current liabilities		$ 60,000
Long-term liabilities		40,000
Principals' advances to corp.		80,000
Total liabilities		$180,000
Capital stock (net worth)		20,000
Total liabilities & net worth		$200,000

As you can see, the technical net worth of the above corporation is only $20,000. No bank could make the $40,000 loan indicated in the statement solely on the basis of that little net worth. However, by obtaining a subordination agreement from the principals of their $80,000 advances, the bank can consider the advances as capital and therefore the loan is quite proper. At the same time, the principals have not had to abandon their tax position of holding notes for 80% of their investment in the corporation. The first profits taken out of the corporation up to a

total of $80,000 can be tax-free to the investors as a repay-
ment of loan. Of course, the purpose of the subordination
is to prevent the removal of these loans, but this restriction
is only temporary. As profits are earned and reflected in
earned surplus, the banks will recognize that they have
other worth to replace the principals' advances and they
will release an equivalent part of these advances from
subordination. Thereafter the investors will be in position
to remove those monies from the corporation on, as we
have explained, a tax-free basis.

USING YOUR CREDIT

Obtaining a line of credit is beneficial, not only for
the direct results which will accrue from the availability
of the capital, but also as a steppingstone toward future
more substantial credtis. For this reason it is important
to establish and *use* working capital credit at the earliest
possible time. Do not wait until the last minute; in fact,
try to obtain your first modest line *even before you need
it.* Obviously, your task will be easier if you seek your
first credit when you are able to show a liquid position,
no matter how small, because you have not utilized all of
your starting equity capital.

Let us suppose that your business has $25,000 capital,
of which $10,000 is in fixed and other assets and $15,000
is reflected as working capital. You may have started this
venture with all of the $25,000 in cash and, even after
purchasing $10,000 worth of fixed assets, and having
operated for a while so that some of your working capital
is tied up in inventory and accounts receivable, you still
have over $4,000 cash in the bank. Despite the fact that
you are having no trouble paying your bills and you feel
no immediate need for additional cash, *this is the time for
you to apply for a bank line.* From a credit point of view,

approval should be almost automatic on a request for a $5,000 unsecured open line. If the banker should ask why you need the money, you can properly answer that you anticipate increased business shortly as you reach your seasonal peak, and want to be prepared for this eventuality.

When a bank does approve a line of credit, it sets up the availability on a stand-by basis. Once you have been informed of approval, you can definitely count on being able to obtain the funds whenever you sign a note. However, you should not allow the bank commitment to sit idle too long. *Even if it turns out you do not need the money, you should borrow it,* at least for a short time. Obviously, the bank keeps a record of each commitment and sets it up on a total control. It is expected that the money will be used and that interest will be earned on it. If you do not use the money, the bank will have frozen funds on which it could otherwise be earning. Since this is undesirable from the bank's point of view, it can lead to a future cancellation of the line of credit. Not only will you have wasted your initial effort, but you will have lost something even more important—*the beginning of your banking history of unsecured borrowing.* Therefore, you should actually borrow the money available to you, preferably within a few months after the credit is granted if you do not use it immediately.

Picking up the actual funds is an automatic function. If you use the line some time after the credit is granted, you do not again have to meet with your bank officer. You merely go to the note teller, sign a note, and receive the funds (usually by getting a deposit slip showing the money has been credited to your checking account). The note teller will have received an authorization slip on your credit and will have kept it on file from the time the line was approved. The bank will not be concerned about when you take the money or check into how you use it, whether it sits unused in your bank account or goes out immediately to pay bills. The real concern of the bank after granting the line is that it is used sometime during the reasonable future and that it is repaid according to agreement.

About the time this chapter was written, I had a brief meeting with a client on a subject which exactly illustrated the point I am trying to make here. The client, who managed the financial program of a fast growing company, had managed to increase a previous year's bank line of $150,000 to $500,000. He had accomplished this, not only by demonstrating a remarkable surge of profit, but also by presenting a projection which postulated that, if growth opportunities were to be taken advantage of, the larger credit would be needed. The anticipated growth did continue; however, so conservative were my client's prognostications, that the cash profits developed far more quickly than he had supposed, and he required only a part of his available credit. He was naturally pleased by this turn of events, but very much surprised when I recommended that he still borrow his full line. *"Even if you use it for only one month,"* I told him, *"take the full amount."* I recommended this because, by so doing, his borrowing history would be enhanced. These histories are kept permanently by the banks for their own use and also —equally important—they must be transmitted to other banks and financial institutions who request credit information. If my client had stopped at his lesser need, the credit history would have read: "Subject has borrowed up to $275,000 and repaid as agreed." Instead, it now will reflect, "Subject borrowed up to $500,000 and repaid as agreed"—certainly an even more impressive record.

There was a further interesting sidelight. The client raised a momentary objection to my recommendation because he was reluctant to incur interest cost on money he did not actually need. But there was a very simple answer.

The loan agreement with the bank carried an informal understanding that deposit balances averaging 20% would be maintained. During the month that the full line was borrowed, the corporate bank account reached 40% of the line of credit; therefore it was possible to carry subnormally low balances for the remainder of the year and still achieve an annual 20% average. Without the need for funds to carry normal balances for the rest of the year, interest expense dropped sufficiently to offset the brief period of higher cost when the full $500,000 was utilized —and the record of half a million dollars successful unsecured borrowing was permanently in the book.

CHAPTER 5

Secured Working
Capital Loans

In the histories of many growth companies are periods when their needs could only have been served by
secured financing programs. At such stages of growth,
other means of obtaining capital would have been either
unavailable or inadequate. Had there been no alternative,
far fewer business successes might have been achieved.
Fortunately, the variety and flexibility of secured financing
have provided what otherwise might have been the missing element required for continued progress.

Modern secured financing methods have made it possible to obtain far greater capital assistance than was ever
considered feasible and proper under earlier criteria. The
justification of this broadening of credit is primarily based
on the use of one instrument—the lien. This lien is usually
granted through a Uniform Commercial Code security interest. As mentioned in the previous chapter, unsecured
lending does not include the creation of a lien; therefore,
secured lending, which does include liens, can go much
further.

We have described a lien as a prior claim on specific assets, given by the borrower to the lender. Liens are not granted lightly, nor can they be created without conforming to certain legal requirements. Today these legal requirements are found in Article 9 of the Uniform Commercial Code, which has been adopted by all 50 states. Whereas formerly, liens were referred to as chattel mortgages, trust receipts, account receivable assignments, etc., under the Code, all liens are now lumped together under the term "Security Interest." The document creating the security interest is called a "Security Agreement," regardless of the type of security interest it creates. The older terms may still be used of course, but they have been eliminated from the statutory terminology.

There are several requirements for the creation of a valid UCC Security Interest. With the exception of a bona fide pledge transaction (where the lender actually takes physical possession of the collateral of the loan), there must be a Security Agreement. This Security Agreement is the major memorandum of the loan transaction, and must be a writing containing as a minimum a description of the collateral and the debtor's signature. Typically it will contain much more (description of the transaction, amounts loaned, provisions for subsequent loans to be made under the agreement, etc.). Banks and finance companies generally have a standard form for this purpose. The security interest will not be considered valid until it has "attached," that is 1) the agreement has been made, 2) the money has been advanced, and 3) the debtor has rights in the collateral he has advanced as security.

The existence of a valid security agreement does not necessarily mean the lender will be protected in a priority contest against the claims of other creditors, and possibly even a trustee in bankruptcy. For this purpose, the Code sets up a filing system for the determination of priorities. The Code requires the secured party to "Perfect" the security interest through filing a "Financing Statement" with the appropriate governmental office. The place for filing will vary, depending on the nature of the collateral, but the most common filing place is generally the Secretary of State's office. The financing statement is another standard form, and its requisites are a description of the collateral and the signatures of both parties. The security agreement may be filed in lieu of a financing statement; however, several cases have held that a financing statement cannot take the place of a Security Agreement. The result is that any person intending to lend money to a borrower can quickly determine other parties who may have an interest in prospective collateral. The filing is of great importance to an unsecured lender, who does not have a lien, for all persons who have filed a security interest will have a prior claim to any assets in the event of insolvency. In this manner, all unsecured creditors are kept informed of the status of the obligation owing to them. If a secured lender does not "perfect" his interest, he is in no better position than the common creditor as far as a claim upon specific assets in the event of insolvency.

There is a great deal of fairness involved in the legal requirements for perfecting a lien. It goes like this. A businessman seeks a credit accommodation which he recognizes is substantial relative to his worth; he is therefore ready to grant a prior claim on some of his assets to the lender. The lawmakers are willing to recognize such an agreement as a mutually satisfactory bargain between borrower and lender; however, they do not want a common creditor of the borrower to become an innocent victim of such an arrangement of which he has no part. Therefore, the lawmakers insist that the common creditor have some means of at least finding out about the existence of a lien. This is the reason for the recording requirement.

Most common creditors are trade suppliers to the borrower. They usually sell on an open account basis and they set their line of credit to their customer based on his worth and payment record. The presence of a lien means that the supplier cannot look to the value of certain assets of his customer for payment of his trade purchases, except subject to the claims of the lien-holding lender. As long as the supplier has a means of knowing this, the lawmakers are satisfied. Actually, the presence of liens has very little effect on the ability to obtain trade credit from suppliers. The majority of such suppliers do not bother to check the recordings. Moreover, the use of liens is now so prevalent, even with large AAA-1 borrowing companies, that they are accepted as commonplace.

One of the largest national credit-card companies achieved its early growth through the use of secured accounts receivable financing. Major motion-picture producers frequently assign liens on film proceeds. Other users of lien financing have included a leading airline, a color-film manufacturer, a nationally advertised food processor, large retail establishments, and many prime defense contractors.

THE ROLE OF COMMERCIAL FINANCE COMPANIES

The most widely used method of providing secured flexible working capital is accounts receivable financing. Although some of the larger banks now provide it, accounts receivable financing as we know it today was primarily pioneered by the major *commercial finance companies*. A few of these firms have been in existence over half a century, yet knowledge about their functions was not widespread in the national business community until the last decade. Their impact is dramatically reflected by a single statistic: In 1956, commercial finance transaction volume was about $4 billion; in 1972, well over $25 billion.

By custom or by regulation, banks primarily serve customers in their immediate geographical areas; the commercial finance companies observe no such limitations. Some of the large national firms, such as A. J. Armstrong, Walter A. Heller, and James Talcott, have clients in practically every state of the union. It is quite usual, as an example, for a business in Arizona, which ships to customers in New England and the Middle Atlantic area, to be serviced by the Los Angeles office of one of these firms. Banks cater not only to businesses, but also to individuals, even going into first mortgage loans on single family residences. On the other hand, the commercial finance companies concentrate almost all of their attention on the business client, and for this reason they have developed specialized techniques which broaden the possibilities of finding satisfactory solutions to financing problems peculiar to commerce and industry. In so doing, the leading firms have become veritable "department stores of finance" for the businessman.

The names of commercial finance companies are listed in the classified telephone directories of the larger cities, usually under the heading of "financing." However, this listing also includes a heavy preponderance of consumer finance companies, and identification may be difficult. If your local bank cannot supply you with a recommendation in this field, you can easily obtain a list of qualified lenders by addressing an inquiry to the National Commercial Finance Conference, 29 Broadway, New York, N. Y.

Significant differences in the services offered by banks, as compared to those offered by commercial finance companies, arise from the dissimilarities in their aims and their capital structures. In the previous chapter we have examined the requirement for banks to build deposits in connection with their lending activities, and how this may influence the fate of an application for credit. The commercial finance companies face no such requirement; in fact, they have tapped an unusual source of funds to build up their supply of lendable capital.

At the base of their capital structure, commercial finance companies have their own substantial investment and net worth, in the form of millions of dollars of common stock and retained earnings. Because of this worth, and also because their loan portfolios have traditionally been diverse and quite liquid, they have been able to secure great numbers of unsecured bank lines at good interest rates. In the past, the total of these lines available to a particular commercial finance company stood at three or more times its own capital. Then came the significant breakthrough to the new source; namely, long-term loans from institutions such as insurance companies. The institutions could provide multimillion-dollar 12- to 15-year loans covered by notes or debentures. Since these placements were always either longer term than, or subordinated to current bank borrowing, additional bank lines became available, and made possible up to an *eight times* leverage on the capital of a commercial finance company. This has provided a unique route by which the tremendous accumulations of money held by such institutions as pension funds and insurance companies can be channeled to serve the capital needs of small and medium-size businesses. Since most major commercial finance companies are public corporations, they can broaden their capital base by issuing additional stock, then obtaining more institutional placements and bank lines, to the extent that they can supply as much capital as they can feasibly place. Therefore, since their prime objective is to increase the total amount of loans outstanding on which they can earn a profit, such finance companies will ordinarily try their best to find techniques enabling them to approve credit applications without unduly jeopardizing their capital.

In a great number of cases, a business in its "middle stage" of growth will utilize a commercial finance company. This is because, when its financing requirements are fewer during its earlier stages, it may be able to satisfy them through modest bank borrowings. Then, when the bank has gone as far as it can, the techniques of commercial finance, including a variety of secured lending methods, become necessary. Finally, if growth has achieved its anticipated goals, the company will have accumulated sufficient net assets and surplus to qualify for some of the more advanced forms of financing —which will normally include new and more substantial unsecured bank credits. Thus does commercial finance fulfill its "middle" function; it is a fact that its arrangements with its clients are of an average duration of only about three years.

There are exceptions to the usual function described above. Certain types of distributorships which, for example, may have very little fixed asset requirements, can involve large-volume sales of standard commodities on short gross markups. Such firms can achieve excellent profits, but must have substantial sales totals to do so. If the sales are to creditworthy customers, and if the commodity dealt in is standard, this is the type of business which may use commercial finance funds on a permanent basis. A coffee broker, a lumber wholesaler, a bulk chemical dealer can easily achieve annual sales of several million dollars—and make profits of over $50,000—with an investment hardly more than the profit he earns yearly. The use of large amounts of turnover money, which commercial finance can provide, is the important element making this possible. Such funds can represent debt far higher in ratio to worth than banks can extend on an unsecured basis. Without their availability, the borrower would be limited in a way that would probably even preclude any profit whatever, because the low gross margins of some of these good basic distributorships make it impossible to operate very long at lower sales volume levels which would be adequate and profitable for other types of operating companies.

Obviously also, certain business activities from their very inception will require secured financing rather than at a middle stage of development. This would be so if you were able to obtain the distributorship of a product which had an immediate sizable sales potential, to be serviced on the basis of repeat orders from a quickly revolving inventory. Right at the outset, your purchasing requirements and accounts receivable carrying capacity would demand a secured financing program. Also, there are cases where, to obtain proper gross operating margins, your purchases must be made on an advantageous cash basis. A small percent differential in purchasing at better prices for cash can represent the major part of your net profit. Secured financing can provide such cash—often at a cost far less than the extra profit it creates.

We can see from the foregoing that there is a higher ratio of working capital requirement to worth in those situations which call for secured financing programs. Concomitantly, therefore, these programs usually involve larger credit lines. For this reason you will find that most of the leading commercial finance companies prefer a minimum loan of about $100,000. They may start with you on a line as low as $50,000, particularly if there appears to be a good chance for future growth of fund employment. At the other extreme, multimillion-dollar lines of credit are not uncommonly granted by commercial finance companies, some of which, in participation with others, have gone as high as $20 million to a single client in the past.

SECURED FINANCING CONTRACTS

Most secured financing arrangements involve detailed contracts. These are necessary because programs such as revolving accounts receivable loans provide high-speed, somewhat automatic handling of substantial sums, frequently many times greater than the entire worth of the borrower, looking to repayment from hundreds of thousands of customers all over the nation. Because the lender deals at arm's length with the borrower, relying on the data which the borrower supplies, there must be complete legal coverage of all the diverse aspects of such an arrangement. Therefore the usual contracts, which are designed to cover a multitude of varying types· of industries and situations, are replete with legal "boiler plate" and may appear to be unduly lengthy. However, most of the stock provisions are only recitations of conditions which a responsible businessman would take for granted, even if they had been unstated. The contract can be divided into the following categories:

1. Intent of the parties—a description of the basic arrangement; for example, that the borrower will assign his receivables and that the financing institution will advance (lend) against them.

2. Representations—the borrower gives his usual terms of sale, states that he will be asigning receivables which arise from bona-fide sales, that there will be no contras or known offsets, etc.

3. Warranties—the borrower warrants that his products and services will be of acceptable quality, and that he will stand behind same and replace if necessary.

4. Rights and remedies—here are covered steps which can be taken by the lender to protect against or recover from circumstances which place the loan in jeopardy.

5. Percentage of advance—this is usually expressed as the maximum percentage of loan against collateral at any one time. It is normally stated, for example, as "*up to* 80% of the total collateral assigned." It is completely impractical to eliminate the words "up to" because the financier may deem certain collateral *ineligible for advance*

(see below) or, equally important, the borrower would have to forego the money-saving advantages of being able to fluctuate his borrowings strictly according to his needs. The maximum percentage of advance must be negotiated between the parties, as no financial institution has one set advance policy for all its clients. The lender will naturally attempt to keep the contract advance percentage as conservative as possible; certain industries having higher possibilities of rejects or offsets obviously demand more prudent advancing policies. On the other hand, the borrower should make sure that the contract provides for an advance percentage which is realistically geared to his gross markup. Obviously, if gross markup is small, the advance against receivables should be higher. This is usually possible because most small markup industries involve standard commodities and a high class receivables portfolio. A wholesale lumber dealer, for example, generally purchases from the mill at a discount of about "five-two-and-two," so that he has less than a 9% gross profit. He must pay for his purchases before his customers pay him; and his purchases will cost more than 90% of his billings to his customers. Since business in this industry is conducted at high levels of volume, even a well-capitalized wholesaler will need financing to carry his receivables. Therefore, it is not uncommon that the maximum rate of 90% advance is made to such firms, particularly if the customers are creditworthy, and because lumber is under the jurisdiction of several industry grading authorities so that claims and rejections are infrequent and quickly settled. In most industries, with gross profits running from 15% to 40%, maximum contract advances are usually set between 70% and 85% of assigned collateral.

6. Term of contract—the greatest majority of financing contracts are written for an initial period of one year. It is important to look for two things in connection with the term; namely, the renewal clause and the penalty

provision. Since the average receivables financing arrangement continues for about three years, a simple renewal is
provided, usually that the contract is *automatically renewed unless the borrower gives written notice before
the end of each contract year*. Normally it is required
that a termination notice be mailed on or before sixty
days prior to the end of the contract year. Any longer
notice period should be considered excessive and should
be changed in the contract. It is also a good idea to flag
your calendar several weeks before the notice deadline
date so that, if circumstances later make it feasible to
cancel the arrangement, the contract is not automatically
renewed for another full year because of failure to notify
in time. Almost all term financing arrangements have
provisions for the payment of penalties if the loans are
paid in advance of the original contract provisions. A
simple mortgage loan on a private residence, for example,
usually contains a penalty of several percent of the entire
loan if it is paid before it is due, although a modest
amount of prepayment per year may be allowed without
penalty. These penalties are based on a circumstance
which is well justified; without them the cost of the loan
would undoubtedly be higher. The reason is very simple.
The lender incurs a definite cost in making and processing new loans. If this cost is not spread over the full
expected life of the loan, and offset against the full
amount of postulated earned interest, the lender suffers
a loss. To protect against this loss, and to compensate
for dislocation of substantial funds without earning the
expected return, a specific minimum is established. In the
case of accounts receivable contracts, the prepayment
penalty will usually be equivalent to a pro-rating of one
year's full interest. For example, if it were anticipated that
the interest for a full year on the average funds borrowed
would be $48,000 and the loan were paid off in full after
eight months, there could be a theoretical penalty of four

months' interest, or $16,000. Actually, the interest paid for the eight months could be subtracted from $48,000 to determine the penalty.

Since most secured financing arrangements are made to accommodate a growth situation, it is frequently true that the loan will have increased over the term—interest paid will also have increased—and there may be little if any penalty to pay in a prepayment situation. In the illustration given above, if $48,000 interest had already been paid by the eighth month, prepayment could have been made without penalty. However, the wording of this section must be carefully checked. The penalty must be stipulated on an *annual* basis; if it is specified on a *monthly* basis (in our example it would be $4,000 per month, or $48,000 per annum) the borrower gets no benefit from increased borrowings and interest, and no cumulative credit toward satisfying the annual minimum requirement. The borrower should be able to obtain the cumulative-average wording and, in a promising growth situation, can frequently get the minimum set at a figure equivalent to two-thirds of the anticipated interest charges.

7. Interest rates—interest rates charged by commercial finance companies (or even banks and other financial institutions) for receivables financing are somewhat higher than ordinary bank interest for unsecured loans. However, it is important to differentiate between *stated interest* and actual *cost of money*. Commercial finance companies charge only for *actual cash use on a day-to-day basis*. No deposits are required, no balances are maintained, loans can fluctuate according to daily need (as will be presently described), and interest is stated as a per diem charge.

A study made at the University of Chicago illustrates how a business which uses unsecured bank borrowings at a *stated* interest rate of 6% can have an *actual* 15% per annum cost of money. This is shown as a possible result of the effect of normal compensating balance requirements, balances maintained during line-resting periods, and the normal build-up in company bank accounts after the tenth day of each month when customers' receivables are being paid off substantially. Frankly, I feel the case cited is a bit extreme; however, I do believe that the average bank loan does have an actual money cost that is at least 25% higher than the stated interest rates, for the reasons given in the University of Chicago study. On the other hand, commercial finance contracts provide for reduction of cost whenever customer payments are received, as in the most liquid period during the middle of each month. To clarify further, we should translate the commercial finance per diem rates of interest into the more familiar per annum charges. This can be done simply by multiplying the stated charges by 365 (the number of days in a year). As an example, let us take a per diem rate (daily interest charge) of 1/30 of 1% per day, one of the very typical rates charged by commercial finance institutions. Converting to a per annum charge by multiplying by 365, we would obtain a resulting factor of 365/30 of 1%—or very slightly more than 12% per annum. In comparison to stated bank interest of 7%, this seems much higher; however, as has been described, such 6% stated interest can represent an actual cost of 9% or more. Moreover, since the per diem interest is charged daily on *actual cash use for that day only,* the comparable per annum charge can be less than stated. This would not be so if the full loan were maintained at a constant level throughout the year. However, for example, a borrower who needs $100,000 during the tightest period of the month can frequently drop to a need for only $70,000 during the mid-month period of liquidity when the accounts receivable come rolling in. As a result, a contract charge of 1/30—which would approximate 12% per annum on a *stated* basis—can actually mean a per annum cost of about 10½% on the full line of credit. Therefore, the actual money cost differential between secured and unsecured borrowing is not as high as it might initially appear to be. As mentioned in the previous chapter, the realistic determination a businessman should make is whether the additional financing he seeks will yield him a greater profit, over and above the cost of the money itself.

I once heard this principle put very simply by a wholesale grocer who said, "I look upon money for financing like I look at a number 2 can of tomatoes. If I can buy it and sell it at a profit, then it makes sense to me."

8. Provisions for "future advances"—The lender and borrower may decide that there will be additional loans to be made at a later unspecified date. For priority purposes, the lender will want the later advances to be secured at the earliest date possible. If there is a provision for future advances in the Security Agreement, then these advances will "relate back" in time to the date of the original security agreement for priority purposes. Therefore, the security agreement will normally state that it covers repayment of any sums that may be advanced, expenditures that may be made, or indebtedness or obligations that may be incurred (including all debts and obligations now or hereafter existing and future advances) to the extent of the maximum amount agreed upon by lender and borrower.

For example, a Security Agreement for a loan of only $100,000 may nonetheless have such a clause securing future advances to a maximum of $500,000 or more.

NEGOTIATING THE CONTRACT

There are many provisions of a financing contract which are unvarying, particularly those connected with the legal aspects, warranties and representations. It would be a waste of time to attempt to modify any of these, as no bank or financial institution is likely to consider even slight changes in the legal verbiage. Those items which are subject to negotiation are the contract provisions dealing with the business aspects of the arrangement. The borrower should attempt to obtain reasonable termination notice requirements and prepayment penalties (sometimes refered to as "minimums" in the contract) which require no more than one year's interest on a cumulative-average basis, as described above, and which give credit for the interest already paid during the portion of the year prior to a later desired prepayment date. It is also very important that the maximum percentage of advance (loan) against collateral be established realistically, based on the standard gross profit of the industry in which the borrower is involved. Normally, the lender will agree to the proper percentage of advance if the industry pattern is clearly presented and understood; no lender knowingly establishes a financing arrangement which, from the very outset, is unworkable.

The final item to negotiate is the interest cost. This is usually done after all credit and legal problems have been solved, as it is only with full knowledge of the situation, to the extent that handling costs can be determined, that the lender can agree upon a rate. Here an important point presents itself; namely, that the cost of *handling* a secured financing arrangement is quite significant. In fact, to the lending institution, the handling cost can frequently be as great as the cost of its own money. This condition was analyzed and dramatically confirmed by a Federal Reserve survey which found that the leading commercial finance companies made no greater profits on their capital investments than did the banks. Yet the stated commercial finance interest rates are definitely higher than normal bank rates. Obviously a good part of this difference in rate is directly attributable to the extra cost of specialized handling which the commercial finance companies must employ in order to satisfy the broader demands of their clientele.

It is because they are not equipped to provide this specialized handling that many banks do not offer secured working capital arrangements such as accounts receivable financing. Some authorities claim that the few banks which do offer these services actually lose money in such activities but engage in them to attract customers who may later become good depositors. For this reason most banks are not overly enthusiastic about offering these services which a commercial finance company looks upon as the mainstay of its business. Also, since the commercial finance company cannot look forward to benefiting through a future depositor relationship, it must obtain its reasonable profit from the financing arrangement itself.

Commercial finance interest charges range from 1/36 to 1/20 of 1% per day. Translating these into the more familiar per annum interest rates, we are talking about a range of 10% to 18% per year stated interest. Since the handling cost for a $50,000 loan can be as great as that for a $400,000 loan it is obvious that the charge will depend largely on the size of the accommodation. Obviously the smaller loans will carry the higher rates. The larger loans, from $300,000 to $1 million, will probably be made at the 12% or 13% level, subject to individual handling requirements. The lowest rates are generally reserved for very large loans, or for those which can be handled on a very standardized basis such as *rediscounts* (to be discussed in Chapter VIII). Then, too, there are always opportunities for enhancement of rate after the contract has been in effect for a while. This is because the lender will then have recovered a good part of the costs of acquisition and investigation, and also, after a reasonable period of *modus vivendi*, handling procedures may be streamlined so that cost is decreased.

COMMERCIAL FINANCE-BANK
PARTICIPATIONS

In many cases where a company financing program has begun with a simple unsecured borrowing arrangement with a bank, a point is finally reached where the bank line will no longer suffice. This may be because the bank has reached its maximum loan relative to its capital. More frequently, however, it is a case of the company growing faster than its ability to increase its unsecured credit. If a commercial finance company is then called upon, it is sometimes possible to persuade the bank to stay in the picture on a participating basis.

Let us assume that a firm enjoys a $100,000 unsecured bank line. The business grows rapidly and it now requires an additional $100,000. However, its financial statement does not justify this increase strictly on an unsecured basis. On the other hand, the credit line can be converted to a secured loan such as in accounts receivable financing. If the bank has no receivables department, a commercial finance company will offer to handle the entire administration of the account in return for receiving its higher rate of interest. The bank is willing because it will continue to benefit from the bank balances and keep its contact with a potentially good customer.

The chief advantage of such a participation is the possibility of a reduction in rate. The borrower pays the *average* of the bank rate and the commercial finance rate. For example, the bank might want 6% interest on its half; the commercial finance company might want 12% on its half. Result: the borrower would be paying 9% on the entire loan. The bank will be perfectly willing to accept the lower interest on its half of the participation because it will receive full benefits from the company bank account balances and because it will be spared all of the cost of handling.

Occasionally such programs are initiated from the other side when, as a means of obtaining more advantageous rates, participations are arranged by the finance companies for their own clients. These are situations where the client is not presently borrowing from a bank, but it is a sufficiently large and sound account to justify seeking a participation. Once again the commercial finance company will handle the administration of the loans, and will receive a higher interest rate. Moreover, in these large situations many banks may be joined in the participation so that the rate may be even more beneficially effected. An example would be the Coburn Credit participation of a $20 million rediscount line. This line was administered by A. J. Armstrong, with $4 million of its own funds in the participation. The remaining $16 million was provided by eleven banks. The banks required 6% interest and 20% constantly maintained compensating balances; and this cost, when averaged against the commercial finance company charges, resulted in an average cost to the borrower of slightly over 8% per annum on a $20 million revolving line. So beneficial was this arrangement to the borrower that ultimately it earned sufficient profit to qualify for low-cost public financing.

ACCOUNTS RECEIVABLE FINANCING CREDIT CRITERIA

Certainly one of the most flexible forms of secured financing is the revolving line of credit advanced against the accounts receivable of a business. These advances— usually from 70% to 90% of outstanding receivables— fluctuate in direct proportion to need. Let us figure on a median 80% advance. If the money your customers owe you, your accounts receivable, stands today at $70,-000, you can count on a $56,000 loan. If you anticipate a $40,000 increase in receivables during the forthcoming month, you can count on obtaining $32,000 more, on the same 80% advance basis, to provide you with the funds to produce or purchase the goods you will sell to create this jump in receivables. When your needs drop, your financing will similarly decline.

In their handling of accounts receivable programs, commercial finance companies establish an almost "open limit" on your credit. The higher your sales and receivables go, the more capital they will provide, with relatively little concern for the mounting debt-to-worth ratio. Rather than basing their credit decisions on the general financial position criteria described in the previous chapter, the commercial finance companies are primarily interested in the *quality of the collateral.*

When you have applied to a commercial finance company and, from a general discussion with them it appears as if there is a generic possibility of their financing your business, an audit will be arranged. This initial investigation, although it can ordinarily be accomplished in a day or two, is unique. Your books and records will be examined, generally by checking from the latest financial statements to the books of original entry; namely, your journals and general ledger. Some of the values on your statement, such as inventory and equipment, may be visually checked to see if they seem fairly reflected. The investigator will want to see that your office systems are efficient and that your detail records are up to date, as the lender is going to have to depend on your handling. Most important of all, however, will be the check of the collateral—the accounts receivable. There the main concerns are as follows:

1. *Concentrations.*   To the lender your customers are known as *debtors*. The debtor must pay his bills so

that the loan made by the commercial finance company against the accounts receivable may be repaid. If a substantial part of the total accounts receivable is concentrated in moneys owing from one debtor, the lender feels insecure because of having too many eggs in one basket. Receivables financiers share a basic tenet with the actuaries of the insurance industry; namely, the principle of spreading the risk. Even if the debtor enjoys a AAA-1 rating, there are risks, exclusive of financial inability to pay, which may impair the collateral. These risks, described below, obviously increase where there is debtor concentration. Normally, if a firm sells to thousands or even hundreds of different customers, no concentration problems arise. It is not uncommon to have a few major customers; if, however, none of their individual accounts exceeds 10% of the total outstanding receivables, there is no concentration problem. Even a single customer who represents as high as 20% of the total receivables may be acceptable, provided this major debtor is creditworthy and the rest of the debtor list is conservative and diverse.

2. *Debtor Credit.* Since a receivables loan may be several times the net worth of a company, the lender will want to see that his client is not accepting orders from too many poor credit risks. Actually the debtor credit criteria are no stricter from a lender's point of view than the borrower should set from the position of his own self interest. It is just bad business judgment to be careless about customer credit; therefore the borrower and lender should have a common interest in this regard. It is true that receivables financing is with full recourse against the borrower (because, although secured by collateral, this type of financing is still a *loan*—which must be repaid, whether or not the collateral liquidates properly). However, recourse can be meaningless to a lender at the point where the borrower's entire worth can be wiped out by excessive debtor credit losses. It is expected, there-

fore, that the borrower's customer portfolio be at least
of a credit quality consistent with normal business
judgment.

3. *Rejections and Offsets.*   Customer remittance ad-
vices and debit memos, as well as the client's credit
memos, are studied to see if excessive deductions are taken
by the debtors in paying their invoices. There are always
a few deductions arising from a predictable small percentage of billing errors; these are not important. More
significant are deductions arising from receipt of faulty
merchandise, or from failure to provide agreed-upon
services. Every debtor has the legal right to offset any
claims he has against an account he owes. Since these
claims can build up before being asserted, a high rate
of rejections can seriously reduce the real value of an
accounts receivable portfolio. Therefore, if your rejection
factor is more than 2% or 3%, you may have difficulty in
arranging a receivables financing program.

4. *Contra Accounts.*   Whenever a firm sells to another firm *from which it also makes purchases,* a "contra"
situation exists. If you are both seller and purchaser to
another company, your invoices to that company will
constitute a contra account. Since your customer has a
full legal right to offset—that is, to deduct what you owe
him in paying his bills to you—a lender cannot even
guess what is ultimately going to be collected against his
asigned contra accounts receivable. Therefore, the opening investigation of your firm will include a comparison
of the names of your creditors (obtained from your accounts payable ledgers) with those of your accounts
receivable debtors. Wherever the same name appears on
both lists, these accounts will constitute possible contras
and will be ineligible for advances under a standard
financing plan. If there is a significant problem raised by
this fact, you can sometimes arrange to obtain a written
agreement from such an account that offsets will not be

taken, but that each of you will make payments in full, on your respective company checks, to each other. Under such circumstances, the receivables from a contra account may be classified as collateral which is eligible for an advance.

5. *Turnover and Collection Ratio.* A very good summary index of the quality of a complete accounts receivable portfolio is its turnover. This analysis is made by using total figures of monthly collections and plotting these against total outstanding at the previous month end. It is simply determining what percentage of the accounts receivable total is collected during the subsequent 30-day period, and averaging this over a year. For example, if your accounts receivable were $100,000 on June 30, and you collected $75,000 during the month of July, your *collection ratio* would be 75%. If you maintained the same average for the next 11 months, your yearly turnover would be 75% of 12 months, or a "9 times turnover." Certain industries which have very short selling terms, such as the food industries, have very high turnovers. However, the greatest number of businesses function on monthly billing terms (30 days, 10th prox., or e.o.m.); and for such normal situations a 10 times turnover is excellent, 9 times turnover is good, 8 times turnover acceptable—slower than these is marginal. Incidentally, since a turnover analysis should be made on real collections (not credit memos), a slowdown in turnover can indicate an increase in rejections, reworks and rebillings.

6. *Agings.* The best detailed picture of the accounts receivable portfolio is an *aging.* Such a report lists each debtor alphabetically and spreads his outstanding account according to its age. The following categories are used:
   a. Current
   b. One to 30 days past due
   c. Thirty-one to 60 days past due
   d. Prior past due

Here is an example of a segment of a typical aging:

	Total A/R	Current	1 to 30 Past Due	31 to 60 Past Due	Prior
Alpha Markets	$ 1,200	$ 1,200			
Baker Industries	400				$400
Cohen & Reilley, Inc.	11,000	9,600	$1,400		
Daylen Corp.	7,500	6,000	750	$750	
Everts Inc.	4,200	4,200			
Foods Chain	3,000	3,000			
Gringo Enterprises	350		350		
Hopping Co.	2,700	2,100	600		
Sub totals	$30,350	$26,100	$3,100	$750	$400

Open receivables in the prior column (more than 90 days old) are generally ineligible as collateral. However, the standard complexion of the aging is gauged by the percentage of the *first two columns* (current and 1 to 30 days past due) as compared to the total outstanding accounts receivable. If, for example, the receivables totaled $200,000, of which $160,000 was in the first two columns (either current or 1 to 30 days past due) this percentage would be 80%. Any aging which shows 80% or more in the first two columns reflects an excellent condition. Seventy-five percent in the first two columns may be acceptable; much lower might be unacceptable.

7. *Consignments and Allowances.*   The presence of a policy which allows consignment sales virtually precludes the possibility of making a receivables financing arrangement. This is because consignment does not constitute a *final* sale; therefore, no true receivable is created and the receivables lien can be tenuous at best. The only exceptions are in those industries where consignment represents almost the entire established trade practice. In such cases, the lenders establish a set of standards, deter-

mining the usual returns on consignments. This return percentage is deducted from the collateral at the outset, and then a partial advance is made against the reduced level. If a magazine publisher had a general return experience of 30% of consigned copies, the expected collectability would be 70% and the lender might advance 80% of this—which would be equivalent to 56% of the gross assigned collateral. However, where consignment is not the usual trade practice, these standards cannot be set. Creating a similar problem are products which must be sold subject to allowances, such as advertising allowances, cumulative quantity discounts, etc. The lender must determine the average effect of these allowances and reduce the gross collateral accordingly, before making his percentage advance against same. A little simple advice—try to eliminate consignments and allowances from your picture if you seek receivables financing.

DETAIL HANDLING AND DOMINION

One of the prime requisites of a secured financing program is the demonstration of *dominion*. This requirement has been greatly relaxed by the Uniform Commercial Code, however. In former years, when a lien was on "Shifting Stock" (ex. accounts receivable inventory), the debtor had to account for all changes in the collateral; otherwise the creditor would lose his secured status. The concept of a "floating lien" has been validated by the "Code." It floats all over a specified class of collateral, without regard to its changing contents. The debtor may now use, commingle or dispose of such collateral without the necessity of accounting to the lender. This does not mean that the lender will still not want to carefully "police" the collateral to protect himself from any possible fraudulent activities of the borrower. Especially in the

field of accounts receivable financing, the lender will want
to keep a close watch on the status of the collateral. Although dominion is no longer a technical requirement, in
accounts receivable financing the lender will want to
exercise some control by keeping "schedules of assignment" and "payment in kind." A discussion of these will
also explain the general operating procedures of a receivables financing program.

The basic collateral in a receivables financing program is the total of invoices covering sales to the customers (debtors) of a business. These invoices are batched
together—generally daily or weekly—and are listed on
the schedule of assignment, a form provided by the
lender. The listing requirement is made as streamlined
as possible, usually calling only for the debtor name and
total dollar amount of the invoice. The schedule is dated
and signed; it is also totaled, and this total represents the
entire batch of invoices which is then being assigned to
the lender as security for a loan. The total amount of each
schedule assigned adds, therefore, to the *collateral account* of the borrower, which has been pledged (or
assigned) to the lender. The borrower then requests the
amount of funds he needs from the lender, who will
advance the funds as long as the amount is within the
limit of maximum percentage advance stipulated in the
basic contract. Along with the schedule of assignment
the lender usually requests a copy of each invoice and
some proof of shipment such as a bill of lading copy or a
delivery receipt. Since these forms are ordinarily part of
the invoice set and related documents which come together at the time of preparing customer billings, this
usually represents no additional work imposed on the
clerical staff of the borrower. In fact, every possible effort
is made to minimize clerical cost. For example, if the
borrower uses bookkeeping machines, it is easy to insert
a carbon copy back of the daily sales journal; and it is
usually acceptable merely to attach this journal copy to

the schedule of asignment, in lieu of making the detailed listing on the schedule.

When remittances are received from customer-debtors, the *exact check* must be given to the lender—which is what is meant by "payment in kind." Here the requirement of dominion requires that the debtor check be given to the lender; it is not permissible to deposit it in the borrower's bank account, even if he immediately issues his own check in exchange for same. However, as you will see in the explanation of "availability financing" below, this is actually not a cumbersome process.

Now let us look at the practical effect of receivables financing, using an illustration that, for simplicity, is somewhat out of context. If the borrower assigns $100,000 total invoice value, and has a contract advance limit of 80%, he can theoretically borrow $80,000. Therefore, 80% of each remittance received from debtors would belong to the lender; the borrower would retain a 20% equity in the remittance. In this example, if $40,000 were received in remittances from debtors, this amount would be forwarded to the lender—but the borrower could make an immediate request for his 20%, or $8,000. This is called "return of equity." It is obvious that, although all remittances are forwarded to the lender, the borrower's funds are not frozen and he can immediately call for his share of any receivables as they are collected. In actual practice, there are continual collections, assignments of new invoices, and calls for advances or return of equities; the combination of these elements into a single procedural pattern is what is known as "availability financing."

AVAILABILITY FINANCING

In accounts receivable financing there are two fluctuating controls which are continually interrelated. These are the *collateral account* and the *cash loan account*. Each

ACCOUNT CURRENT

No.	Date	Adv. by Lender	Assign Sched.	Cash Receipt	Rec. Debit	Collateral	80% Advance	Cash Loan	Available
1	2/3		$100,000			$100,000	$ 80,000	—	$80,000
2	2/4	$60,000				100,000	80,000	$60,000	20,000
3	2/7		25,000			125,000	100,000	60,000	40,000
4	2/8	30,000				125,000	100,000	90,000	10,000
5	2/11			$40,000	$40,000	85,000	68,000	50,000	18,000
6	2/12	12,000				85,000	68,000	62,000	6,000
7	2/14		20,000			105,000	84,000	62,000	22,000
8	2/15	7,000				105,000	84,000	69,000	15,000
9	2/16			22,000	25,000	80,000	84,000	47,000	17,000

is maintained as a running balance, fluctuating as the result of detail transactions. The collateral account is affected as follows:

1. When invoices are assigned, the collateral account increases.

2. When payments are received from debtors, the collateral account decreases *in the amount of the bill being paid*—not necessarily in the amount of the cash received. If, for example, a debtor owed $500, but paid only $450 because he claimed credit for damaged goods in the amount of $50, this would wipe out the entire receivable and therefore would reduce the collateral by $500 although only $450 was received.

3. When credit memos are issued, the collateral account is reduced (because the receivable is being reduced).

The cash loan account is affected as follows:

1. When cash is advanced to the borrower by the lender, the cash loan account increases.

2. When remittances are received from debtors, the cash loan account decreases.

3. When returns of equity are made to the borrower, the cash loan account increases.

The collateral account reflects the daily total of security pledged by the borrower; the cash loan account reflects the daily total of money lent to the borrower. A complete picture of these accounts is given to the borrower once a month on a form known as the "account current." However, since this form is received only after the month end, the key to a receivables program is an *availability control,* such as the one shown on the table opposite. The availability is the amount of cash the borrower can call for any time he desires. This table illustrates the actual working of a receivables financing program on an availability basis.

In the table it is assumed that the program is opened with an initial assignment of a total $100,000 of invoices.

The table is keyed with numbers to show various types of transactions as follows:

1. On date of 2/3, $100,000 invoices are assigned, reflected as a transaction under the "schedule" column, and added to the total collateral. Assuming an 80% contract limit of advance, 80% of collateral would amount to $80,-000. Since no cash loan yet exists, the availability is also $80,000.

2. On 2/4 the borrower calls for an advance of $60,-000, which increases the cash loan by that amount. Since the availability was $80,000, there still remains an additional $20,000 availability after the lender advances the $60,000 requested.

3. On 2/7 the borrower assigns new sales invoices in the amount of $25,000. This increases the collateral to $125,000, 80% of which would be $100,000, increasing new availability to $40,000.

4. On 2/8 the borrower calls for $30,000 additional cash. This increases cash loan to $90,000, with an availability of $10,000 still remaining.

5. On 2/11 debtor remittances are received in the amount of $40,000 and forwarded to lender. This reduces both collateral and cash loan by a like amount but *increases* availability to $18,000.

6. On 2/12 borrower calls for $12,000 "return of equity"; availability of $6,000 still remains.

7. On 2/14 $20,000 new invoices are assigned, increasing collateral. Availability rises to $22,000.

8. On 2/15 borrower calls for $7,000 additional advance out of availability.

9. On 2/16 debtors pay $25,000 worth of invoices. However, one debtor claims a deduction of $3,000 for shortage in shipment, so only $22,000 cash is received. Therefore collateral is reduced by $25,000; cash loan is reduced by $22,000. Yet, despite the customer deduction of $3,000, the availability increases to $17,000 because of the remittances received.

As can be noted from the above, an availability program—which is a true *revolving loan*—presents the most flexible type of financing possible. The borrower only calls for money as he needs it; he is only charged for the money he uses (as reflected in the cash loan balance column) on a day-to-day basis.

ELIGIBLE COLLATERAL

In computing daily availability, there is one further element which must be applied; namely, the qualification of *eligible* collateral. Usually any receivables which are more than 90 days old are ineligible for advance; also ineligible are overconcentrations in a single debtor, or receivables which are in dispute or which are contras. The lender will periodically supply a list of these ineligibles, the total of which the borrower will subtract from the collateral balance before multiplying by 80% to determine availability.

LENDER MONITORING PROCEDURES

Because the credit granted is frequently high in ratio to the net worth of the borrower, the secured lender must perform certain monitoring functions. The borrower is required to submit regular financial statements prepared by his own outside accountant. Approximately every ninety days, auditors on the staff of the lender will make detailed examinations at the place of business of the borrower, auditing from the financial statement or trial balance to the books of original entry and subsidiary ledgers. The detailed collateral records, such as the individual customer accounts receivable ledger cards, will be spot checked. Regular analyses will also be made in the offices of the lender of the cash collections and trends in re-

ceivables turnover, customer claims for rejects and short-
ages, etc. In addition, all secured lenders conduct a
continual *verification* program by mailing what appear to
be routine accountant verification statements to randomly
selected debtors. If such debtors reply that the receivables are incorrectly stated, the lender will so advise the
borrower and adjust the collateral account accordingly.

NON-NOTIFICATION

It might appear from the foregoing explanations that
receivables financing would interfere with the customer
relations of a business. This is not so at all. Almost all
receivables financing is carried out on a *non-notification*
basis, which means that the customer of the lender's
client is not even made aware of the existence of such a
financing arrangement. The invoices sent to the customer
are not marked in any way; the customer-debtor mails
his remittances direct to the client of the lender. The
lender does not even endorse the debtor checks forwarded
to him by his client-borrower. The client's name is en-
dorsed on the debtor checks under an arangement whereby the lender can still deposit them in his bank account.
When verifications are mailed, they are done so on the
standard forms of an accounting firm, in the name of the
borrower—as if it were part of a routine audit being made
by the borrower's own outside accountant. As a result of
all these special procedures, the client-customer relationship is rarely disturbed.

BULK RECEIVABLES HANDLING

To certain substantial clients, lenders extend the use
of a bulk handling receivables financing arrangement.

Under such arrangements, no detail listings or journals are required in connection with the schedules of assignment. The schedules themselves are special short forms containing a warranty that the mere adding-machine tape used in totaling the invoices to be assigned accurately represents an increment of bona-fide receivables. If large numbers of remittances are received monthly, arrangements may even be made for the borrower to deposit them in his own bank, usually in a separate trust account for the benefit of the lender in order to satisfy dominion requirements. Obviously the borrower must have a fair net worth and reasonably good financial condition to qualify for bulk handling. He must have CPA statements prepared quarterly and must also supply monthly receivables agings to the lender. By spot checking these agings in regular auditor visits, by correlating the audits with a good verification program, and by making careful analyses and comparisons of the quarterly CPA statements, the lender is able to exercise sound credit judgment on a bulk-handled account.

OLD LINE FACTORING

Factoring can be considered as another way of obtaining working capital in ratio to the accounts receivable of a business. Yet, technically, there are several material differences between factoring and receivables financing. In factoring, another dimension is added—the assumption of credit risk by the financial institution. Factors do not lend against receivables as collateral, they actually *purchase* the outstanding receivables without recourse to their client. It should be noted that this non-recourse arrangement is limited to the credit risk, the financial inability to pay on the part of the debtor. If a factor purchases an invoice covering the delivery of faulty merchandise, he can charge back the "reserve account" (see below) of his client. This is because the contract between factor and client carries the usual warranties which would invalidate the sale of such an invoice and the individual transaction would be rescinded.

The technique of factoring is the oldest form of what we now know as commercial finance. Factoring began over a hundred years ago when the founders of what is now James Talcott & Company were engaged in the business of selling Scottish woolens to manufacturers in the United States. As the manufacturers grew and increased their output, their needs for woolens increased, but the mills in Scotland were unwilling to extend higher levels of credit to their faraway customers in a relatively young country. Therefore, the Talcott firm, which had more firsthand knowledge of its customers, agreed to purchase the American accounts receivable of the Scottish mills and thereby assume the credit risk. From this beginning, the practice of factoring grew until, in itself, it became a substantial industry.

Since it deals primarily with accounts receivable, factoring shares most of the credit criteria and contract provisions we have described above in connection with receivables financing. However, the main differences in these two techniques clearly point out why factoring has its own special advantages to particular types of industry. Those industries which the early factors first served, the "soft goods" industries such as textiles, wearing apparel and leather, were so influenced in their growth pattern by the factoring techniques that such financing is today still almost basic to these industries.

Textile converters who sell to garment manufacturers are faced with the problem of being major suppliers to a group of customers who, although capable of buying in large volume, can have serious fluctuations in their worth based on the success or failure of each year's new designs. For conditions such as these, ordinary credit-checking services are inadequate and too slow in reporting material changes. In a number of fields, however, the factors can provide the necessary protection. They are able to keep their fingers on the pulse of certain industries because, through handling a number of clients in a particular trade, they are daily observing payment patterns of the debtors in that trade. They can quickly detect any material changes in payment practices of a debtor. Also, factors exchange credit information freely among themselves. Not only do they make direct telephone queries to one another, but the credit men of various factoring companies, particularly those in New York, lunch together at least weekly and exchange information and attitudes. From such activities the client of a factor benefits in that he is enabled to make the greatest possible sales to customers without risk of bad-debt loss.

The factor also fulfills functions in areas where, even though credit information might be available, the client either cannot easily obtain it or readily evaluate it. For this reason some Japanese trading companies, financial giants in their own right, use the services of factors to take credit risks for their United States offices. The Japanese companies frequently rotate their key personnel between Japan and their various foreign offices. Whereas well qualified in their own particular industry, these executives, when transferred, are thrust into a local economy with which they are not familiar. Therefore, rather than risk bad-debt loss on their substantial orders, they use the credit services of a factor without even borrowing in this connection.

Widespread use of factors is also made by European manufacturers. Such manufacturers will submit to their factor all orders they receive from customers in the United States. When the factor "checks" (okays) the credit, the factor will issue a "maturity guarantee" to the bank of the European manufacturer stating that, for example, the factor guarantees to pay to the bank 90 days after invoice date the entire face value of the invoice covering shipment of the particular order. The factor will collect directly from the United States customer and will assume this credit risk. Meanwhile the bank, located near the European manufacturer and knowing well his ability to perform, will frequently advance to the manufacturer a large percentage of the working capital he needs to complete the order. In this way a financing device based solely on the creation of an account receivable can indirectly produce production financing for a manufacturer.

FACTOR PURCHASE GUARANTEES

The extension of guarantees by factors is not limited to international transactions; frequently a factor will assist a client to make key raw material purchases from suppliers by issuing payment guarantees. The payment guarantee of a factor is accepted by all suppliers and, by performing this function, a factor can enable his client to make excellent buys, to obtain assured raw material deliveries in sufficient quantity to fill order backlogs, and therefore to make profit far in excess of the cost of the factor's services.

MATURITY PURCHASE PROCEDURE

Considering that a complete assumption of credit risk is involved, detail handling procedures under a factoring arrangement are quite streamlined. Prior to shipment, the client will submit a list of orders received from customers. The factor will check these orders, thereby making a commitment to buy the invoices and assume the credit risk. Actually, it is unnecessary to submit every order received from each customer because the factor, in checking a first order for each new customer of the client, will "set a line" on that customer. Until notified otherwise, the client then knows that his factor will continue to buy all invoices up to that limit at any one time.

When shipments are made, the covering invoices are listed on a schedule and, if all items are within the credit limits set, the factor agrees to buy them on a *maturity date*. In other words, there is a contract between client and factor for a purchase at a future date. This date is set simply on the basis of standard industry billing procedure. For example, in the e.o.m. billing practice prevalent in the soft-goods field, all billings up to the twenty-fifth of one month are due after the tenth of the following month. In actual experience, most of the checks come in between the eleventh and twentieth of the month. Therefore the factor sets the twentieth of the month as the maturity date and agrees to pay on that date his cash purchase price for all invoices "factored" up to the twenty-fifth of the previous month. (This explanation is slightly simplified but it accurately expresses the basic procedure.)

Now, at the time the invoices are factored, the client does not automatically receive any money (because a *future* purchase is involved) but the client *has the right* to request—and obtain—funds if he needs same. In other words, the client can draw an advance against the money the factor has promised to pay to him on the maturity date. This advance can run as high as 90% of the total purchase price; in fact, under special circumstances a factor may occasionally *overadvance*—actually lend more than 100% of the purchase price. This is done based on the close relationship between factor and client, and knowledge that such spot accommodations are economically feasible. Advances are actually loans for which slightly more than bank interest is charged, strictly on a pure daily cash basis over the period from the date the advance is made until the maturity date. They are automatically repaid on the maturity date out of the factor's purchase price of the now mature invoices. It is important to note that the factor pays *in full* for the purchased invoices on the maturity date *whether or not payment for same from the debtors has been received by the factor.*

At the time schedules of invoices are assigned, a "client reserve" is created on the factor's books. This reserve consists of funds due the client from the factor. If no advances are requested until the maturity date, the reserve will practically consist of 100% of the value of the factored invoices, and this reserve account is therefore paid in cash to the client on the maturity date. If advances are taken by the client, the difference between the total due on future maturity dates—less the amounts borrowed on advances—constitutes the client reserve. The factor can offset against this reserve any debtor claims of faulty goods received or improper billings; however, the factor cannot charge his clients' reserves for credit (bad debt) losses from the debtors.

Because the factor assumes full credit risk and must therefore take the responsibility for follow-up and collection, he must be in direct contact with the debtor-customers of his clients. Therefore the whole process, differing from receivables financing, is on a *notification* basis. All invoices bear a rubber-stamped legend stating that they have been assigned and that payment must be made directly to the factor. Statements are issued monthly in the name of the factor and mailed directly to the debtors. In the industries where factoring is widespread, notification is accepted without question as a standard procedure. The federal government also accepts assignment readily on government contracts, and in fact—in the "Assignment of Claims Act"—*insists* on notification. However, there will occasionally be found in certain industries a few firms which do not readily accept assignments and this can cause a problem under the usual factoring arrangement.

On the positive side of the coin, however, the full notification system of handling obviously presents many cost-saving opportunities to business firms. Since the factor keeps detailed records of every individual debtor of each client, the client is spared the expense of a credit department, an accounts receivable bookkeeping department, and a statement and collection department. The factor lends money on advances at rates close to bank interest; and these rates do not include such extra services. When you realize that the factor supplies all these services—absorbs all of the debtor bad debt losses as well—and usually charges only between 1% and 1½% of the value of invoices assigned, you can readily see why this arrangement continues to be widely used.

HYBRID FACTORING

In California, at the end of World War II, a form of factoring developed which was somewhat of a hybrid between receivables financing and old line factoring. Credit checking was performed for the client but the factor would not make non-recourse purchases over such a broad range or to the extent or limit to which an old line factor would go. Debtor accounts were handled on either a notification or non-notification basis.

The hybrid factor provides a service for the smaller accounts which do not have sufficient fund employment to qualify as clients of major national commercial finance companies. The rates are necessarily higher, because of cost of handling in ratio to the size of funds employed by individual clients, as the usual total client loan account in this category of finance varies from $10,000 to a maximum rarely exceeding $50,000.

Hybrid factoring does not utilize the maturity-purchase arrangement offered by the old line factors. Credit information is always made available to the clients but schedules are often assigned without prior credit approval. If this is done, the factor will rate the schedule and will mark all unacceptable accounts, usually with the initials "D.R." (Department Risk). The factor will make an agreed advance but will charge the client reserve for any unpaid debtor accounts, usually after 90 days. On the other hand, under the hybrid arrangement, schedule advances (with exception of a nominal reserve) are paid as soon as the schedule is processed; there is no necessity for an interim loan made prior to a maturity date, so there are no loan interest charges. The factoring fee is deducted from the schedule advance, usually from 2% to 3% of the total face value of the invoices assigned. Hybrid factors also maintain detail records of debtor accounts, which saves expense to the client. In fact, a business doing a volume up to $300,000 or more can probably not perform the same functions for any less cost, and still get the benefit of receiving the working capital advanced against assigned invoices.

LOANS ON WAREHOUSING

Like accounts receivable, the inventory is a current asset which generally fluctuates in ratio to the activity of a business. Therefore, borrowing programs made to coordinate with inventory movement represent a valid form of working capital financing. Since most inventories involve commodities which are somewhat standard in nature, they qualify readily as collateral for secured lending. Once again, the lender may be faced with a requirement for demonstration of dominion in order to perfect his lien on the collateral. Warehousing is an arrangement whereby the inventory which is to be the collateral for the transaction is physically pledged to the lender. This is done by the physical segregation of the collateralized goods, with a third party warehouseman taking dominion over them.

WAREHOUSE ADVANCE CRITERIA

The percentage of advance is negotiated on the total amount of collateral placed in the warehouse. This percentage is always based on *cost* of the goods involved although, if freight and other charges (such as duty, in the case of imports) are significant, then they can be added to price of the items to obtain *landed cost*, or the total delivered cost laid down in the warehouse. Most important in the mind of the lender is that the borrower should have a reasonable equity in the inventory. This is required not only as a possible buffer against loss but also because the requirement of even a nominal equity on the part of the borrower will restrict excessive inventories in proportion to the total amount of equity the borrower is able to provide. For example, if an arrangement were made for loans of 75% against an inventory of sheet aluminum, one of the limiting factors would be how much money the borrower could provide on his 25% equity. If the borrower had $50,000 for this purpose, the financing would be limited to $150,000, since this would handle a total inventory of $200,000 of which the borrower's 25% would equal the maximum of $50,000 he had available for this purpose.

Usually, however, the maximum loan is set on the basis of sound business principles. The chief consideration is the annual turnover which should be normal to the industry and which should also prevent the cost of financing the inventory outweighing the profit to be made from sales. Generally, slow-moving inventories are justified only where there are higher gross markups on sales to compensate; chinaware, which turns over only two or three times a year, is a good example. On the other hand, low-markup items, like foodstuffs, paper, metals, etc., should have a fast turnover, sometimes as high as ten to twelve times a year. Probably an average inventory turnover is about five times a year; therefore, for example, the maximum inventory loan should be one-fifth of the cost of goods sold annually. Let us postulate a hypothetical aluminum baking-pan manufacturing company with sales of $1 million per annum, in which the cost of aluminum in the product is 60% of selling price. Annual cost of goods sold would be $600,000. On a five times turnover, maximum inventory loan should be 1/5, or $120,000. Actually, the limit might be set to accommodate seasonal fluctuations; for example, setting the limit during the slow season at $90,000 but during the peak season at $150,000. These limits when set are known as the "inventory line."

As we have mentioned above, in addition to the line, the other limiting variable is the *percentage* of advance against cost. This is usually governed by the estimated ease of disposal in case the lender must liquidate the collateral, which in turn is established by the market for the collateral itself. The highest percentages of advance are made against true commodities, items such as coffee, cotton, vegetable oils, which are actually traded on the world commodity markets daily. The lender knows that the market for these items is so widespread that he can in an emergency practically dispose of them through a few telephone calls. For this reason advances on true commodities can run as high as 95%. Rated immediately below these are standard raw materials such as brass, paper, standard pipe, lumber, etc., on which inventory advances can run up as high as 80%. Once again, the criterion of disposal is important. For example, standard plywood sheets, which have a widespread use, nevertheless can require as much as a 25% discount in order to move quickly in a distress situation; therefore, a lender will be reluctant to advance more than 75% on cost against a plywood inventory. Framing lumber generally falls into the same category, and because of its bulk, is a good example of an item for which the element of *landed* cost is important. Douglas Fir lumber which costs $78 per MBM in Oregon where it is milled, may cost $102 in San Diego because of freight charges. Since these charges determine the local market, a lender may advance $75 per MBM in San Diego on the same lumber on which he could only lend $55 per MBM in Oregon.

PUBLIC WAREHOUSING

Many financial inventories are stored in *public* warehouses which are established as ordinary storage facilities by independent companies which engage in the warehousing business for the profit they make on their services. Although the special functions they provide for the financial industry may also be lucrative, originally most of these warehouses were erected for storing and handling goods for clients without such facilities on their own premises. For this reason, besides general storage depots, there are lumber warehouses, cold storage warehouses for perishables, and so on. Regardless of the type of warehouse, it can serve a valuable function for financing purposes. Since the warehouse company is a disinterested third party and has no affiliation with the borrower, the placement of goods in a warehouse is an excellent demonstration of dominion. Trade suppliers of a company will

not assume that the warehoused inventory is an unen-
cumbered possession of a company being financed. This
is because the law assumes that a creditor will check his
customer's premises before extending substantial credit
—and that such a check will not hold forth the inventories
which are located elsewhere. Further, the lender appoints
the warehouse as his agent, who takes certain control
steps which clearly establish the fact that the lender is
behaving like a secured lender, qualified to have such an
inventory financing arrangement properly interpreted.

When goods are placed into a public warehouse, a
warehouse receipt can be requested. This receipt, when
prepared by a recognized, responsible warehouse, can be
presented to financial institutions as collateral for inventory financing. Under arrangements to be described
below, the warehouse will control the release of goods
from its custody in accordance with instructions of the
lender. The warehouse is completely responsible for the
safekeeping of the merchandise entrusted to it, and, if an
insured receipt is issued, this coverage is extended to fire
loss. Excellent records are kept and periodic physical
inventories can be obtained by borrower or lender at
slight cost. Often, because of its handling facilities, a
public warehouse can receive, store, and ship inventories
more economically than can many firms on their own
premises.

FIELD WAREHOUSING

For some business firms, the storage of inventory
at a distant location in a public warehouse presents problems of cost and inconvenience. This is particularly true
of manufacturers who must process raw materials into
finished goods before shipment, or for other businesses
which must pack a selection or variety of items from
inventory to fill orders. For such firms *field warehousing*

provides an excellent alternative. There are only a few field warehousing companies with offices in major U. S. cities, but they are able to render their services in any location. These companies, like Lawrence, Hazlett, and New York Terminal Warehouse companies, to name a few, are well recognized by financial institutions for their competence and financial responsibility. Whereas public warehouses were primarily established as storage depots, field warehouse companies were formed to provide dominion and control in inventory financing. Because of their constant alignment with financing, or of possible incorrect inferences drawn from their advertising, many businessmen assume that they are sources of working capital funds. This is not so. However, they do perform a valuable *service to lenders.*

First, field warehousing satisfies the legal requirement of dominion in a unique way. As we have seen, the lawmakers want trade suppliers to have the opportunity of ascertaining the presence of secured financing arrangements between a business and a financial institution. One acceptable satisfaction of this requirement is the establishment of an *ostensible* warehouse *on the premises of the borrower.* The theory is that a prudent supplier would visit the premises of a customer before extending credit and would actually *see* the field warehouse. Actually, practically no suppliers take this trouble, and so prevalent is the use of field warehousing by many fine large companies that it is well accepted by most sophisticated suppliers.

To establish the ostensible warehouse, a clearly delineated area is set aside on the premises of the buyer. If possible, a separate partitioned section is used; if not, a chicken-wire barricade may be strung for appearances. Sometimes the entire area except offices can be considered as the field warehouse, as in lumber yards. In any event, a simple plan is drawn, usually on a piece of 8½ x 11-inch paper, and posted near the warehouse entrance, to show the approximate limits of the field warehouse. The borrower then executes an actual sublease of the warehouse section to the warehousing company, usually for $1 a year. A few metal signs of nominal size are posted around the warehouse stating that the goods stored therein are the "property of" the warehousing company. Finally, an employee of the borrower is selected to act as "field warehouse manager." This employee is transferred to the payroll of the warehousing company which bills the borrower for the wages it has been paying the employee, so that no additional expense is incurred. In fact, the warehousing duties may take very little time on the part of this employee so that he is free to continue his previously appointed duties. However, through this arrangement, the warehousing company is able to take full responsibility for the stored inventory through the bonding of the warehouse manager. On this basis, *bonded warehouse receipts* are issued to the lender. Certain other services are also rendered to the borrower, including monthly inventory reports, showing movement as well as balances, all prepared on central installations of electronic computing and tabulating equipment. The cost of this entire service is usually nominal, based on a fraction of 1% of the inventory value in the warehouse.

WAREHOUSE RELEASE METHODS

The regular operational procedures of both field and public warehousing are essentially the same. As has been previously mentioned, when goods are put into the warehouse, a warehouse receipt is issued and the lender will advance funds to the borrower. At this point the warehouseman, as agent of the lender, controls custody. It is necessary, therefore, to have methods of removal from warehouse. This is accomplished by one of the following release techniques:

1. Pre-delivery payment
2. Blanket release
3. Minimum hold

Since choice of releasing technique is the lender's, the borrower should attempt to negotiate the method best suited to his operation. Once agreed upon, the lender will issue a written *delivery* instruction to the warehouse and this will govern future functioning until changed.

If *pre-delivery payment* is stipulated, the warehouse manager is required to obtain full payment at cost for the goods he releases. This payment may be in cash, or in the form of an assignment of receivables created from shipment of the goods to be released. Sometimes, instead of making payment to the warehouse manager, it may be made to the financing institution which will in turn advise the warehouseman how much he can release.

The second method, involving the use of a *blanket release*, is more flexible. Under this system, the delivery instructions originally given to the warehouse manager provide that uncompensated releases may be made up to a certain limit; this limit is the "blanket." For example, a blanket of $25,000 may be set. This means that the warehouse manager may, on request of the borrower, release up to $25,000 in cost of goods from warehouse. (Note that goods are put into warehouse and shown on the receipts issued at their true cost—and further, they are released on this same cost basis.) As releases are made to use up the blanket, there is a method of *reinstatement*. When a release is made, the warehouseman issues a *confirmation of delivery* to the lender. When the lander receives payment from the borrower (which can be cash or assigned accounts receivable) he signs the confirmation and returns to the warehouseman, thus reinstating that part of the blanket. Using the example of a $25,000 blanket, let us assume that the borrower has obtained releases of $10,000, $8,000, and $5,000. At this time he has only $2,000 open on his blanket. Therefore he pays $18,-

000 to the lender who in turn signs the first two confirmations of delivery and sends them to the warehouseman, thereby reinstating this amount which, added to the unused portion of the blanket, provides a new $20,000 releasing availability. The money for payment by the borrower to the lender can come not only from cash receipts or proceeds of assigned receivables, but also from loan proceeds on new warehouse receipts issued as additional goods from suppliers are put into the warehouse.

The most streamlined releasing procedure is the *minimum hold*. Here the delivery instructions merely advise the warehouse manager that he may continue to make releases on requests from the borrower, provided the total value of the goods in warehouse does not fall below a certain figure. Should the total inventory drop to this minimum the warehouse is temporarily "closed." Obviously this method is used where there are not only frequent releases, but equally frequent inputs of new merchandise. Therefore this procedure is excellent for a fast-turning inventory which is maintained at a fairly consistent level. Should it become possible to reduce the inventory level requirement, the borrower would have fewer accounts payable due to suppliers, which would provide him with funds to reduce his inventory loan from the financial institution. Therefore, the lender could issue a new delivery instruction to the warehouse specifying a lower "minimum hold" because less collateral would have to be maintained under control to justify the lower loan.

INVENTORY—OR "FLOATING"—LIENS

The Uniform Commercial Code greatly expanded the scope of secured financing. Under pre-code law, a lender could not have a valid security interest in property unless

he could show some exercise of "dominion" over the collateral. Vice versa, as soon as the borrower exercised
dominion over the property, the security interest took on
doubtful validity. This greatly frustrated the needs of
modern commercial financing. Banks had to elaborately
"police" their collateral, for fear that should the borrower
commingle proceeds from sales with his personal funds,
the security agreement would be ruled a fraud on unsecured creditors. There was a hard and fast rule that
the borrower had to account in some manner for all proceeds arising from the disposition of any collateral. The
net result made it very difficult for a lender to get a
valid security interest covering large amounts of "shifting stock."

The Code changed the entire picture by allowing the
lender to take a security interest in "inventory" and its
proceeds. The term "inventory" should cover all items
held for sale, present and future, in a business which has
rapidly turning-over stock. The lender's agreement may
also state that the security agreement will cover inventory
"whenever acquired." This relieves the necessity of drawing a new security agreement every time new inventory is
acquired, or having to account for each piece of inventory
as it is acquired. The proceeds clause in the security carries the security interest automatically to any proceeds
of the sale by the borrower. The borrower may deal with
the collateral proceeds in any manner he wishes, without
the danger of the bank's secured position being ruled invalid. This arrangement takes care of legal protection of
the lien; however, from a credit point of view the lender
will want his agreement with the borrower to include
certain procedures and reporting requirements. Normally,
a bank will want to receive sales and collection information, as well as periodic inventory reports, to insure that
the total outstanding loans are adequately secured by
inventory and/or receivables.

The borrower may re-invest the proceeds in more

inventory as the bank's security interest covers all inventory, past, present, and future. As long as the value of the collateral is sufficient to cover the obligation, the credit position of the bank is satisfactory.

Another concept validated by the Code is a provision for "future advances" in a security agreement. Such a clause provides that obligations covered by the security agreement shall include future advances of money or other value that may be given by the lender in the future. The collateral will secure such advances, even though the lender and borrower have not at the present time agreed that they be made.

The combination of an "after-acquired" property clause and a "future advances" clause produces a "cross-security" agreement under which collateral acquired at any time may secure advances whenever made. Such a provision allows two parties to engage in continual financing over an extended period with only the original security agreement. The bank's right to a security interest in all proceeds is not impaired by such an agreement.

There is one important exception to the use of the floating lien. It does not apply to any security arrangement based on possession of the collateral by the lender. The most significant example would be a warehousing arrangement. The floating lien serves its greatest utility in financial arrangements involving manufacturing and sales of inventory.

Inventory lien financing is based on the same credit criteria as are warehousing loans. However, because of the looser control, lenders will tend to make lower percentage advances against liened inventory than they would against warehoused goods. On the other hand, since the lien can extend across all the inventory of a borrower, including that which is in process, the total collateral can be higher.

An inventory of warehoused lumber in a furniture

factory could warrant a 75% advance; the same lumber as part of an inventory lien might receive only a 60% advance. However, this might be offset by the fact that the lumber in process and finished furniture could build up more collateral value for the lender; therefore, the total advance could be the same in both cases.

It is important to analyze the general *mix* of the inventory into the following three categories:

1. Standard raw materials
2. Inventory in process
3. Finished goods

Knowledge of the above analysis will encourage the lender to make an optimum safe advance; when the inventory is not broken down for him in this way he will tend to be more conservative. The usual level of raw materials will deserve the highest advance percentage. This drops for inventory in process because the raw material is no longer standard or wholly recoverable after it has been worked on. Finished goods are usually not too significant in an inventory lien because they are to be shipped out imminently. Therefore, in the example we cited of the wood furniture manufacturing company, the lender might establish the advance according to the following table:

Category	Advance (%)		Cost Total	Advance
Raw materials	70		$ 90,000	$63,000
In process	40		50,000	20,000
Finished goods	60		25,000	15,000
		Total	$165,000	$98,000
		Advance against total:		60%

From the above analysis, the lender obviously establishes an over-all advance percentage of 60%. He will check periodically to see if this category mix remains the same.

The conservative lender will always prefer warehousing to an inventory lien arrangement. The borrower will prefer the lien because it is less cumbersome, but he must be reconciled to the possibility of a lower advance. In some cases the best interests of both parties may be served through a *combination of lien and warehousing*. The raw materials would be separated in one part of the premises in a field warehouse, the rest of the operation would be covered by lien. An 80% advance might be set for the warehoused materials, and a 60% advance on the items covered solely by lien, so that the average advance of 70% might be higher than if only a lien were used. Where the inventory consists of many diverse items or large quantities of low-cost items, liens are preferred because field warehouse handling would be impractical. Also, it should be obvious that keeping in-process items under warehouse would be virtually impossible; here again, the lien is the only solution.

When an inventory lien is created it is necessary to submit a detailed physical inventory listing to the lender. Lenders will normally insist on semi-annual submission of physical inventories. In the interim, dominion and control are usually satisfied by filing monthly *designations* which look like this:

Jones Manufacturing Co.
Inventory Lien Designation

Beginning inventory March 1:		$280,000
Purchases, month of March:		90,000
Sales—March:	$150,000	
Inventory cost of goods sold	× 50%	(75,000)
Ending inventory March 31:		$295,000
Certified correct from our records	(signed and dated)	

Note that these interim designations are based merely on summarized book figures. They are corrected at the end of any month when an actual physical inventory is taken. An adjustment of the loan will be made between borrower and lender to conform to the new designated total. If the total decreases from the previous month the borrower will have to repay the percentage advanced on the decreased portion. If the total rises, the lender will increase his loan (subject, of course, to the inventory line limit).

CHAPTER 6

Secured Growth
Capital Loans

In Chapter II, growth capital was differentiated from working capital by the function it was meant to perform. Whereas working capital borrowing is usually coordinated with the cyclical aspects of a business and its loan reduction comes primarily from annual liquidations, the repayment of growth capital loans is postulated to come from profits of a program extending several years into the future. This differentiation applies on a consistent basis to the collateral which each type of financing utilizes. As we have seen, working capital loans are usually secured by assets which turn over rapidly and fluctuate seasonally—*current* assets such as inventories and receivables. Growth capital, which extends over a longer term, is more normally secured by collateral which remains unchanged in the possession of the borrower; namely, the non-current or *fixed* assets such as machinery and equipment.

CHATTEL MORTGAGES

The chief instrument used in establishing the lien required by the lender in making growth capital loans is the *chattel mortgage*. Although this term no longer appears in statutory language, it is commonly used by lenders out of custom. A chattel is any piece of personal property, and it is made the collateral of the loan in much the same manner as a mortgage on real property. The chattel which is the collateral for the loan remains in the borrower's possession, until there is a default on the obligation, in which case the lender has the remedy of repossession.

A chattel mortgage is created by drawing a security agreement between the parties. This agreement will state that the specified chattel is security for the debt. To perfect his security interest, the lender will have to file a financing statement documenting the transaction at the appropriate public office specified in the commercial code of the state. The transaction is usually handled on standard forms drawn specially to meet the legal needs established by the Uniform Commercial Code. Any creditor wishing to inquire whether particular chattels are encumbered can simply request the information from the public office where all chattel mortgages are filed. If the chattel mortgage is not filed in that office, then it can have no effect with regard to other lenders.

The chattel mortgage can be given great flexibility by the inclusion of a future advances clause. Where such a clause is included, the agreement will state that the chattel stands as security not only for the initial loan, but also for later loans unanticipated at the time the initial loan was made. Where there is no clause providing for future advances, loans after the initial advance will be considered unsecured. The legal theory in chattel financing is that a single loan is created with the chattel property as security and that, as this loan is paid down, the chattel is proportionally free of the indebtedness it was advertised to secure. Therefore, with an ordinary chattel, any additional funds advanced after amortization has begun will be considered *unsecured* loans. Take, for example, a chattel mortgage of $120,000 which is specified to be repaid over four years at the rate of $2,500 per month. At the end of two years, when the unpaid balance is down to $60,000, borrower and lender agree it is feasible to *increase* the loan $25,000 to cover an unanticipated increase in business. Even though both the circumstances and the present value of the collateral justified the new cash advance, this additional $25,000 would *not* be secured by the existing chattel mortgage unless the mortgage had contained a "fluctuating" provision at the time of original filing, and this fact alone could interfere with the lender's making the new accommodation to which he was otherwise agreeable.

FLUCTUATING CHATTEL MORTGAGES

Utilizing the method described above, some loan arrangements are designed to be fluctuating with the prior knowledge that this is to be an integral part of the program, rather than as the result of an unexpected future development. For example, I once arranged the financing of a company in the computer leasing field, using as chattel security the computing equipment. There was also an assignment to the lender of $8,000 monthly lease income on the equipment. The financing consisted of a six-year loan to be repaid at the rate of $3,000 per month. The effect of the receipt of the lease income was that the lender was being paid off faster than required;

therefore, he *lent back* to the borrower the extra $5,000 per month which the borrower needed for operating expenses. Legally, each time this was done it constituted a new loan which could not have been secured by the equipment had not the original chattel contained a fluctuating provision.

Another type of loan arrangement can call for an underlying amortization which is less than normal, to accommodate financing needs which do not parallel a straight-line reduction over the term of the chattel mortgage note. To understand the foregoing, one must first realize that a standard part of all chattel mortgage growth financing is the reduction of the borrowings over a fixed period through regular monthly payments—until the loan is fully repaid. Now, although it can sometimes be clearly projected that such a program can be fully liquidated at a certain future date, the repayment funds may not be available on a straight-line basis. For example, where a 36-month term loan is involved with equal monthly amortization payments stipulated, 1/36 of the repayment funds would theoretically have to become available each month on a straight-line basis in order to "live with" the amortization requirements comfortably. Too often this is not the case; however, the lender, in recognizing this, can still be quite confident that the loan can be fully repaid at the end of the term. Let us say that a firm wants to borrow $90,000 for three years to make production improvements which will yield profit of more than that figure. However, it will take a learning period on the use of the new facilities so that the added profits will not begin to be realized cash-wise until after the first year. Therefore, most of the repayment funds will accrue to the borrower during the latter part of this financing arrangement and he will have to rely on his present profit flow during the earlier stages.

To accommodate such a situation, the chattel loan

can be written with a rate of amortization which does not parallel the term of the loan. In other words, you could have a three-year term with a "five-year" amortization. This means that, although the entire loan is due in three years, the amortization is set up *as if* it were a five-year loan (instead of repaying 1/36 of the principal each month, only 1/60 per month is required); therefore the amortization requirement is subnormal to the term of the loan. Obviously, when the entire loan is to be repaid at the end of the third year, 40% of the loan still remains unpaid. This unpaid portion is referred to as the *balloon*.

CHATTEL LOAN BALLOONS

The use of final balloon payments, although it may appear gimmicky, is accepted as a respectable procedure in the financial community. As we have explained, it is frequently employed to tailor a financing program to the operating projections of a particular business; this is certainly economic feasibility. On the other hand, some loans involving balloons are also arranged with full knowledge that they *cannot* be repaid in full at the end of the stipulated term; but this format is still used to satisfy certain requirements of the lender.

It is a basic credit concept that loan risk increases with the length of the loan term. Long-term business loans are considered riskier than short-term loans because the lender must extend his forecast of creditworthiness farther into the future. Whereas first mortgages on residences can be long-term based on the stability of the housing market and practical lack of real depreciation, a going business is subject to many future uncertainties of marketing, technology, and competition. The introduction of new types of machinery can render obsolete even well-maintained equipment. For this reason, an institution which makes equipment chattel loans would prefer to project only three or four years into the future, then "take another look" to see if it is safe to continue the financing. At the time of the second look the loan will probably be well secured because of the intervening paydown, and, if other phases of the borrower's picture remain satisfactory, the loan will undoubtedly be renewed, possibly on an even easier basis than the original amortization.

There is another point to be realized by a businessman seeking long-term growth capital; namely, the requirements the *lender* must meet with regard to the liquidity of *his* portfolio. Most financial institutions in the commercial field have liquidity requirements imposed upon them, either through banking regulations, indentures to debenture holders, or agreement with investors. The liquidity requirement usually refers to the average term of loans outstanding, which is supposed to be the collectability of the portfolio. One lending institution might have, for example, a liquidity requirement of 180 days; since this is to be the average of all loans outstanding, it would be assumed that, should the necessity ever arise, 50% of the portfolio could be liquidated in six months. Because many institutions do the bulk of their lending on a very short-term basis (e.g., 90-day lines of banks, monthly receivable financing by commercial finance companies) they can also take longer-term paper, usually from two to seven years. This is because, averaged against the short-term borrowings, these longer loans will not throw the portfolio beyond the liquidity limit. Most equipment loans range from two to five years in term; six- and seven-year terms are also possible. However, it should be obvious that a lender will make fewer seven-year than five-year loans, and will lean toward the shorter-term fund placement opportunities when the liquidity limit average is neared. Further, there are other institutions which have maximum time limits on their loans, many of these being at the three- and five-year level.

For the above reasons a businessman is ill-advised to charge into a lender's office with demands for the longest-term loan possible; he may be asking for something which is simply not available. On the other hand, the same final results may be obtained by seeking a shorter-term financing with a balloon, which will probably be renewed as a new term loan if all has gone well when the balloon payment becomes due.

CHATTEL MORTGAGE CREDIT CRITERIA

Unlike the case of secured current asset financing where the primary credit emphasis is placed on the quality of the collateral, sound secured growth capital lending is predicated somewhat equally on several criteria. These are:

1. Justification of the loan purposes
2. Value of the collateral
3. Cash flow or source of repayment

If it can be demonstrated that growth capital can be used to achieve production efficiency, cost savings, or increase of markets, the expected enhancement of profits and worth are the usual justifications for a financing program. Whereas machinery and equipment will probably be the collateral for the borrowing, the use of the funds is not necessarily limited to purchase of additional equipment unless this is the indicated application. Any general business purpose is eligible as long as it promises possibilities of success. If $50,000 borrowed on equipment is used to launch an advertising campaign which increases profits far beyond this figure, the loan purpose is equally justified as if the same money were invested in some new machines to create the same profit increase. Normally, a fairly simple description of the purpose and explanation of the way the benefits are to accrue will suffice in the case of most small or middle-size applications. If a growth capital loan of half a million dollars or more is desired it is advisable that this subject be covered more thoroughly as part of a detailed cash-flow projection (see Chapter XI, Private Placements).

EVALUATION OF COLLATERAL

Every item in the fixed asset category of the balance sheet has worth; however, some will not qualify as collateral for growth capital chattels. "Leasehold improvements" are ineligible. Special patterns, molds and dies, although they may represent sizable investments, are rated fairly low because they may have limited use outside of the borrower's business. Standard machinery and equipment—productive, handling, office, or even rolling stock—are highly acceptable. There are further qualifications, even in the eligible collateral category, depending on the present condition of the equipment and its *local* resale value. Note that the location does have some bearing on the value; equipment located in a remote area may require costly shipping to dispose of it, whereas in metropolitan Los Angeles, for example, where the growth of small industry is heavy, any equipment auction is assured of drawing good crowds who buy at top prices.

To establish the loan value of equipment, an *appraisal* is usually required. There are certain companies whose entire business is making appraisals, and their estimates will frequently be acceptable. However, because the appraisal companies work primarily for insurance and legal purposes, some lenders prefer appraisals from auctioneers whose primary function it is to dispose of the equipment they appraise. Further, all lending institutions tend to work with a few local appraisers with whom they have had previous experience. It is advisable, therefore, to obtain the names of such appraisers from banks or financial institutions with whom you may hope to establish a relationship.

There are three types of appraisal evaluations:

1. "Replacement Value"—the cost of going out to purchase new equipment on today's market, to replace the used equipment being appraised.

2. "Sound Market Value"—the theoretical going market value of a piece of used equipment if one sought to purchase it from a dealer, or, if there were a "willing buyer" immediately available for the equipment in its present condition.

3. "Auction, or Liquidation, Value"—the present distress value of the equipment—as is, where is; in other words, what it could bring on the block, under the auctioneer's hammer.

Whereas the first two evaluations above are meaningful for insurance purposes, it is the third valuation, the *Auction Value*, which influences a lender. This does not mean that the other valuations—which the appraiser will usually supply in parallel columns—should be eliminated; they serve a good psychological purpose. If a lender notes, for example, that the auction value is considerably lower than the "Sound Market" value, he will feel more confident about the realistic possibilities of disposal. A good example of such comparisons can be found in the following appraisal totals which were submitted to me by a large machine shop as this chapter was being written:

Replacement value	$1,267,515
Sound market value	828,307
Auction value	472,481

The above relationship is fairly typical of a business which has purchased substantial equipment over a period of years so that its total fixed asset amount is quite large

before deducting depreciation. However, it was interesting to note that, on the balance sheet of the company
whose appraisal appears above, the depreciated value was
only $295,630, or far *less* than the auction value. This was
the result of accelerated depreciation being taken, and
therefore this company was actually able to borrow *more
than 100%* of the book value of its equipment.

From experience I have found that there is a fairly
standard relationship between auction value and depreciated book value; knowing this may be helpful if you wish
to estimate the auction value of your equipment before
bothering to make an appraisal. If a business has been in
existence more than five years, and has taken normal
depreciation on its equipment, the *net* book value of this
equipment *after* deducting depreciation is usually roughly
equivalent to the auction value (assuming that the equipment has been maintained in decent condition).

LOAN RATIOS TO APPRAISALS

Although occasional spot advances may be made in
fairly high ratio to cost of individual pieces of newly
purchased equipment, a substantial growth capital loan
will usually be made on the security of all of the machinery and equipment of a business firm and, if the
latter be the case, the percentage of advance will run
anywhere from 25% to 75% of the book value. The availability of an auction appraisal will resolve this wide
disparity of advance percentages. Very simply, you should
be able to obtain a loan at least *equal* to your auction
value appraisal total. If the lender had to make a disposal
on very short notice thereafter, he should still come out
whole.

In fact, a lender will usually advance from 100% to
150% of auction appraisal in a *going business* situation.
Here again we see evidence of the principle of *limited
future forecasting*. Let us say that a three-year loan is

arranged for $120,000 with equal monthly repayments of $3,000 (plus a balloon of $12,000). Since auction value is determined to be $100,000 in this example, the lender is making a 120% advance. At the time of approving the credit, the lender feels he understands his client's business sufficiently well to postulate its continuing on an even keel for at least a year. At the end of the year the borrower will have reduced the loan by $36,000 (12 months × $3,000) so that the balance would stand at $84,000—a figure surely not in excess of the auction value, even including the realistic additional depreciation during the intervening 12 months. Therefore, in this going-business situation, the lender has not violated any conservative lending principles.

GUARANTEED APPRAISALS

In some instances an entrepreneur may have difficulty convincing a lender to rely sufficiently on an auction appraisal to approve a particular financing program. This difficulty can arise when the lender is located in another city so that he feels unsure of local conditions in the borrower's area; or when the lender is unfamiliar with the category of equipment to be chatteled and without trade contacts for its disposal in the event of a default; or simply, as it sometimes happens, when the lender cannot perform many of his functions of evaluation within an urgent time limit set by the borrower. To overcome these difficulties, the use of a *guaranteed appraisal* is very effective. In some cases of marginal applications, where a lender is "on the fence" about granting credit approval, a guaranteed appraisal can provide the positive margin.

The guaranteed appraisal is provided only by an auctioneering firm; in fact, it is doubtful that a lender would accept it from any other source. In making such an appraisal the auctioneer *guarantees* to purchase the chatteled equipment for a specified price at the time demand is made, and to make payment directly to the lender. Usually the appraisal guarantee decreases over the life of the loan, parallel to the amortization of the loan.

For example, a three-year loan of $400,000 might be sought with $100,000 per year amortization and a $100,-000 balloon payment at the end of the third year. To cover this situation, an auctioneer would issue a guarantee which, in effect, would say: "I will buy this equipment now for $400,000; at the end of the first year for $300,000; at the end of the second year for $200,000, and, when your loan is fully due at the end of the third year, for $100,000." Since the lender realizes that, if demand is made, the auctioneer is responsible for repayment of the loan and, by virtue of being actively engaged in the auctioneering business, will be capable of holding a liquidation sale to meet his obligation, he has confidence in the arrangement. Also, the fact that an auctioneer will not put his guarantee on the line without being familiar with the equipment and its local market is quite reassuring.

These guaranteed appraisals are necessarily more costly to the borrower. Generally the fee runs several percent of the amount being guaranteed. Considering the seeming risk of the guarantor, and the benefit to be gained by the borrower, this is actually quite fair. The reason some auctioneers are willing to perform such services for a relatively modest charge is they feel that, if called upon to fulfill their guarantee, they will do so through an auction about which they feel confident and well-qualified, and that they will earn the auctioneer's fee which is the bread and butter of their regular business.

CASH FLOW REQUIREMENTS

With a good purpose established, and with ample collateral as security for a growth financing program, all responsible lending institutions ask one further question: What is the source of repayment? No lender wants to own equipment; that is not his business. Despite all the legal protections and provisions he makes to hedge against possible foreclosure in the event of forfeiture, the lender probably would not approve the credit in the first place if he thought, from the outset, that a forfeiture was likely. For this reason the *cash flow* must be shown to be sufficient to meet the obligation.

The cash flow of a business is the profit plus depreciation. Many credit analysts will figure profit before taxes because they feel that, if the profit lessened, the tax would likewise decrease, and also that the taxes paid in previous years can be carried forward against a loss year to provide a cushion. In any event, depreciation is always added back to the profit in a cash flow computation because it is a *non-cash* expense; it does not remove dollars from the company bank account as it is merely a bookkeeping entry. Therefore, a business which shows a profit of $30,000, after all expenses including depreciation of $12,000, actually has a cash flow of $42,000 per annum. Against this cash flow will be applied all sums which are required for the repayment of indebtedness, such as the type of loan we are discussing, or existing contracts for purchase of equipment made on an installment basis. These are the only significant items, since all operating expenses have already been deducted in arriving at that increment of cash flow represented by the profit. If the total of these items—plus the amortization requirement of the new financing under consideration—does not exceed the *demonstrated* cash flow, loan approval should be easy. If sufficient cash flow is not demonstrated by financial statements reflecting the current operation, then the borrower should be prepared to show how the new financing program will provide the needed extra increment. This can be best accomplished by detailed cost figures showing comparisons between present and future operations which reflect production efficiencies, or by a delineated marketing analysis and projection showing how increased sales will create profits by spreading the administrative expense and increasing the gross income.

DISCOUNT AND ADD-ON

Although the financing cost of many chattel mortgage loans is expressed in terms of simple interest charges, there is also a great prevalence of writing this type of loan with *discount-interest* or *add-on*. The practice of discounting interest was inherited from the English banking system. In England (and later also in the United States) many banks followed the practice of deducting (discounting) the interest for the full term at the time of funding a loan. For example, if a loan of $100,000 at 6% interest were granted for one year, the bank would discount $6,000 in full payment of one year's interest, and advance $94,000 to the borrower. The bank was receiving $6,000 income on $94,000 which, instead of stated interest of 6%, was actually income of almost 6½%. For short periods of time like one year, and particularly where there is no amortization, the difference is slight. However, where regular monthly payments are made over the life of a loan, the effective interest cost changes considerably.

If you have ever financed the purchase of an automobile through a bank or other institution, you have undoubtedly been given a type of discounted loan. A slight difference has evolved, however; the interest, instead of being deducted from the total loan amount, is *added*. Handled in this manner, the interest charge is known as an *add-on*. The usual car loan calls for monthly payments over a term of several years, and it will therefore illustrate the true differential of add-on interest.

Take, for example, a bank auto finance loan of $2,000 for two years at 6%. The bank will charge 6% of $2,000 for each of the two years ($120 × 2) and therefore make an add-on of $240 so that the loan will have a total face value of $2,240. The loan will be repaid in equal monthly payments. The total amount of money advanced, however, is $2,000 and—since it will be repaid down to zero at the end of the term—the *average* advance during the entire life of the loan is $1,000. Now, if you note that the bank has charged $120 per year for this average loan of $1,000, it then becomes obvious that the actual interest rate is about 12% on a "6%" auto financing contract. (Actuarially, it is claimed that the rate is closer to 11%.)

The above example has been used not only to explain the function of an add-on, but also to illustrate the widespread use of this type of interest charge—and at the level cited. There is good reason; namely, the handling cost involved in making the equipment chattels, evaluating them as collateral, and processing the monthly payments. An add-on of 6% is probably the pivotal rate charged on good quality chattel financing. Some very prime situations may qualify for an add-on as low as 4%, others require 7% or more. The add-on rate may go as high as 10%; however, this level is usually found only in consumer financing involving contracts with relatively low face amounts.

CONDITIONAL SALES PURCHASES

The purchase of production equipment or other physical assets on a time-payment basis is now a commonplace practice in American industry. The seller of machinery will accept a nominal down payment and make delivery upon the execution of a *conditional sales contract*. Legal ownership of the property is retained by the seller until the buyer has made all the required monthly payments over the term of the contract, which usually runs from 12 to 36 months. Because this procedure is primarily an implement of sales stimulation through financing, we will defer a full discussion of it until a later chapter. However, it is obvious that conditional sales contracts provide a form of financing equipment purchases in addition to the methods already described. There are several specific differences, among which are the following:

1. Conditional purchasing usually involves no legal recordings.

2. Whereas title is retained by the conditional seller under contract, the purchaser has ownership of property under a chattel mortgage, subject to forfeiture.

3. The financing of a conditional sales contract is almost always *with recourse to the seller.*

The third point explains why a businessman who has obtained financing from a bank on one piece of equipment is sometimes later unable to obtain from the same bank financing on a second similar piece of equipment. There might have been only one difference in the two transactions; namely, that the first purchase was made from a machinery dealer whereas the second piece of equipment was obtained from the surplus stock of another manufacturer. In the second instance the bank or financing institution would not have been presented with acceptable "dealer recourse."

No lender wants to own equipment through the forfeiture of a contract, because he is not in the equipment-selling business. Therefore, the presence of a machinery dealer in the picture, whose day-to-day activities keep him in the machinery market, is necessary to the lender. This is true whether new or used equipment is involved, and explains why, even if you have made a very good buy on a piece of machinery at an auction, you may have more difficulty in financing the purchase than if you had paid 30% more for the same machinery from a dealer. It is true that dealers may be on recourse on contracts many times their net worth, but it is not solely the repayment guarantee the lender seeks. Rather, he wants assurance that, if the contract is forfeited, the dealer, who is well qualified to do so, is responsible for stepping into the picture and reselling the equipment elsewhere. This fact has occasionally given rise to an unusual practice wherein a business firm which desires financing on existing equipment, and which also requires some additional new items, will sell some of its equipment to a dealer and repurchase it on a contract that includes the additional new pieces desired—the entire transaction being financed by an institution on the basis of the dealer recourse.

LEASING

The technique of leasing certainly qualifies as one of the basic methods of equipment financing although, technically, no borrowing is involved in its format. Under a leasing arrangement, the financial institution will actually own equipment which it leases to a business firm for its exclusive use over a specific number of years. Originally, the concept of leasing as a major business financing tool was limited to isolated very large applications, such as the leasing of railroad cars and engines to railroad companies by equipment trusts, or to manufacturers who preferred to lease patented and special machinery (such as IBM and U.S. Shoe Machinery Corporation), rather than selling it. From such beginnings a much broader scale industry has evolved which leases such heterogeneous things as office machines, traffic barricades, turret lathes, motel furnishings, display equipment, offshore oil-drilling barges, etc.

Instead of lender and borrower, we have here a

leasing company (lessor) and its customer (lessee). The legal requirement for demonstration of dominion is quite different because the lessor is not truly a lender or creditor. In fact, the lessor's primary requirement is to show that he is the actual *owner* of the equipment of which the lessee has exclusive use; and this is done simply by affixing a nameplate or label to each such piece of equipment, identifying its ownership by the leasing company.

The classic advantages claimed for leasing are:

1. Facilitation of purchase of needed equipment
2. Release of funds which would otherwise be tied up in ownership of fixed assets
3. Possible tax advantages
4. Improvement of the financial statement

The first two of the above reasons are obvious; and, since the funds of the leasing company replace those of the lessee invested in certain pieces of equipment, working and growth capital are made available in much the same way as by the other methods of equipment financing, such as chattel mortgage lending.

TAX ASPECTS OF LEASING

The possible tax advantages of the use of industrial leasing may or may not apply; this is a question which is governed by the facts involved in each individual situation. No modern leasing institution will make sweeping claims of tax advantages, yet there is no question that, to a number of companies, substantial tax benefits have accrued. Even situations which parallel earlier beneficial cases cannot be accepted as providing a firm indication of present benefits because the applicable tax laws and interpretations are constantly changing in this field. It is not fitting to go into a discussion of tax aspects of leasing in this book because of the breadth of the subject; however, the basic question concerns the allowability of all the lease payments as a tax-deductible expense when the underlying equipment can be purchased at the end of the lease for a fraction of its value (thereafter continued to be used by the lessee, or sold by him for a profit which might only be taxable on a capital gains basis).

There are, indeed, certain leases which might qualify easily for tax write-offs. A typical case is where equipment is required for a particular project with a known finite period of usage; for example, construction machinery needed for a long-range dam project where the entire life of the equipment will probably be spent on the project. Defense industries will lease certain production machinery for particular application to specific contracts —particularly if it is a cost-plus contract. This gives the defense contractor a much better write-off than the government-allowed depreciation. Leasing contracts which tie in closely with the normal life of the underlying equipment are more likely eligible for tax benefits. For example, I have seen repeated acceptance of deductibility of some supermarket equipment leases where the individual items on the lease were set up according to normal life usage, varying from four to eight years, Of course this meant that the lease payments were higher in the earlier years of the lease, instead of being uniform throughout, but the total payments were unchanged and the tax objective was attained.

While the tax aspect has some significance, in the greatest number of cases where leasing is being used *as a tool of business finance,* there is little materiality to the tax avoidance. However, as we will see below, there is a definite possibility of *deferment* of taxes which presents management with the advantage of having more money to use for growth and retained surplus prior to the time the tax liability must ultimately be squared away.

LEASING CREDIT CRITERIA

There is great similarity between leasing credit criteria and the standards involved in the granting of chattel mortgage loans. As described earlier in this chapter, the prime considerations are the intrinsic value of the equipment, justification of the purpose, and source of repayment or cash flow of the borrower (in this case, the lessee).

The lessor shares with a chattel mortgage lender the policy of avoiding repossession of equipment, therefore he must be satisfied that the cash flow of the lessee is, or will be, sufficient to cover all of the lessee's annual payout requirements including the new lease under consideration. You will recall that cash flow consists of net profits plus depreciation; and, since lease rentals payments are tax deductible, the net profits are computed into tax flow *before* taxes. The general financial strength requirements of a leasing client are also similar to chattel lending standards, but when specialized equipment of restricted general use is involved, a leasing arrangement may demand somewhat higher creditworthiness. On the other hand, leasing companies seem to have easier credit criteria where the leased equipment has widespread use.

LEASING ADVANCE LIMITS

It is almost general that the financing of equipment through leasing makes possible a higher ratio of fund advance to collateral value than by any other technique. As you will presently see, almost 100% financing is achieved in purchase-leases. The most obvious reason for this practice is that ownership of the equipment is retained by the lessor; it is not necessary to defend a prior lien against other creditors, nor is any involved legal proceeding like a foreclosure required for repossession. The lessor is in position to take his property whenever the lease terms are not met—and his claim to it is unchallenged. Because earlier leasing was done primarily with substantial lessees, and because of the equipment ownership aspect, the more liberal advance principles have carried into the entire leasing field.

Leasing is available primarily from specialized leasing companies. In addition, a number of the major commercial finance companies and banks have leasing subsidiaries or divisions. It is interesting to note that the commercial finance companies which may restrict chattel loans to 60% to 75% of fair market value (100% to 125% of auction value) will, in their leasing divisions, follow the higher advancing practices of the leasing industry. This leads us into what is probably the major advantage of leasing: the benefits which can accrue from the availability of larger working capital.

PURCHASE-LEASE FUND AVAILABILITY

When leasing is used to purchase new equipment from a supplier, there exists a typical purchase-lease arrangement. In such a procedure a prior agreement is reached between lessor and client (lessee) relative to the terms of the leasing contract, including approval of the new equipment to be bought. Thereafter, the lessor will issue its own purchase orders to the manufacturers of the desired equipment and will pay for this equipment in full when it is delivered to the lessee. Since new equipment is purchased at its standard price, this means that the leasing company is making a 100% advance on market price. Actually, the lessor will require that the lessee put up a *lease deposit*—usually the first month's rent plus one additional month's rent for each year of the contract life of the lease. For example, a five-year lease might call for a total deposit equivalent to six months' rent payments. The lessor can view this as a reserve, however, an advance of approximately 90% of *market value* is still being made on the equipment—and this is certainly a high level of advance compared to other methods of equipment financing.

Whereas other techniques of equipment acquisition may cost less than leasing (certainly cash purchases without financing cost the least) they represent money savings on the financing of the purchase only. Offsetting this saving can be the loss of opportunity to make a profit on the additional capital which leasing makes available. This is demonstrable particularly when a business which needs capital is making a fair return on its investment. Take, for example, a company with an investment of $100,000, doing an annual sales volume of $500,000 at a net profit, after all expenses, of 5% of sales, or $25,000. Such a company is earning 25% annually on its investment and, if its growth merely requires the use of more capital, it can be assumed that the money freed by leasing will also create a 25% annual profit return for the business. Under such circumstances, using a normal five-year leasing program and projecting the cumulative earnings effect over a ten-year period from the beginning date of the lease, there can be demonstrated the possibility of earning approximately $50,000 more on the freed capital than if a cash purchase had been made. Such a saving does not include the cost and profit advantages which could arise from the actual use of the new equipment. Of course, this reasoning does not apply to a company which has all the money it can use, so that the employment of freed capital would not create additional 5% earnings (however, it is obvious that it was not for such firms that this book was written).

Most of the earnings advantages of freed capital come from the fact that a leasing program provides greater fund availability *during the early stages* of the contract. This is illustrated by a study reported in the *Harvard Business Review* [1] which analyzes comparative cash availabilities under several methods of acquiring equipment. These methods include five-year leasing, full cash purchase, 75% bank loan at prime interest, and installment plan with very nominal 4½% add-on. The comparison is based on the theoretical purchase of $100,000 of new equipment, as follows:

Method	Year End	Excess Freed Cash Through Leasing
Cash purchase	1	$79,026
"	2	58,999
"	3	39,913
"	4	21,773
"	5	4,580
75% bank loan	1	20,466
"	2	16,591
"	3	13,369
"	4	10,805
"	5	8,900
Installment purchase	1	20,281
"	2	15,424
"	3	10,241
"	4	3,121
"	5	—3,236

As the table shows, there is an early freeing of additional capital funds under leasing programs which can be significant when there is a potential good return on such funds if they can be made available.

1. Pros and Cons of Leasing, Frank Griesinger, Harvard Business Review, March 1955.

SALE-LEASEBACKS

Whereas purchase leases primarily involve new equipment, it is possible to obtain leasing accommodation on equipment which is not purchased from a machinery supplier. In such cases, the equipment is sold by the prospective lessee to the leasing company, then *leased back* to the lessee. A variety of situations can qualify in this category. For example, a user of hot-forming exotic metal presses designed and built his own presses, sold them at his cost to a leasing company, then leased them back. In acquisitions, many acquiring companies have had a leasing company buy the equipment of the company being purchased, the equipment then being taken back on a lease by the acquiring company. In some instances, a going business will sell all of its presently used equipment to a leasing company, then lease it back, usually when its needs most closely parallel the financing aims prevalent in normal chattel mortgage borrowing. It is possible that such transactions will not yield as high an advance on the equipment value as do purchase-leases involving new equipment; however, they will probably equal the advance which might be obtained through chattel mortgage borrowing.

LEASING CONTRACT TERMS

The great majority of leasing contracts range in term from two to eight years. Longer leases are usually special situations and call for lessees of major financial stature. Actually, leases running less than three years are not too frequently seen except when covering automotive rolling stock. Three-year leases can be written to cover lower value items which depreciate quickly, such as office and apartment house furnishings. Electric office typewriters, for example, are widely written on four-year leases. The greatest number of industrial leases are, however, written on five-year terms, with much of this type of standard equipment being put on leases which run from five to eight years. Now, here is an important point: when we speak of the term of the lease we are referring to the *basic lease term*. After this term expires there are the following types of options:

1. Outright purchase of the residual
2. Lease renewal options at reduced rent

Under the first method, an option is given to the lessee to purchase the equipment at a price which almost totally discounts the original cost. The leasing company refers to this price as the *residual value*. There are no fixed practices by which residual values are set, although they do not vary widely. The usual residual is about 10% of the original cost of the equipment. Obviously this gives the lessee the opportunity of purchasing the equipment for a fraction of its real value at the end of the basic lease term. However, the use of purchase options is being widely discontinued because such stipulations can remove some of the depreciation incentives which make it possible for the leasing company to extend such reasonable rates to its lessees. From the lessee's point of view, the value of the purchase option has also realistically been seen to lessen. If there were to be any tax advantages, the exercise of a purchase option should certainly erase the façade of a true lease with deductible rent payments. Moreover, the *renewal option* can be as economical, if not more, to the lessee.

Most renewal options run from 2% to 5% *per year* of the original list price of the equipment. (Typically, they may begin at 5% the first year, then drop to 4% the second year, 3% the third, and 2% thereafter.) For example, a usual $100,000 five-year equipment lease might require

$25,000 rental per year, but, after completion of the basic lease term, the subsequent rental would average only about $3,000 per year. This rental is so low that most firms find it less than having to pay the purchase option price, and, since the renewal options are for only one year at a time, the lessee is not "locked in" with investment in an older piece of equipment for which he may find a better, more modern replacement.

LEASING RATES

Leasing charges vary widely, which is only natural because this form of financing is being extended into situations of varying risks and amounts. The traditional and most generally used format of leasing charges is the add-on, the percentage of which ranges primarily from 4½% to 7%. As described earlier in connection with chattel mortgages, this percentage is multiplied by the contract term in years to get the total charge. For example, a 5% add-on for a $100,000 five-year lease would be $25,000 ($5,000 times five years), and the total lease contract would be $125,000. From this figure is deducted the lease deposit, to obtain the remaining balance. Usually the add-on is quoted as a separate increment to the contract, in other instances the lease is set up as, for example, 2% of the equipment cost per month (which could be roughly equivalent to a 5% five-year add-on).

Some of the more substantial leases made to very well-rated companies are written on a simple interest basis, usually ranging from 7% to 9% simple *stated* interest, which is not too significantly lower on an actual money-cost basis than the more conservative add-ons. It is true that there are a few additional sources of lease financing which are unusually inexpensive, but these are applicable only to special situations. Such arrangements are offered by leasing operations which are part of larger companies which have substantial taxable income. These companies have gone into leasing because, by owning the equipment which they lease, they may benefit taxwise from the depreciation and also, possibly, from the "investment tax credit." As a result of these tax savings, rates which run even slightly below 6% *actual* simple interest (as opposed to stated interest) can be stipulated in a lease. However, the lessee must be quite financially strong, the equipment must be new and have a widespread general use, and the leases must be at last $100,000. In such cases, also, there can be no purchase option as it would defeat the reasoning which has made the arrangement available on such an attractive basis.

At this point, I would like once again to discuss the materiality of the presence of a purchase option. As was noted earlier in this section, renewal lease options are usually given on such reasonable terms that practically all advantages of purchase are eliminated; also, the lessee is freed from having an investment locked into the purchase of equipment which was probably rapidly obsolescing. Despite knowledge of these reasons, some businessmen worry about not being able to purchase the leased equipment if they later desire to do so. Other businessmen say, "After I've practically paid for the equipment by completing the lease, I'd like to be able to own it." There are satisfactory answers to both of these positions. Actually, no leasing company wants to wind up with equipment in its possession. It is in the business of leasing, not manufacturing, distributing, or oil drilling. As long as lease payments are met, no lessor wants to remove equipment and embark on an uncertain quest for a new lessee or buyer. Therefore, it is possible that, if approached after the termination of a lease, a lessor will, under special circumstances, agree to make a sale. I have known other special cases where lessees were allowed to negotiate purchases midway through a lease contract. The provision for such possibilities obviously cannot be pre-agreed or inserted into the lease contract as it would surely negate the façade of a true lease which can be necessary to serve purposes of the lessor and/or the lessee. Most businessmen now realize the fallacy of becoming "equipment poor"—having their profits absorbed in a persistent build-up of equipment, some of which is even incapable of continuing to earn. Therefore the older "pride of ownership" attitudes are disappearing. Either through very nominal lease renewal options, or through later negotiated purchases, a lessee can be assured of continued use of leased equipment as long as he desires, and of still being able to benefit from the other advantages which induced him to execute the leasing contract in the first place.

BALANCE SHEET ADVANTAGES

The two major forms of growth capital financing—chattel mortgage lending and leasing—provide special opportunities to re-structure the balance sheet of a financial statement so that the picture is reflected more advantageously. Discussing this will provide a partial explanation of why I think it is well to delineate the broad concept of "working capital" into the two categories of *working* capital and *growth* capital.

As explained in the early chapters, one of the characteristics of working capital is that it is used to accommodate cyclical needs over the period of one year, therefore it is typically short-term. In fact, true working capital loans are usually arranged on terms of one year or less (as in the standard unsecured bank borrowing programs described in Chapter 4). As a result, these borrowings are reflected under the *current* liability section of the balance sheet because all monies technically due in one year or less must be so reflected.

If, indeed, a loan under our definition of growth

capital is intended for a term of several years, it is sometimes helpful to see that it is set up differently—not, for
example, as a series of renewable 90-day unsecured bank
credits, but so that only *the first year's* indebtedness is
reflected under current liabilities on the balance sheet.

In our earlier discussions of financial statement
analysis to determine creditworthiness of a company seeking financing, we saw that the *current ratio* (ratio of current assets to current liabilities) and net current asset
position (current assets minus current liabilities) were
regarded as significant criteria. These two indices are
definitely affected when leasing and chattel mortgage
financing are substituted for current borrowing. The following three balance sheets of the same hypothetical
company illustrate why this is true.

In the first balance sheet the statement reflects the
use of a $250,000 unsecured bank line, $180,000 of which
was needed to finance additional equipment:

Assets

Cash	$ 40,000	
Accounts receivable	160,000	
Inventory	120,000	
Total current assets		$320,000
Machinery & equipment (net after depr.)		$450,000
Other assets and prepaid items		80,000
Total assets		$850,000

Liabilities

Notes payable, bank	$250,000
Accounts payable	60,000
Total current	$310,000
Other liabilities	70,000
Total liabilities	$380,000
Net worth	470,000
Total liabilities & net worth	$850,000

In the above illustration, current ratio is barely 1 to 1. Net current assets (working capital) appear to be $10,000. Now, let us assume this same company arranges a $180,000 five-year chattel mortgage loan. Since only one-fifth of the loan is due in any one year, $36,000 is all that must be reflected as a current liability; and, since out of the $250,000 bank line, $180,000 will have been switched into the chattel mortgage loan, the remaining $70,000 will constitute the only part of the unsecured bank loan which will be reflected under current liabilities. This appears as follows:

Assets

Cash	$ 40,000	
Accounts receivable	160,000	
Inventory	120,000	
Total current assets		$320,000
Machinery & equipment (net)		$450,000
Other assets and prepaid items		80,000
Total assets		$850,000

Liabilities

Notes payable, unsecured, bank		$ 70,000
Current portion, chattel mortgage note		36,000
Accounts payable		60,000
Total current liabilities		$166,000
Chattel mortgage loan	$180,000	
Less current portion	—36,000	
		$144,000
Other liabilities		70,000
Total liabilities		$380,000
Net worth		470,000
Total liabilities and net worth		$850,000

As you can see, net worth remained the same, yet now the current ratio has changed from 1 to 1 in the first example to a quite healthy approximate 2 to 1. Net cur-

rent asset position has improved from $10,000 to $154,-
000. On both counts, the statement reflects drastic
improvement.

Finally, let us assume this same company substituted
a $180,000 sale and lease-back for its chattel mortgage
loan in the same amount. To compare the three statements simply, we will also assume that the equipment involved in the loan (then sold and leased back in this
final example) had a book value of $180,000 also. There-
fore, in addition to the removal of the chattel mortgage
loan from the statement, the book value of the equipment
will be removed from fixed assets, as follows:

Assets

Cash	$ 40,000	
Accounts receivable	160,000	
Inventory	120,000	
Total current assets		$320,000
Machinery & equipment (net)		$270,000
Other assets & prepaid items		80,000
Total assets		$670,000

Liabilities

Notes payable, unsecured, bank	$ 70,000	
Accounts payable	60,000	
Total current liabilities		$130,000
Other liabilities		$ 70,000
Total liabilities		$200,000
Net worth		470,000
Total liabilities and net worth		$670,000

Note that the net worth still remains the same, yet
current ratio is now nearly 2½ to 1 and net current
assets have increased to $190,000. Of course, in the final
picture reflecting a leasing arrangement, the debt-to-
worth ratio is by far the lowest of the three arrangements
illustrated.

Actually, this does not reveal the whole picture. Lenders and the better accounting firms now insist on adding footnotes to financial statements indicating the presence of a leasing contract and the obligations to pay under same. Further, there is increasing pressure to reflect one year's rent payments in the current liability section of the balance sheet. This would make the second and third examples above reflect identical current ratios and working capital positions. Some leasing proponents claim that lease rental payments for the next twelve months should not appear in the curent liability section, and they point out that normal rent on a building being occupied under lease is never reflected as a liability. However, the payments do have to be made on a current basis on the equipment lease, and here the parallel draws more closely to the chattel mortgage loan situation. For this reason, bank and financial institution analysts of today will tend to treat both obligations in the same manner. Therefore, as far as realistic improvement of the balance sheet is concerned, leasing will create no further advantages over chattel mortgage borrowing, but both techniques do provide definite improvement over the type of open line borrowing illustrated in the first balance sheet illustrated above.

CHAPTER 7

Package Financing

The foregoing chapters of this book have covered elementary and intermediate techniques of business finance. Before moving ahead to more advanced and specialized procedures, it may be wise to review the basic techniques in the context of familiarity with every variation so far described. Now that you have been presented with a number of alternatives, you should begin to think about how to select the financing methods best for your specific business needs.

This is particularly true when more than one tool of finance must be used. And here we return to the distinction made in Chapter II between short- and long-term capital requirements. Taking a slightly different approach, you should be able to determine whether what you seek is best obtained on a secured or unsecured basis. If your needs are high in ratio to your worth, secured financing will be the indicated route to take, particularly if the increased growth and profits anticipated will justify the higher cost of such financing. On the other hand, you should consider unsecured borrowing first if your statement will justify it to the extent that your needs are properly met. Many situations can be satisfactorily accommodated by a single unsecured bank line, based on the criteria described in Chapter IV. This is particularly true of needs which develop during the early stages of a business when a modest amount of money is needed. It is also true much later in the game, when a company has achieved a strong financial condition.

UNSECURED COMBINATIONS

There are a number of instances where the single unsecured bank line of credit, extended on the regular 90-day renewable notes, may be unsuited to the needs of a business. As was mentioned earlier, this type of credit line is appropriate for a cyclical fluctuation over a one-year period. Because of the requirement for an annual "resting" of unsecured 90-day note lines, the businessman must be confident that, during his yearly slack period, he can function without any outside financing whatsoever. In many instances this is true; in others, only partly true. If the latter is the case, the financing need should be *broken down* into its short-term and long-term components.

A typical situation would involve the usual requirement for financing yearly build-ups to peak sales activity —plus a specialized need for specific funds to purchase equipment (or enlarge a selling operation, launch a new promotional campaign, etc.). The specialized need is justified by expectation of greater profits; however, several years of profits will be required to repay the financing of the project. It is obvious that such an increment of the total financing program must be arranged, not as 90-day renewable note credits, but as a term loan. Let us say that a distributor requires a total of $136,000 credit for all his needs, and that his statement qualifies for an unsecured credit in this amount. Included in this requirement is an expenditure of $36,000 for new material handling and packaging equipment which will take several years to pay for itself. The proper approach would be to ask the bank for an unsecured line of $136,-000, *broken into two loans*. One loan, in the amount of $100,000, to cover peak seasonal needs, would be structured on 90-day notes with complete payout for at least one month during the slack period. The other loan would be covered by a $36,000 term note, payable over three years at the rate of $1,000 per month.

If the total financing requirement of such a situation is somewhat in excess of the total unsecured line the bank feels it can grant, the desired end may be achieved by suggesting that the $100,000 open line be set up for seasonal fluctuations on an unsecured basis, but that the equipment purchase increment of the loan be switched to a secured transaction by use of a chattel mortgage note. Another combination—which would still maintain the unsecured borrowing position—would be the arrangement with an outside leasing company of a purchase-lease contract for the new equipment. If the company qualifies for the $100,000 unsecured credit, the bank should have little concern about the lease arrangement because the encumbered asset—the new equipment to be purchased —would not have been part of the company assets to which the bank looked in granting the unsecured credit.

SECURED COMBINATIONS

When management realizes that its financing needs are so diverse and so large that the proper solution is the use of secured financing, more complex combinations are possible. These combinations, extending to a number of asset categories for collateral, are usually involved in the *package financing* programs more often supplied by commercial finance companies rather than by banks.

Some of the usual package financing combinations are:

1. Receivables financing and warehouse lending
2. Receivables financing and inventory lien financing
3. Receivables financing and chattel mortgage lending (and possibly plus inventory or warehouse financing)
4. Any of the above in connection with letters of credit for imports

You will note that, regardless of the combination, the presence of receivables financing is a necessary element in the package. This is because the lender will want to have some dominion over the ultimate source of repayment of his loans, which is usually the accounts receivable. Moreover, this requirement also provides the most flexibility for the borrower as, by using proceeds from receivables assignments, the revolving aspect of inventory financing can be expedited. This is demonstrated in the following examples:

(1) A field warehouse with 70% advance on lumber, plus an 80% advance on accounts receivable. The warehouse loan has a maximum of $150,000 and a $25,000 release blanket. When lumber is released from the warehouse, the blanket is reduced in an amount equal to the cost of the released lumber. However, the reductions are quickly reinstated by proceeds from accounts receivable financing, so that the warehouse can continually be drawn from. For example, if $10,000 worth of lumber at cost is released from the warehouse, the 70% loan against it would amount to $7,000. To repay this amount from receivables financing would be simple. The $10,000 cost value lumber would be marked up, e.g., 15%, and sold to a customer for $11,500—an 80% advance on the customer invoice would make $9,200 available, obviously providing more than the $7,000 required to reinstate the warehouse release.

(2) An 80% receivables financing program is pack-

aged with a $250,000 maximum loan against a 60% inventory lien and a three-year chattel mortgage of $72,000. The mortgage is to be reduced $2,000 per month. The company for which this package is arranged averages sales volume of $75,000 per month. An analysis of the cost of goods sold reveals that the products of the company contain a cost of materials averaging 50% of the selling price. Since there is a 60% advance against the inventory lien, it is decided that an amount equal to 30% of sales (60% advance × 50% of selling price) will be required to repay the lender for his advance against the inventory which has been converted into sold merchandise. Therefore, on sales of $10,000, the amount of $3,000 (30% arrived at as described above) would be withheld from the 80% receivables advance of $8,000. On the monthly volume of $75,000, it can be assumed that 20% or $15,000, will become available monthly from a return of equities arising from receipt of customer remittances —$2,000 of which the lender will be authorized to deduct for monthly amortization of the chattel mortgage. Purchases of new inventory will be financed by the revolving inventory loan arrangement and, as you can see, the normal functioning of the accounts receivable financing program will automatically repay the inventory loans and the monthly chattel loan amortization.

A specific case, covering a program arranged for one of my clients, provides an interesting illustration of package financing. My client had the opportunity of buying carloads of imported carpet wool on the East Coast for resale in original cartons to carpet manufacturers in the West. His entire gross markup was only 7%; yet he was able to do an annual volume of $800,000 and make a profit of $30,000 per year *on an investment of only $7,500.*

To obtain the distributorship, a $50,000 letter of credit was dangled under the Eastern wool importer's nose (we will discuss letters of credit in a subsequent chapter). We arranged with a New York bank to provide the letter of credit for 15% cash margin—the $7,500 which constituted the entire cash investment in the deal. A bank in Los Angeles agreed to advance 85% of *landed* cost against the wool if placed in a public or field warehouse. Since this warehouse loan was against landed cost, it not only provided a takeout of the letter of credit loan from the New York bank, but also virtually financed the cross-country freight cost. To save establishing an accounts receivable bookkeeping department, a notification factoring arrangement was made on an 85% advance basis (which provided more than enough to repay the 85% of cost warehouse loan because of the 7% markup of cost to selling price). The Eastern importer would ship a freight carload, then present the invoice and bill of lading to the New York bank. Since a carload of wool would be invoiced for about $42,000, there was always ample coverage in the $50,000 letter of credit; therefore the New York bank would pay the importer upon presentation of his draft, then forward the order bill of lading to the Los Angeles bank, which would use this as authority to the railroad to release the wool to the local warehouse. The warehouse, in turn, would issue a warehouse receipt against which the Los Angeles bank would advance 85% to the New York bank to repay its letter of credit payment to the Eastern importer. The $7,500 originally put up as margin remained intact with the New York bank to provide for the unadvanced 15% increment of cost of the wool in warehouse, and the letter of credit was constantly reinstated by repayment with funds obtained from the warehouse loan. Working capital (and ultimately, the profits) came from return of equities from the factor as customers paid their bills. In summary, here was a beautifully flowing financing program which, on a revolving basis, used two $50,000 bank credits turning over a sufficient number of times to create an $800,000 annual volume. From this resulted a profit of $50,000 before financing cost. The cost of all the financing was $20,000 and, although this was the major expense of the operation, was really quite a bargain considering that it made possible a $30,00 yearly profit on a $7,500 investment—a sweet little return of 400% on capital!

CHAPTER 8

Time Sales Finance

The role of installment selling in business is well recognized for its massive contribution to increased sales volumes. Not only have installment contracts constituted the great majority of transactions in certain fields, such as the automotive industry, but their use as a selling tool has continued to spread over a broad range of varying activities. This is particularly true of "big ticket" items—goods or services whose cost runs from $200 up to several thousand dollars. From home appliances and grand pianos, the list has stretched to such diverse items as carpeting, dental work, intercommunication systems, mink coats, raw land sales, etc. A new type of color camera, which sold poorly in retail stores at $200 each, became a fast-moving item when promoted by a direct-selling sales force for $276 each on a 36-month contract. This was just one of many products whose true potential was not reached until offered on a time-payment basis.

The success of installment selling has been reinforced by its widespread acceptance, both on commercial and consumer levels. Whereas in earlier times it was considered prudent to save in order to make purchases, the modern purchaser tends to feel there is little difference

in accumulating the savings by making time payments
while benefiting from the use of the acquired goods. In
such an atmosphere of thinking, the growth of installment selling—and of the concomitant requirement for
financing of time sales—has resulted in the development
of a massive segment of the financial industry. Obviously
a great deal of money is required to "carry the paper," in
other words, to finance the installment contracts. Very
few businesses, including many very substantial firms, are
in a position to do this for themselves. Frequently a firm
will advertise, "We carry our own paper," which, frankly,
is only partially true. The customer may only have contact with the selling firm (through arrangements to be
described below) but there is almost inevitably a financial institution in the background. Funds for financing
installment contracts can be obtained from the following
sources:

1. Consumer finance companies
2. Industrial banking and general finance companies
3. Rediscount divisions of commercial finance companies
4. Banks

The choice of the source of funds will often influence
the type of arrangement between the seller of the goods
and the financing institution. For this reason we will
devote the following paragraphs to some of the different
formats.

OUTRIGHT PURCHASE OF CONSUMER PAPER

The first source of financing mentioned above—the
consumer finance companies—are, as their name implies,
primarily interested in contracts of sale to individuals.
In this group are included the familiar "small loan" companies whose branches are ubiquitous. The small loan in-

dustry includes many giant national companies in a highly competitive field. Large sums are spent for advertising in the quest for potential consumer borrowers. The small loan companies have found that an excellent way to build up volume is through the introduction of new potential borrowers by business firms who have made time sales to such consumers. For this reason they are interested in purchasing consumer installment contracts.

Actually, the business which makes an installment sale on this basis in a sense serves merely as a referral agent for the small loan company. When the sale is concluded, the customer is put into direct contact with the finance company which approves his credit. Furthermore, all installment payments are made by the customer to the finance company on what is called a *direct collection* basis.

For a small business which generates nominal amounts of installment paper, the consumer loan companies may offer the only funding source. There are both advantages and disadvantages to their use. Generally, there is very little cost to the seller. He makes his sale, transfers the paper to the loan company, and has no responsibility for follow-up, collection, or other servicing of the contract. Moreover, the finance company will usually pay full value for the paper. It hopes to earn the carrying charge in the contract and, if it is attractive, may even kick back a small percentage to the dealer. For the finance company there is always the additional possibility that the purchaser may eventually find it difficult to carry this contract along with other obligations and then can be "flipped over" into a debt-consolidating conventional form of small loan, which is the main business of the consumer finance company.

On the negative side, the dealer (seller) loses continuity of contact with his customer, thereby possibly losing the opportunity to make additional sales in the future. Occasionally, also, the buyer may lose some of his enthusiasm for the purchase when he goes into the finance company to complete the credit application or sign additional papers. There are even other customers who, although perfectly willing to enter into installment contracts at the dealer's premises, balk when they learn they will be involved with an outside finance company on a direct collection basis.

DEALER RESERVE PURCHASING

The use of small loan companies for installment contract financing is, as we have described above, primarily a contract-by-contract arrangement. Each deal is viewed on its individual merits; much more emphasis is placed on the specific individual consumer credit. Frequently it is more desirable to work within the framework of a more standardized over-all arrangement between dealer and fund source when the individual consumer credit, although significant, is not as heavy. There are a number of institutions which provide this type of financing. Pioneers in the field are the *industrial banking* firms, many of which, such as Morris Plan banks and *thrift and loan* banks, accept savings deposits from the general public under state charters and regulations. A list of many of these institutions can be obtained from American Industrial Bankers Association, 813 Washington Building, Washington 5, D.C. Also in the same category are many "general" finance companies which have their own funds and do not take public deposits. In some larger cities banks make dealer arrangements for assignment of consumer or commercial installment contracts, but the specialized industrial and general finance companies which make this their chief business are usually able to provide a broader, more flexible service. These lenders will be concerned with the stability and reputation of the dealer and with the reliability of the goods or services he sells on installment contracts. In dealing with such lenders, the dealer can usually write his contracts on his own premises. If he knows his customer's credit, the dealer can easily get the new contract approved by submitting a short credit application form to the lender. It is not necessary to bring the customer into contact with the lender, nor to have the customer visit the offices of the finance company. In many cases an *indirect collection* method is used; in other words, the customer sends his payments to the dealer, who in turn remits them to the lender. Direct collection is also frequently used; however, a customer usually has no objection when given a payment book calling for installments to be remitted to a bank or finance company (which is quite different from having to deal with the finance company in signing the contract in the first place).

Installment contracts are purchased by the specialized lenders, usually on a continuing arrangement covered by a basic agreement with the dealer. The purchase may be on a recourse or non-recourse basis. In any event, there is generally recourse to the extent of the *dealer reserve* held by the lender. This reserve is created at the time the paper is purchased by the lender. The lender will agree to purchase installment contracts at a specific price below the full value of the contract, which is the *discounted* amount. If the dealer has added sufficient carrying charges to justify handling of the contract by the lender (including a reasonable profit to the lender) the discounted price will probably be the full amount of the dealer's sale to his customer, prior to his adding the carrying charge. A number of considerations will determine how much the lender's discount will vary—above or below the fair value of the contract, exclusive of the carrying charges. We will go into this matter more thoroughly later.

After agreeing on the purchase price, the lender will advance the entire payment with the exception of the dealer reserve. This reserve, which may be as small as 5% (but which can be much larger depending on the relative risk quality of the paper and its underlying collateral) is usually held until the entire contract balance is fully paid by the customer. There is therefore an effective increase in the reserve percentage as the contracts are paid down. For example, a dealer might sell $100,000 of installment paper for full value, with 5%—or $5,000—reserve withheld. When this batch of contracts is paid down to a total of $25,000, the original $5,000 reserve, if undiminished, will stand at 25%. From the lender's position there is some justification on the premise that the most creditworthy customers will pay the most promptly—and even prepay in some cases—so that the residual outstanding contract balances will have had the "cream" removed and should call for a larger reserve.

There is no automatic reserve reduction under this method and the lender can hold the entire amount until all contracts are paid off, but there can be some modification. In a continuing relationship the dealer will usually agree to substitute new good paper for any contracts which turn sour; in return, the lender will frequently agree to certain reserve repayments to his dealer before all contracts are fully paid off, particularly if he feels the remaining reserve is adequate. It is also possible for a dealer to enter into a prior agreement with the lender on this subject. Envisioning a continuing relationship with frequent assignments of new contracts, it might be agreed that the lender would hold 5% reserve on all new contracts but that, as a result of customer payments received, when the reserve held against all the unpaid contracts of this dealer reached an average of 20%, no further reserves would be required. The total reserve would be maintained at 20% and the lender would regularly remit overages. Normally, if such an arrangement is made, the lender has the right to hold all reserves in the event of a termination whereby he will be taking no further new contracts.

TIME SALES CONTRACT REQUIREMENTS AND RATES

Before going into the last major category of installment financing we should examine the lender requirements as to the paper to be financed. Too often I have seen companies which have gone into installment selling on a basis which precluded proper financing. It is understandable, of course, that a business is thinking primarily in terms of increasing sales when it embarks on an installment selling program and, for this reason, does not build into the program satisfaction of potential financing requirements. On the other hand, the financing source must be able to make its normal profit and be satisfied that it is conforming to all legal requirements when it steps into the shoes of the business whose contracts it has assumed. It is necessary, therefore, that the following points be covered:

1. Are the carrying charges sufficient to provide for the financing cost?

2. Are the down payment, contract term, and repayment acceptable on sound industry principles?

4. Does the contract include an acknowledgment of receipt of the goods or services in good order?

4. Does the form of contract conform in every way to legal requirements?

While the first point appears obvious, it is surprising how many times installment programs have been prepared without provision for ample financing cost. Usually the cost is covered by the carrying charges. In the installment selling field these charges are stated as the *Time Sales Price Differential*. The use of a "differential" instead of an interest charge is interesting. In legal theory a difference exists between what an item can be bought for with 100% cash as opposed to buying it on the installment basis. Assume, for example, that a large lot of mixed steel sheet and strip were for sale. It might be proposed that the lot be sold in increments, which might take several months. Now, let us suppose that a would-be purchaser asks for a price on the entire lot, and is told he can buy it for $40,000, $10,000 down and $10,-000 each month for three months. The buyer counters with an offer of $35,000 cash on the spot, and the seller agrees. The time sales price differential in this example was $5,000. It is the result of a difference in the deal itself, not a function of interest. A time sales price is different from a cash price—and the lawmakers usually agree. In California, for example, where there is a maximum annual interest rate of 10% chargeable to the consumer on certain contracts, it is perfectly allowable to use a 10% time sales price differential (which is nearly 20% interest) on the same contracts. It is, of course, essential that the seller be consistent; that he is willing to sell his goods for cash at a price which would be exactly equal to the installment contract price less the differential.

As we will see shortly, it is sometimes possible for the business to make a profit on the financing itself. However, since the prime incentive for the adoption of an installment contract program is usually to derive more profit from increased sales, the first consideration should be assurance that the financing costs will be covered. Time sales price differentials are applied exactly the same as *add-ons* (see Chapter 6). Although various differentials may be used, they usually vary from 6% to 10% per year. Sales of industrial equipment, such as lathes and presses, to commercial users will stay closer to the 6%

level. Sales of lower priced items to consumers will generally call for the 10% add-on differential because of the extra handling cost of the smaller contract. Normally these differentials will be all that are required as discounts by the financial institution. In fact, as I said, there may be room for a kick-back to the dealer. For example, one of my clients sold an intercommunication and hi-fi radio system to homeowners for $600 cash. On an installment basis he received $60 down payment, leaving a *contract balance* of $540. The installment program called for a three-year contract with 10% time sales price differential ($54 per year × 3) of $162. The total time contract called for $702 ($540 plus $162) to be repaid in 36 equal installments. These contracts were assigned to a specialized lender who was satisfied with 9% on this kind of transaction; so he rebated to my client 1% of the differential, or $16.20.

It may be wise to talk to potential financial sources to predetermine what discount they require. Then, if you wish to embark on an installment selling program, you can take this information into consideration.

Some firms do not add the entire discount to the differential, as they may have provided for some of the financing cost in their basic selling markup. This is particularly true with companies who sell *almost entirely* on the installment basis. Such companies are little concerned about their cash sales price as they expect practically no cash sales. However, they must establish a cash price in order to add legally the time sales differential. Therefore, a good part of the financing discount cost will be "packed" into the cash price and—as a selling point—the time sales differential will be shown as only a very nominal charge. This procedure was followed by the distributors of a widely sold automatic color camera which originally retailed in camera stores for $200. Distribution was switched to direct selling on an installment basis and the cash price was increased to $240, packing in $40 for financing. Added to the new $240 cash price was $1 per month carrying charge for 36 months—$36—a differential calculated to create no resistance whatsoever on the part of the customer. However, combined with the $40 packed into the cash price, there was an ample $76 to cover financing costs for the three-year contract. The new $240 cash price was adhered to as established and, of course, the company was delighted to sell its camera at that price to the few purchasers who preferred to pay cash.

The second area to clarify in advance concerns the length of time the contract is to run and the amount of down payment. These must be related realistically to the size of the transaction and the anticipated useful life of the product being sold. It is obviously improper to sell a two-year supply of a particular type of goods on a four-year contract. The commodity sold should certainly provide benefits considerably beyond the time at which the installment contract has been paid in full. A piece of industrial equipment can be placed on a two- or three-year contract, some substantial machinery contracts running even longer. Home study courses have been sold on 12- to 18-month contracts; yet somewhat permanent home improvements can be placed on three- to seven-year contracts. Whereas automobile finance contracts are generally limited to two or three years, mobile home installment contracts—which were originally governed by the same limits—have now been found satisfactory by lenders to be placed on seven-year contracts.

The down payment and monthly installments will be influenced in several ways by the substantiality of the contract and the value stability of the product sold. Ideally, most contracts call for a 25% to 33⅓% down payment, but this standard is frequently waived. Down payments of 10% are fast becoming acceptable to many

SECURITY AGREEMENT

The undersigned Seller hereby sells, and the undersigned : **Mr. & Mrs. John Smith** , Purchaser, hereby purchases for the time sale price and subject to the terms and conditions hereinbelow and also on the reverse side hereof, the following property, delivery and acceptance of which, in good order, is acknowledged by Purchaser, viz:

New/Used	Model	Serial No.	DESCRIPTION OF MERCHANDISE	Sales Price		
New	1964	TA-9181	High fidelity stereophonic radio phonograph	$ 895	00	(A)

To be installed at the following address: **25 Maple Lane** Brief description of Trade-in (if any): **None**

SALES TAX 35 80

TERMS OF AGREEMENT

The undersigned Purchaser agrees to pay the TIME PRICE BALANCE designated herein in **36** successive monthly installments of $ **28.89** on the **fifteenth** day of each succeeding month beginning on the **fifteenth** day of **January** , 19 **65** , at the office of Seller or Seller's assignee, all sums to draw interest after maturity at the highest lawful rate. Any accrued default or delinquent charges shall be payable with the final installment. Purchaser further agrees that said chattels shall be kept and/or installed on or in the premises above described and shall not be removed therefrom without the written consent of Seller or Seller's Assigns and that Purchaser shall not transfer any interest in this Agreement or in said property and shall not make any material change therein without Seller's consent; that title to said chattels shall not pass to Purchaser until all payments hereunder, including collection charges, and attorney's fees, if any, are fully paid; that the Seller, in entering into this Agreement, has accepted as true and relied upon the information in "Purchaser's Statement," which Purchaser warrants to be true and complete.

If Seller is unable to verify within seven (7) days after date hereof the representations contained in said "Purchaser's Statement," or if within said period Seller verifies that Purchaser's Credit is not as represented in said statement, he may promptly notify Purchaser of that fact, and thereupon, at the option of the Seller, this Agreement may be cancelled and rescinded.

If Purchaser defaults in the performance of his obligations hereunder, Seller at his option may accelerate payment of all or part of the amount unpaid as permitted by law, (1) sue for the same, or (2) repossess said property, and (i) retain it and all payments in satisfaction of the balances or (ii) sell it and pay the balance owing under said Agreement, paying the surplus, if any, to Purchaser. (See Additional Terms of Agreement on the reverse side hereof).

TOTAL CASH SELLING PRICE	$ 930	80	(B)
DOWN PAYMENT — $ 130.80			
TRADE-IN $ -0-	$		(C)
(SEE DESCRIPTION ABOVE)			
INSURANCE TO BE PROCURED BY BUYER ☐ SELLER ☐ BALANCE	$ 800	00	(D)
CREDIT LIFE $ DISA- BILITY $	None		
FIRE $ THEFT $	$		(E)
OFFICIAL FEES	$ None		(F)
AMOUNT CASH PRICE UNPAID	$ 800	00	(G)
TIME PRICE SERVICE CHARGE	$ 240	00	(H)
TIME PRICE BALANCE (G plus H)	$ 1040	00	(I)
TIME SALE PRICE (Total of B, E, F, & H) $	1040	00	(J)

Seller may at his option add subsequent purchases of goods or services made by Purchaser to this Agreement, and add the price thereof to this contract as provided by law, in which event all terms and conditions hereof shall apply equally to such subsequent purchases, (See additional Terms of Agreement on the reverse side hereof).

ALL OF THE "ADDITIONAL TERMS" ON THE REVERSE SIDE HEREOF HAVE BEEN READ BY PURCHASER WHO UNDERSTANDS AND AGREES THAT ALL OF SAID "ADDITIONAL TERMS" ARE PART OF THIS AGREEMENT AS THOUGH FULLY SET FORTH AT THIS POINT.

NOTICE TO THE BUYER: (1) Do not sign this agreement before you read it or if it contains any blank space. (2) You are entitled to a completely filled-in copy of this agreement. (3) Under the law you have the right to pay off in advance the full amount due and under certain conditions to obtain a partial refund of the service charge.

DATE **November 20, 1964**

RECEIPT OF A COPY OF THIS AGREEMENT IS HEREBY ACKNOWLEDGED BY PURCHASER

SELLER **Clark Radio Company** PURCHASER *John Smith*

SELLER'S ADDRESS **1510 Main St., Los Angeles** PURCHASER *Marjorie Smith*

BY: *R P Sloane* TITLE: V.P. PURCHASER'S ADDRESS **25 Maple Lane, Los Angeles, Calif.**

NO. 184 (REV. 9/20/63) — LAW PTG. CO., LOS ANGELES - BURLINGAME financial institutions, particularly if the dollar amount seems sufficient to represent a stake which the customer will not want to abandon and lose. It is true that some contracts are written on a no-down-payment basis; however the seller must be prepared to carry these himself, as they will probably not be acceptable to a lender until some equity has been created by the purchaser's having made several monthly payments. On balance, the length of contract, monthly installments, and down payment are interrelated. A modest contract must be of fairly short duration; otherwise the monthly installments will be too small to handle economically.

Finally, the contract must conform to all local state requirements and must include elements on which lenders will insist. The lender wants to see evidence of receipt of the goods purchased and an acknowledgment of the obligation on the part of the buyer to pay the full amount of the contract. The legal requirements which are also important to the lender (since he stands in the shoes of the seller) include: proof that the customer has received a fully executed copy of the contract, a stipulation that the type shall be large enough and easily readable, a specific delineation of the time sales price differential, etc. On the following page is a sample of a conditional sales contract which meets all these requirements.

REDISCOUNTING

The methods we have previously described for financing time sales—through the use of small loan offices and general and industrial banking institutions—place the handling of the contracts almost totally with the fund source. These methods are used by most firms at the inception of their installment selling programs and, whereas the subsequent use of industrial banking companies may provide the ideal answer on a continuing basis, there is another arrangement to which certain businesses turn: the rediscounting of their *own* time sales finance operation.

Rediscounts are provided by some of the larger banks and commercial finance companies. Rediscounting is a procedure whereby one financing agency finances another —on a secured basis—by the method of assignment or reassignment. A small finance company can obtain additional funds by rediscounting collateral which originally was assigned to it by its clients. With the growth of installment selling this arrangement has now been extended to business firms which create a continuing flow of time sales paper through their own merchandising operations. The early cases of this kind involved operating companies which established *captive finance companies;* that is, wholly owned subsidiaries formed for the purpose of acting as a finance company for the time sales paper generated by the operating divisions of the same parent company. The finance subsidiary would be given a cash capital of its own and would make arrangements with outside financial institutions to obtain leverage borrowing. In the financial industry there are some purists who insist that a rediscounting arrangement is only possible with a separate finance company, and not with a financing division of an operating company. This reasoning is based on the fact that a subsidiary is a separate corporation—a specific legal entity engaged solely in financing, whereas a division of an operating company is not. However, recent experience has developed that has resulted in outside financing institutions treating both in the same manner in a rediscounting arrangement. I will therefore discuss the topic as equally applicable to both. The outside financial institutions originally preferred rediscounting a corporate subsidiary entity because the corporate form—restricted as to withdrawals of its cash capital by subordinations from the parent—gave assurance of the continuity of the buffer equity which is desired in rediscounted paper. However, it has been realized that, on a properly structured rediscount providing for such equities through limitations on the percentage of advance, even a non-corporate division cannot create new paper without having some equity in same. Moreover, since the parent company may be required to guarantee the rediscounting of a finance subsidiary with modest capital, the differentiation fades even more. In such cases the outside financing source will be looking toward the *tangible worth* of the entire company.

REDISCOUNT LINES

The over-all limiting factor in a rediscounting arrangement is the maximum *rediscount line*. This line of credit is established as a ratio to the tangible worth of the applicant. Where a corporate subsidiary is capitalized with an original cash investment of, say, $100,000, the tangible worth is that same amount. When, however, a rediscount line is sought for a mixed financing and operating company, an analysis must be made primarily to determine the liquid assets, eliminating such items as leasehold improvements, good will, receivables from affiliates or officers, and so on.

Once the tangible worth has been determined, the line is set. Normally, the line is initially established on a very conservative basis; such as a ratio of 1½ to 1 (for example, $150,000 rediscount line to $100,000 tangible worth). After confidence is established in the arrangement, the line will be periodically increased so that ratios of 3 to 1 or even 4 to 1 can be achieved. Obviously the use of such a leverage—where $4 can be obtained for every $1 invested—is one of the chief attractions of a rediscount arrangement.

REDISCOUNT ADVANCES

Another limiting factor in a rediscount is the percentage of advances made against the time sales paper. Here arises a very important difference between regular accounts receivable financing and rediscounting. As was described in Chapter 5, the advance against receivables is a percentage of the *collateral,* namely, of the face value of the assigned invoices. Proper rediscounting, however, cannot postulate advances strictly on collateral; instead, the rediscount must realistically relate to advances against *cash* equity in the paper. The reasoning behind this policy is based on the make-up of the time sales paper itself.

Let us take, for example, the sale of a water-softening equipment package for a $1,000 cash price—on a three-year contract with an add-on time sales price differential of 10%. The differential will be $300 ($100 × 3 years) and, when added to the cash price, will result in a total contract of $1,300. This contract is assigned to the outside financial source which, it is true, is then the prior lien holder of $1,300 in collateral. However, the $300 differential is *unearned* at the outset, and—more important—it represents no investment whatsoever on the part of the seller. Therefore, if an 80% advance were made on the total value of the contract, this advance—$1,040—would actually give the seller more than his entire investment and profit in the contract. As mentioned above, the rediscount requires some cash equity on the part of the assignor. As a general rule the level at which cash equity begins is determined by subtracting the add-on and seller's profit from the face value of the contract. Assuming the profit on the $1,000 sale to have been $60, the seller would have $940 in direct cost and overhead (also a valid cost) in the transaction. Most financial institutions recognize they must advance costs so that the seller can continue doing business at the same level; however, it is felt that a lender should not go so far as to advance the profit—the seller should receive his profit as a return of equities which develop from the payoff of the contract by the customer. Moreover, as mentioned above, it is also felt that the seller should have some of his own investment in each contract so that he has a positive interest in the full payment of the contract by his customer. This creates an incentive to screen customer credit carefully as, in event of nonpayment, it is the seller's equity which is the first to be lost.

In a typical arrangement, the sample contract described above would be assigned by the operating company to its captive finance subsidiary or division for a price which would eliminate the unearned time sales differential, and also in many cases, less a nominal financing discount of about 5%. In other words, the financing entity would acquire $1,300 in collateral for $950 as follows:

Total face value of contract		$1,300
Less: unearned add-on	$300	
internal financing discount	50	350
Cost to captive finance company		$ 950

The captive finance company, which is now the assignee of the contract, in turn reassigns it to the outside financial institution which, on a rediscounting basis, may, for example, advance 80%. This 80% advance is made against the $950 cash equity of the captive finance company, or a total rediscount loan of $760. At first glance, the advance of $760 may not seem very high against $1,300 in collateral. However, let us analyze the transaction further to obtain the true picture.

First of all, the $300 add-on represents no investment by the seller, as we have said. There was probably $60

net profit earned by the operating company in the sale
which is reflected by the contract. Therefore the company
has an actual invstment of $940 which, after subtracting
the $760 advanced through rediscounting, results in the
final investment in each such similar size contract being
$180. As you can see, the rediscount ratio here is slightly
better than 4 to 1. With $100,000 cash equity to work
with, there would be over $400,000 available through
rediscounting.

Now, here is an even more remarkable fact. In the
above example (which represents a fairly conservative
advance from the outside financial institution), you can
see that $180 investment by the captive finance company
can create collateral in the form of time sales contract
paper amounting to $1,300. This is a ratio of over 7 to
1. Therefore, on a rediscount basis, you can create more
than $700,000 worth of paper with only a $100,000
investment!

STARTING A REDISCOUNT WITH PAPER

Because of the requirement that, in a rediscount, you
must have some equity in the paper, a certain amount
of cash is allocated to a captive finance division or subsidiary. Generally, a minimum of $100,000 is advisable,
although I have seen rediscounts begin with hardly half
that amount. The possession of sufficient unused cash
for this purpose makes it possible to begin the program
with relative ease. However, if retained earnings or funds
from available credit are insufficient, the starting of a
rediscount may still not be precluded.

Most captive finance operations are found in companies which have begun their installment selling by
discounting their paper with outside financial institutions,
as described earlier in this chapter. Not only is valuable
experience gained this way, but also, as the contracts pay

off, reserves become available to provide a return of earned equities. As a result, the operating business can begin to hold some of its own paper, rather than discounting all of it on the outside. At the same time a working credit and collection department can be initiated, sometimes with only one qualified employee, so that, when the time comes to go into a full-scale rediscount, the source of rediscounting funds will be satisfied with the internal credit controls. It is true that, prior to obtaining a rediscount arrangement, it may only be possible to carry 25% or less of the paper generated while the other 75% or more must continue to be discounted with outside finance companies to provide a steady flow of working capital. However, the relatively minor portion of the paper which is retained will have 100% of its equity provided by the operating business. It is through this *equity in paper* that the possible inception of a captive finance rediscount can be created.

Suppose, for example, a retailer of pianos created new paper at the rate of $40,000 per month on three-year installment contracts. Approximately $10,000 would be represented by the time sales differential which, since it would be an unearned financing charge at the time of original sale of the pianos, would represent no investment on the part of the retailer. For the retailer to carry 25%, or $10,000 of the paper, he would have a theoretical equity of about $7,500 (as the result of deducting the unearned financing charge). However, this total amount would not be made up entirely of out-of-pocket cost. The gross profit would probably have been approximately $3,000, consisting of net profit plus overhead which might be spread over the other sales, once monthly breakeven point was passed. Therefore if, out of the $40,000 new paper created each month, $30,000 were discounted with an outside financial source to provide continuing working capital, the retailer could carry the remaining $10,000 with a cash investment of $4,500 per month. To maintain such a program for one year would appear to require $54,000; however, this amount would be provided not only by retained profits during the year, but also by the conversion of unearned financing charges to earned income on the contracts being carried. (Three-year contracts held for one year actually earn considerably more than ⅓ of the financing charge for that year, as the greatest interest is earned at the early part of any installment contract. This can be demonstrated by the *rule of 78;* in the example being used here, about $7,000 interest would be earned during the first twelve months following inception of the retailer's program of retaining 25% of his own contracts.) Furthermore, some of the equity can be provided through reporting income from the retained contracts on a cash basis for taxes, thus deferring payment of taxes until the rediscount has been established.

Now, let us suppose the above program has created $120,000 in retained paper at the end of twelve months. Adjusting this face value for customer monthly payments received, and for the unearned time sales differential, a rediscounting source might advance between $60,000 and $70,000 as a loan against the paper. True, this is too small a line for the financial institution to entertain for a rediscount on a regular basis; however, it can easily be shown that this was created by retaining *only* 25% of the retailer's contracts. Obviously, once begun on a basis of involving 100% of the retailer's contracts, this rediscount would represent a loan of about $400,000, which will certainly qualify as to minimum requirements. The problem of which comes first, the chicken or the egg, has been solved. The rediscount is established as sufficiently large on an early potential basis; and the first advance of $60,000 to $70,000 will provide the retailer with sufficient cash to satisfy his equity requirements in making the potential of a $400,000 rediscount line an actuality.

COST AND PROFIT IN REDISCOUNTING

Usually, the basic incentive for establishing a captive finance company is to facilitate growth of sales on an installment basis. The primary benefit sought is the enhancement of profits from volume increases. Many businesses have found that, if they can present a standardized financing package in all their markets, their representatives can do a better selling job. A standard financing package integrated into a national merchandising plan is usually only possible when there is a captive finance company in the picture. Also, other types of businesses, particularly retailers and distributors, find that carrying their own paper maintains a closer contact with customers, resulting in continuing sales on a repeat basis.

However, there is the additional incentive of making profit from the financing itself. There are a number of well-known illustrations of this possibility; for example, GMAC, the captive financing operation of General Motors, which turns in a very healthy financing profit. The earnings which truly arise from the financing activity itself will depend on a number of variables. To make a realistic analysis, the rediscount should be equated against the cost of discounting paper with an outside fund source. In other words, if you postulate a 5% discount as the basis on which your captive finance company purchases paper from your operating divisions—but an outside source would purchase your contracts at face value less only the time sales price differential—you are not realistically earning an extra 5% (of course, the opposite can be true if your paper *is* being discounted beyond the differential).

Usually, the financing profit arises strictly from the excess of add-on income earned in comparison to the cost of money and handling. It is therefore a netting-out of the following variables:

1. Time sales price differential (add-on)
2. Handling cost
3. Rediscount interest cost

As has been mentioned previously, the add-on can run from 6% to 10% per year, depending on the commodity sold and the category of customer. Most consumer goods will carry the maximum add-on of 10%, yielding the captive finance company an income of approximately 20% interest on its money. (Actuarily, it is slightly less, but this is offset by the fact that money borrowed in a rediscount is never 100% of the face value of the paper.) The physical handling of the paper—preparing payment books, entering payments, checking credit and making collection follow-up—can cost 1% to 3% of the contract sale price. Where the handling cost is higher, the add-on is usually higher to compensate for the added expense. Finally, the cost of rediscounting funds will vary from 6% to 12%, simple interest, depending on the source of funds and the application itself. Taking the high range of figures—both income and expense—a typical consumer sales rediscount with 10% add-on would have gross income of 20% interest less costs of 15% (interest 12% plus handling 3%) for a net profit of 5% *on volume*. With the leverage of four times or more obtained in rediscounting, this earning rate could lead to a yield of 20% net profit per annum on investment.

There is, of course, one further cost factor involved; namely, bad-debt loss. Customer credit loss in rediscounting is usually not as significant a factor as it might be in an ordinary operating business. Not only is a captive finance company run according to the more prudent credit policies of a typical finance operation, but the receivables, instead of being on an open account basis, are covered by a contract of conditional sale. With the possibility of repossession confronting him, a customer will make strong efforts to avoid losing the equities he has created through making a down payment and subsequent installment payments. A fairly conservative reserve for bad debts would be about 1½% (which a rediscounting source of funds will want to see reflected on your balance sheet). You can frequently carry higher reserves for tax purposes.

REDISCOUNT CREDIT CRITERIA

Earlier in this chapter we briefly mentioned certain criteria related to individual contract credits. Whether the customer is a commercial account or a consumer, normal credit precautions are expected in ratio to the size of purchase. The down payment and total term of contract must be sensibly proportioned to the commodity sold, its usage and depreciation. The financial institution supplying rediscount funds will want to satisfy itself that your method of processing individual credit applications is sound and normal. However, after checking these elementary requirements, emphasis is switched to a major extent to the quality of the over-all portfolio, as reflected in the monthly aging.

In time sales financing, the basis of advance against eligible collateral is a *contract aging*. The determination of eligibility of collateral differs slightly from the method used in accounts receivable financing as described in Chapter V. Receivables are aged according to the number of days past due from the due date; time sales contracts, however, are aged on the basis of the *number of payments missed* per the terms of the original contract. No purpose is served by setting forth the date of the last payment received, or the number of days it is past due; the status of the entire contract is much more meaningful. Therefore a typical time sales contract aging would appear as shown in the table.

You will note from this aging that the *entire unpaid*

balance of the contract is placed in the column which correctly reflects the status of payments. If one payment were two months late and the other payments followed at regular monthly intervals, the entire contract is still running two months behind its scheduled repayment terms. Generally, the outside financing institution will make a rediscount advance on all collateral represented by contracts with customers who have missed no more than two payments.

The above eligibility requirement sometimes causes problems which arise with customers who, although they may fall a few months behind because of temporary reverses, are later able to pick up and maintain a schedule of steady monthly payments. Some financial institutions will still classify such accounts as ineligible, but others can be induced to advance once again on what is known as a "two-thirds of contract" provision. This provision allows a formerly delinquent account to re-establish its eligibility if it reaches a payment schedule that is two-thirds of the original contract terms—and if a recent steady payment history has been demonstrated.

To illustrate, let us take a $3,600 contract, payable in thirty-six equal monthly installments of $100 each. The customer makes three payments, reducing the unpaid balance to $3,300, then misses the next four. At this point the account would be ineligible for advance. However, conditions improve and the customer is able to continue his monthly payments. When he has made five such payments, the account will once again be eligible for a rediscount advance. Here is the explanation. The original contract called for twelve payments to be made each year—once each month. The customer made three payments, missed four months, then paid five consecutive months—which accounted for the twelve months of the first year. The contract called for twelve payments, and, since the customer had made eight, he had returned to

A Typical Time Sales Contract Aging

Name	No. of payments made	Original contract amount	Monthly installment	Date of contract	Current	Missed one payment	Missed two payments	Prior (missed more than 2 payments)
Alberts	18	$1,080	$ 30.00	3/63	$ 540			
Baker	15	3,600	100.00	7/63		$2,100		
Chase	2	1,800	50.00	8/64	1,700			
Dean	4	900	25.00	5/65		800		
Everts	15	1,800	50	6/63	1,050			
Fox	3	720	20.00	9/63				$660
Green	1	2,880	80.00	10/64	2,800			
Hoyt	5	1,440	40.00	5/64	1,240			
Jones	5	1,800	50.00	3/64			$1,350	

a position of being within two-thirds of original contract terms. The remaining unpaid contract balance was therefore again eligible for advance.

Other than the difference in determining eligibility, the handling of a rediscount arrangement with an outside financial institution functions in very much the same way as does accounts receivable availability financing. The explanation and table in Chapter V on the use of an availability line can be consulted for additional information.

FLOOR PLANNING AND TRUST RECEIPTS

Many companies which sell on an installment basis function as distributors of such standard items as refrigerators, television sets, machine tools, compressors, etc. Such distributors perform no processing on their inventory, merely stocking it for resale in its original form as purchased. These firms frequently have the availability of *floor planning,* or *flooring,* as a means of financing the inventory bought for resale. One of the earliest uses of flooring—and now certainly the most widespread—was the financing of automobiles and trucks for the retail dealer. From that beginning, flooring has spread to major appliances and the other items mentioned above. It should be noted that flooring is only found where the inventory consists of specific items of major individual value which are easily identified and, because they are standard brand merchandise, turn over quickly in a wide established market.

Although flooring is another form of inventory financing, we are covering it in this section because it is usually interrelated with installment selling. The institutions which supply flooring credit—the banks, and specialized finance companies—will only do so if they are

also assured of the opportunity of financing the installment paper which is generated. In other words, few
lenders are interested in floor planning unless there is
some potential time sales financing in the picture.

The parties to a "flooring" arrangement are generally
(1) the supplier, (2) a bank or finance company, (3) the
dealer and (4) the customers. The dealer will enter into
an agreement with the bank whereby the bank will take
a security interest in all inventory of the dealer. The term
"inventory" is all inclusive, covering all items the dealer
holds for sale, present and future. This agreement will
further provide that all proceeds from the sale of the financed inventory must be turned over to the bank, less
the dealer's profit. The result is that the dealer pays for
only a very small percentage of the cost of the inventory,
yet retains a good percentage of the profits arising from
the sale. The bank will pay the cost of the inventory
directly to the supplier, rather than to the dealer.

In practice, it works like this: The dealer will order
the inventory from the supplier, by presenting evidence of
the financial arrangements with the bank. The supplier
will then ship the goods to the dealer, and send the invoice to the bank for payment. When the dealer sells the
goods to the public, payment will be made in one of two
ways: (1) cash or (2) *chattel paper* (this is a note
coupled with a security interest in the goods). According
to the agreement with the bank, the dealer must either
pay over the cash or assign the chattel paper to the bank
within a very short period (usually 3 days). The bank
generally prefers to get chattel paper, due to the attractive interest it can collect on the obligation.

A sample transaction would be as follows: Supplier
sells a car for $3000 to the dealer—the bank paying 90%
($2700) and the dealer $300. The dealer then marks up
the car $500 and adds finance charges of $700, selling
the car for a deferred payment price of $4200. The

dealer will then keep his investment in the car ($300) and his mark up ($500) and turn the remainder (usually in the buyer's chattel paper) over to the bank. The bank earns the interest on the payments from the consumer.

The bank is generally well protected in this arrangement, as its security interest will also extend to all proceeds of the sale of the inventory. Thus, if the dealer takes a trade-in as part payment for a sale, the bank will have a secured interest in the trade-in under the original security agreement.

Under the new Uniform Commercial Code, the filing of a "financing statement" by borrower and lender takes the place of the earlier intent to engage in trust-receipt financing. The transactions are covered contractually by a *Security Agreement*. However, some of the elements of trust-receipt financing are retained because flooring is still a trust arrangement and the secured collateral originates in a tripartite, or "three-cornered" transaction. There should always be three entities involved: namely, the outside supplier, the borrower, and the lender. The borrower then re-sells the collateral in the manner described above. The lender may advance his funds directly to the outside supplier, or may provide a *sight draft* envelope for the supplier to present to the bank for payment with the invoice and shipping documents and receipts included. In this three-cornered transaction the borrower receives the goods in trust while the lien has come into existence simultaneously with the purchase.

CHAPTER 9

Acquisition Financing

In the field of finance there is probably no activity which fires the imagination more than the financing of acquisitions or buy-outs. For one thing, the very transaction itself—acquisition—represents a dynamic and relatively recent trend in our economy. As an adjunct to progress through orderly growth, a giant leap ahead is obtained by purchase of another operating company. The resultant news releases can frequently impart glamour to the acquirer, particularly if it is a public company.

Moreover, the financing techniques used in acquisitions have, until recently, been quite esoteric. As a result, they became potent tools in the hands of those versed in their use. More than a few deals were made possible through ingenious combinations of legal, financial, and tax know-how, sometimes resulting in leverages which, even in very substantial situations, called for little equity contribution by the purchaser. This possibility is being modified somewhat as financial institutions learn more about the pitfalls of improperly planned acquisition programs. Nevertheless, there is still broad financial availability for this purpose and each individual situation can present its own specific opportunities for the takeover of substantial assets with the use of relatively little equity capital.

GENERAL ACQUISITION PURPOSES

It should be unnecessary to go into detail about basic motivations for making acquisitions. The reasons are well known: diversification, increase in asset strength and profit potential, better market coverages, and, in general, an acceleration in the progress of the acquirer. For public companies there is also frequently the psychological impetus in the stock market, resulting in a higher multiplier being placed on the company stock so that it reflects more than the mere addition of the profits of the acquired company. Ideally, an acquisition should result in "one plus one equals three"; in other words, the resultant combination should yield more than the sum of the two parts. Frequently this does happen. Two companies each earning $100,000, for example, could merge and yield a profit of $250,000—the additional earnings resulting from savings in a single overhead where duplication of cost is eliminated.

Purely from a financial point of view, acquisitions can be constructive by supplying elements which will enhance and round out the balance sheet and earnings picture. A fast-growing company with good profits, yet with working capital needs high in ratio to its net worth, can benefit by merging with a company having substantial asset value. Conversely, a company with substantial assets but with slower growth in profits, which requires continuing investment in fixed assets, may benefit by acquiring a high-earning low-worth company to provide better cash flow needed to justify additional growth capital financing.

WHY ACQUISITIONS ARE AVAILABLE

Since most of the benefits described above accrue to the surviving company (the buyer), many people wonder if there are any sellers. Most assuredly there are. The reasons for selling are always interesting to an acquisition financier—as they should be to a potential buyer—at least to the extent that it can be determined that the seller is not attempting to unload a deteriorating situation. If this is not the case, the reasons for selling are usually the following:

1. Retirement of principals. The sellers may not immediately intend to retire (sometimes they do wish to do so) but they are thinking in terms of consolidating their gains, putting their individual finances in order, and diversifying their investments.

2. Tax purposes. While operating a business, the principals are usually able to earn only on a basis subject to ordinary income taxes. By making a sale, the potential earnings of a going business are capitalized, so that the sellers have the possibility of capital gains, or even deferred taxes (see below).

3. Lack of sophistication. This is, indeed, a strange reason; but it does occur with surprising frequency. Many sellers, because of unfamiliarity with acquisition techniques, do not realize they could just as easily be the buyers. For this reason we see cases where the "mouse swallows the elephant." Small companies, which logically could have been acquired, have emerged as the buyer in a merger with much larger firms.

The first two of the above incentives can be used in inducing the principals of a potentially good acquisition to agree to sell. As to the third condition, obviously this must exist when the buyer makes his approach, and thereafter the less said the better.

ACQUISITION PRICING

In Chapter III we discussed methods of evaluating equities. These same principles apply in determining the price of an acquisition where seller's equities are being purchased. Of course, there are some cases where only specific assets are being purchased at their cost or market value; such evaluations are simple, but they are not always encountered. Just as frequently a going business as an entity—or the stock of a corporate business—must be bought. As has been mentioned, the evaluation of a going business can be book value or an earnings-multiplier, but not both.

Book value is obtained simply from the net worth on the balance sheet. It may frequently be readjusted upward if rapid depreciation has caused certain physical assets to be reflected lower than their fair market value. It may also be lowered to correct for obsolete tooling, dead inventory, and the like.

Much more frequent in today's acquisition picture is evaluation of a going business by an earnings-multiplier. In other words, a business is evaluated by a total price representing a certain number of years times the *present* level of profits. If a firm is evaluated at five years' earnings and it is presently earning $100,000, the price would be $500,000, or a "five times multiplier." Remember, the profit is always *after* taxes. If the seller is a corporation the after-tax figure will be available from the corporate earnings statement. If the seller is a proprietor or a partnership, the profits will have to be translated into a pro forma corporate after-tax figure. The pro forma tax is usually figured at 40% to 50%, so a partnership which reported $100,000 profit, would actually have a pro forma corporate after-tax profit of $50,000 to $60,-000, to which the multiplier would be applied. Also, in

232 How to Finance a Growing Business

non-corporate entities like partnerships, there are no principal's salaries, so these must be deducted from the pro forma to get true profits (however, the deduction will only be about half the postulated amount, because corporate salaries are pre-tax expenses and are tax deductible).

Any financing source involved in an acquisition will want to see that the price paid by the buyer is proper. There are guidelines which have begun to appear as a result of the increasing tempo of acquisition activity in the recent past. The multiplier, which is frequently referred to as the *Price-Earnings Ratio,* has been charted as follows:

		P-E Ratio
1.	Business with long existence and established good will among many customers—like a milk business with established routes	10
2.	Businesses established for some time with proven ability to survive or manufacturing companies with large capital investments	8-7
3.	A business established less than ten or twelve years or grown up around a single personality	6
4.	Industrial corporation requiring management skill but not unusually rare special knowledge, without particular patent or trademark protection where capital requirements are not great	5
5.	Small special character businesses—like local flour mills, shoe shops or bakeries	4
6.	Highly specialized businesses dependent on the skill of a small group, or seasonal, or dependent on weather	2-1

7. Businesses of a personal service character
   or business dependent on the skill of a single
   person like an author's agency or an animal
   hospital[1]   1

The earnings multiplier will usually prevail over the book value. In a well-balanced business, the price based on the multiplier will exceed the book value, so the higher evaluation is used. Occasionally the book value is slightly higher than the multiplier and, if the difference is not significant and the assets can serve as financing collateral, the purchase may be made on the book value basis. (Note: More sophisticated acquisition evaluations are described in Chapter 13.)

REMOVAL OF NON-OPERATING ASSETS

In some cases there are legitimate book values present which are simply too high for the earning power of the business. Occasionally this has resulted from outside activities of the seller which have been thrown into the business for convenience, even though they had no connection whatever with the business. A large trucking company, for example, had used surplus funds to buy land which, though valuable, created no income for the company. There is a simple solution to such conditions; the seller can be asked to buy back (or deduct from the selilng price) such assets at his own book value. Alternatively, if the seller refuses, they may be included in the purchase if the buyer knows he can *spin off* these assets by selling them quickly in the open market for the book value he paid for them. (Frequently spin-offs can be made at good profits.)

Another very common situation is where the selling

1. Dewing, *The Financial Policy of Corporations*, New York, The Ronald Press, 1953.

company owns its own plant or premises. If there is a big equity in the property relative to the total value of the business, this can cause a pricing problem. The property may be a good real estate investment but real estate investment returns are lower than returns on equities in operating businesses. For example, one of my clients was interested in acquiring a company earning $100,000 after taxes, but with a book value of $1 million, of which $600,000 was an equity in the plant building. An eight times multiplier was as high as the buyer would go, but the seller would not accept $800,000 on his $1 million net worth. The deadlock was solved by removing the building from the deal. The buyer agreed to pay $50,000 a year rent as a tenant of the building. This made a pro forma $50,000 increase in rent expense (none had been paid by the seller since he owned the building) but there was a decrease in depreciation of $20,000 (since the buyer would not own the building)—which netted out to $30,-000 more expense *before* taxes, or $15,000 less profit after taxes. The seller's profit figure was therefore adjusted from $100,000 to $85,000 and the buyer paid eight times, or $680,000, for the business excluding ownership of the building. The seller agreed because in his mind he was receiving $1,280,000 (his $600,000 building plus $680,-000 cash from the seller).

USE OF SECURITIES FOR PAYMENT

After the evaluation of a proposed acquisition has been made, the method of payment must be determined. Obviously an all cash purchase is the simplest approach, but this may not be possible or desirable, for the following reasons:

1. Tax considerations of the seller (see below).
2. Buyer's lack of sufficient cash.

3. A recognition of the need to tie in the sellers by means of stock ownership after the acquisition. Frequently the sellers may agree to merger in order to pocket some personal gain, but with an announced intention of remaining with the company. If such sellers are vital to the continuing progress after acquisition, they can be given stock holdings in the resultant entity as incentive for continuing affiliation and effort.

The securities which may be used in connection with acquisition include common and preferred stock, debentures, notes—indeed the entire gamut of securities found in corporate structures. If common stock is used, there is greater *dilution* of the resultant entity's earnings, and therefore the buyers will sometimes attempt to limit the amount of common stock used for this purpose. In fact, where the buyer is a profitable company with ample funds, it will prefer to make cash purchases and avoid any earnings dilution whatsoever. Conversely, the sellers may not want to take their chances on future appreciation of the buyer's stock and may insist on the greater safety of a senior security, such as preferred stock or debentures. Between these two extremes there can be mixtures of common stock and senior securities, debentures convertible into common stock, notes with stock purchase warrants—or a mixture of these with some cash. The form of payment used is most frequently set to satisfy the sellers' wishes in a desirable acquisition as follows:

If the seller merely wants to sell out—and get out—he will want all cash or a substantial cash down payment with subsequent installment cash payments evidenced by notes.

If the seller desires safety, but wants a "kicker" to sweeten the deal, it may be necessary to issue debentures which are convertible into some stock, or which have some stock purchase warrants attached.

If the seller is predominantly interested in obtaining a strong equity position in the resultant entity, and if he is bullish about future stock prospects, he will want either very heavy conversion rights or all common stock.

If the seller has strong aspirations for common stock, but his assets include some buildings or non-operating assets, senior securities may be granted for such assets, with the purchase being rounded off by common stock on an earnings multiplier basis.

The buyer will be influenced in his method of payment by a somewhat different set of criteria as follows:

If the buyer wants to build up equities so that the resultant entity represents a combined worth, he will use as much common stock as possible.

If the buyer desires to acquire assets but needs time to pay for them, he will issue debentures or notes to the greatest possible extent.

If the buyer wants to lock in some key principals of the seller he will issue warrants or conversion rights in connection with the senior securities used for payment.

If the buyer has ample funds and wants to enhance his own profit picture without dilution of his stock, he will try to make the purchase for cash.

Each situation differs, not only with respect to the seller's desires, but also in regard to the aims of the buyer. Later in this chapter we will cite some actual examples to illustrate mixes of purchase methods.

FORMS OF ACQUISITIONS

Before examining the tax aspects which will frequently influence the method of payment, it is necessary that we understand the difference between the basic types of merger or acquisition. These procedures create differing tax situations. They are:

1. *Asset Purchase.*   The assets of the seller are pur-

chased as individual items. No liabilities are assumed. Usually the company cash is retained by the seller, who sometimes also retains the accounts receivable so as to reduce the cash which the buyer must show. The going business, as a single entity, is not purchased (although good will may be paid by the buyer); the individual assets are bought.

2. *Statutory Merger.* Two corporations are consolidated in accordance with the laws of the state in which they are located. Usually these laws require approval of the stockholders of *both* the buying and the selling corporations. The statutes vary; some states, for example, demand approval by two-thirds of the stockholders. In a statutory merger the acquirer is called the *surviving company.*

3. *Acquisition of Stock.* The purchase of the controlling stock of one company by another. This differs from the statutory merger in that approval does not have to be obtained from the stockholders of the buyer—board of directors approval is sufficient. The shareholders of the selling corporation will show their individual approvals by accepting the *tender* (offer to buy) of the buyer.

Other than the differing tax considerations which we will presently discuss, there are obvious advantages to each method. While the stock acquisition involves a broad-brush purchase of a complete going corporation, it is sometimes not as simple to implement as a merger. The merger, on the other hand, requires the most stockholder approvals, which may be cumbersome to obtain, particularly if the buyer's stock is widely held. The asset purchase is loose and requires more definitive legal work in the purchase documents, but it is sometimes used where the buyer is concerned about being subject to some unknown liabilities of the seller. Also, as we will point out, some financing problems in corporate acquisition can be solved through an asset purchase.

TAX AIMS OF THE SELLER

A great number of acquisitions involve sellers who wish to make a complete sale and step out of the picture entirely. Such sellers know they are faced with a gain which is taxable immediately upon receiving payment and they are prepared to pay the full tax at the same time. No tax angles will appeal to them, nor does the buyer who is prepared to make full payment have to contend with any further tax considerations.

Another type of seller, although he wishes to sell out completely, may be in such a position that he does not need all his cash immediately and wishes to *defer* some of his taxes. This is particularly true if the seller does not anticipate a high taxable income after the sale of his business. Under tax law, if the seller receives *less than* 30% of the total price during the calendar year in which he sells, he will only have to pay taxes computed on the money he receives that year, and similarly computed only on the installments he receives in each subsequent year. This is the *29% installment purchase* plan, so named because it is the maximum below the 30% level at which this tax treatment becomes unavailable. This tax ruling is helpful in persuading certain sellers to accept partial payments. Further, it establishes a relatively reasonable down payment—29%—as the maximum which can be paid to qualify for the special tax treatment. In subsequent years, the balance can be paid off in any agreed amounts, with payments spread over any number of years. For example, if the purchase price is $100,000, a down payment of $29,000 might be made with five subsequent annual payments of $14,200 each.

Installment payments are a very useful tool in the financing of acquisitions because, in a sense, the seller helps finance the acquisition of his own business. Often there are definite profit advantages, based on the return the buyer earns on his invested capital. Let us say that a buyer has $200,000 invested in his business earning $40,-000 per annum; his return on capital is 20%. Therefore, any capital he can retain (particularly if he needs all the capital at his disposal) can earn 20%. Using the above example of a $100,000 acquisition, the buyer would have the use of $71,000 of the seller's money (after the down payment of $29,000) for five years. Actually, since there are annual repayments of $14,200 required the buyer does not have use of the full $71,000 for five years, but rather the average of $35,500 (the average between $71,-000 at the time of purchase and zero at the time of complete payout). The buyer earns 20% return on available capital, but must pay 6% per annum interest to the seller on the unpaid portion of the purchase price. However, this still leaves the buyer with a 14% advantage (20% minus 6%) accruing from the use of the seller's money. On $35,500 this 14% advantage amounts to $4,970 per year, or a total of $24,850 for the five-year payout. Therefore, if the negotiating for acquisition becomes tough over the question of selling price—or over the possibility of an installment purchase—the buyer has nearly $25,000 leeway to increase his purchase offer if he can obtain an installment payout.

TAX-FREE EXCHANGE

One of the most powerful incentives for sellers to accept corporate securities (and thereby help finance the acquisition of their own companies) in payment for the equities they are selling, is the possibility of accomplishing a *tax-free exchange*. Transactions which qualify for this type of treatment result in no taxes having to be

paid on sales negotiated with securities rather than cash
—at least not until some later time when the securities
received might be sold for cash. A seller might own stock
in his company which originally *cost* him $5,000. After
building his profits he sells his stock to a public company
in return for $500,000 worth of its stock at true market
value. Despite this tremendous gain, the seller has to pay
no taxes. At a later date, if he finally does sell the acquirer's stock, he will then be taxed on the basis of what
he receives in cash from such a sale versus his *original
cost basis* of $5,000. Obviously, the tax-free exchange
offers a fine opportunity to build up equities—or to capitalize earnings of a business being sold—without paying
taxes. There is a further advantage related to the creation
of an estate for heirs. Without going into tax detail
which is not the purview of this book, it can be simply
said that the tax-free exchange allows a *stepped-up basis
of cost* which provides substantial inheritance tax benefits.

The sale of the assets of a business for securities of
the buyer qualifies as a tax-free exchange, as to that part
of the purchase price which is not in cash—provided at
least 90% of the purchase is in stock.

The sale of the stock of a corporation in an acquisition, in return for stock of the buyer, is much more
restricted. In order to qualify for tax-free exchange treatment, at least 90% of the seller's stock must be acquired
and the payment must be made solely in common stock.

Tax-free exchange in statutory mergers is much
less restricted. Whereas acquisition of one corporation by
another, using the acquirer's stock for payment, requires
that only common stock can be used to qualify for tax-
free treatment, any form of security—common or preferred stock, debentures or notes—can be used in a
statutory merger while still qualifying as a tax-free
exchange. Moreover, a nominal amount of cash or
property can be made part of the payment without dis-
turbing the tax status of a statutory merger. From a

financing point of view, therefore, the merger can present the greatest variety of possibilities in using the "paper" of the acquirer to constitute payment of the purchase price.

TAX CONCERN OF THE BUYER

The buyer is usually not in conflict with the tax aims of the seller. In fact, the buyer will frequently stress tax advantages in an effort to accomplish an installment purchase or to persuade the seller to accept some of the buyer's securities in lieu of cash. The only place where the tax considerations of the buyer and seller may not coincide is in the *allocation of value* to the assets. The seller wishes to value inventory at a lower price because higher evaluations of this stock-in-trade can create gain taxable on an ordinary income basis. The seller may want to allocate a larger portion of the price to good will, which the buyer cannot later depreciate as a pre-tax deduction. The buyer will prefer to place higher values on assets like machinery and equipment, which will give him a higher basis for depreciation and subsequent tax savings. Bear in mind that these problems arise from allocation of values within the structure of the agreed purchase price, and do not change the price itself. From a financing point of view, the higher evaluation of depreciable assets is beneficial because it allows for higher cash flow (through reduction of taxes after the acquisition), available for amortization of the debt which might have been created specifically to finance the acquisition.

BUYING A BUSINESS WITH ITS OWN ASSETS

Occasionally there are mergers which involve the combination of two business entities on an exchange of stock basis with the sole purpose of achieving a resultant company which benefits all stockholders for the reasons enumerated in the early part of this chapter. Such mergers take no money out of the business, and the possibilities of getting together depend primarily on negotiating an agreement between the two original companies as to the evaluation of the stock of each in the reorganization which creates a single entity. More frequently, however, one company acquires another in a transaction requiring at least some *cash payout* to the selling shareholders. This is true whether the route of statutory merger or stock acquisition is followed. In such cases the role of acquisition financing becomes vital.

The acquiring company will easily know what financing is available to it on its own resources. More often than not, the buyer will be fairly close to full utilization of its own borrowing ability. In fact, strange as it seems, the company being acquired often has more potential financing leeway than the buyer, but has not used it either because of lack of sophistication or simply because it has had no need of additional funds. In the buyer's eyes, however, the sellers' assets are a possible source of additional capital; therefore, they will be examined very carefully to see what they can produce. In other words, an acquirer can use money which he borrows on the seller's assets (subject to some restrictions mentioned below) to provide part of the cash purchase price he must pay to the seller.

EVALUATING FINANCING POSSIBILITIES

The financial statement of the selling company must be examined very carefully to determine the financing possibilities. The key, of course, is the balance sheet, because it reflects all of the major asset categories as well as the encumbering liabilities. From an over-all point of view there may be unused unsecured borrowing potential. For example, a seller may be borrowing only $75,000 from his bank for working capital, yet may have a net current asset position of $300,000. The buyer has an unsecured bank line equivalent to 50% of his net current assets; therefore, he can obtain $75,000 cash for payout by bank borrowings on the additional net current assets created by the acquisition.

Another simple blanket form of financing is through the pledge of the seller's stock by the buyer to an outside source of funds. There are certain financial institutions which will make term loans against stock, particularly if they are given a modest "kicker" in the form of options on a few percent of the stock. It must be noted, however, that lending on pledges is usually limited to the stock of public companies, or to the stock of well-established privately held companies with proven profit stability. The acquisitions of small banks or savings and loan companies frequently utilize borrowings secured from large banks or other financial institutions on a pledge of stock.

If neither of the above approaches will yield sufficient cash to complete the acquisition (and this is often the case) the buyer must look to the individual assets of the seller, usually in the following sequence:

1. *Real Estate.* Real property owned by the seller has usually been in his possession for some time prior to the acquisition. Normally there is a mortgage on the property; however, there is also an excellent possibility that the equity in the property has increased since the time it was mortgaged as a result of amortization payments and property appreciation. The buyer should consult a real estate lending institution to see how much money he can obtain by increasing the mortgage based on current valuation. The buyer may allow the existing mortgage to stand, but, on the basis of being able to

demonstrate the possibility of a higher mortgage loan, may obtain a second mortgage loan from a commercial finance company in a package financing deal including other assets. In other words, if the existing mortgage is $100,000—but could be increased to a new first mortgage of $150,000—a commercial finance company should be willing to increase its package loan on other assets $50,000 on the basis of a second mortgage.

2. *Machinery, Equipment and Fixtures.*   This category of assets presents ideal collateral for a medium-term loan. The net depreciated value of fixed assets on the balance sheet will give an approximate basis for loan values (see Chapter 6); however, it is very important to get an accurate and realistic appraisal because some significant borrowing potential may otherwise be overlooked. A successful selling company may have followed accelerated depreciation and expensing procedures which have resulted in a material understatement of its fixed assets. I have previously cited the example of a recent acquisition where the net depreciated book value of the fixed assets was $196,000, yet the auction value appraisal was $375,000 (on which the buyer obtained a loan of $450,000). While the seller could not increase the value of the equipment on his books (and would have had to pay far more taxes if he had not depreciated it so quickly) the buyer was able to obtain over $250,000 cash acquisition financing on it, over and above its reflected value. With a good demonstrated cash flow the buyer might have obtained an even higher price on a sale-leaseback.

3. *Accounts Receivable.*   The receivables should be checked to see if they are encumbered. If unsecured bank borrowing is used—even in addition to some chattel borrowing—there should be some leeway for additional financing. To make a quick evaluation you should assume 10% of the gross receivables reflected to be ineligible for

one reason or another, then postulate an 80% receivables financing program on the balance. Later in the negotiations you will want to review carefully the accounts receivable detail aging, to arrive at a more specific availability.

4. *Inventory.* Although low on the scale as collateral for borrowing, substantial inventories are frequently free of lien and can therefore contribute to the total package of available financing. The buyer should analyze the inventory into raw materials, work-in-process, and finished goods (see Chapter 5) in order to determine potential borrowings.

As a result of analyzing the above categories of assets, the buyer should be able to determine how much he can count on obtaining through borrowing on the seller's own assets. The only limiting factor may be the ability to demonstrate sufficient cash flow after the acquisition so as to meet the repayment schedule required by the lender. Of course, this is a criterion of all term lending; moreover, the resultant entity will have the benefit of both the buyer's and seller's cash flow combined.

Let us analyze an example of acquisition financing availability by referring to the following hypothetical balance sheet of the seller:

Assets		
Cash	$ 50,000	
Accounts receivable	250,000	
Inventory	300,000	
Total current assets		$600,000
Fixed assets	$400,000	
Less depreciation	250,000	
Net fixed assets		150,000
Real estate, net		125,000
Prepaid and other items		100,000
Total assets		$975,000

Liabilities

Accounts payable	$200,000	
Bank loans payable	150,000	
Taxes and accruals	75,000	
Current portion long-term debt	50,000	
Total current liabilities		$475,000
Advances from stockholders	$100,000	
Chattel mortgage loan	40,000	
Real estate mortgage	60,000	
	$200,000	
Less current portion above	50,000	
Total long-term liabilities		150,000
Total liabilities		$625,000
Capital stock		50,000
Earned surplus		300,000
Total liabilities & net worth		$975,000

In the above example about $180,000 should be realized from accounts receivable financing (80% of the 90% eligible for advance). The raw material inventory is found to be $150,000 which is placed in a field warehouse for a 70% loan of $105,000. The balance of the inventory ($150,000) is subject to an inventory lien on which another $50,000 is loaned. An appraisal is obtained on the machinery and equipment which reveals an auction value of $200,000—against this a chattel mortgage loan of $250,000 is obtained. A mortgage banker currently appraises the real estate at $150,000 on which he can arrange a 60% first mortgage loan of $105,000. However, the buyer decides to retain the existing first 6% mortgage and, instead, arranges for a commercial finance company to advance the $45,000 excess loan availability against a second mortgage as part of the entire package. The buyer then totals all these availabilities, less the present encumbrances to be paid off, as follows:

Receivables financing	$180,000	
Warehouse loan	105,000	
Inventory lien	50,000	
Equipment chattel	250,000	
Real estate second mortgage	45,000	
Total availability		$630,000
Less: Bank loan payable	$150,000	
Existing chattel mortgage	40,000	190,000
Available for acquisition financing		$440,000

Obviously a nice leverage can be developed in a situation such as this! The selling corporation earns a profit of $120,000 net after taxes and is willing to sell for $700,000 (which you will note is nearly double his net worth, the price having been determined on an earnings multiplier basis). He agrees to take $500,000 in cash and a ten-year note for $200,000—$20,000 per year. Therefore, the buyer needs only $60,000 to complete the transaction, the balance of which will pay itself out from its own earnings. However, the lender insists that the buyer come up with at least $100,000 of his own as a minimum equity. This he does willingly, and, along with the $50,000 cash the seller shows on his balance sheet, is assured of adequate working capital for the future. This deal, almost identical to an acquisition I recently financed for a client, made it possible for the buyer to acquire *for only $100,000 of his own* another company making $100,000 profit after taxes annually! The additional interest is tax deductible, and profits plus depreciation create a cash flow sufficient to service the debt handily.

ROUTE PROBLEMS

In many cases a corporate purchase is the most highly desirable form of acquisition, the business being acquired by a purchase of 100% of its common stock. However—even when all the financing is available as we have illustrated—there can be one serious obstacle: *how to get the money out of the corporation and into the hands of the sellers.* Corporations are subject to laws governing the removal of their assets, including cash. Cash may be used to pay corporate obligations; but it is *not* a corporate obligation to pay for stock a shareholder sells to an outside buyer. The only other way money can be taken out of a corporation (which is to continue in business and not be liquidated) is by declaring dividends. But—here we have another restriction—dividends may only be paid out of *earned surplus.* Therefore, the amount of earned surplus will limit the amount paid out of the corporation to its selling shareholders, regardless of how much can be borrowed on the corporate assets. After all, the money borrowed on the corporate assets must go into the corporation bank account. The corporation is the borrower, not the stockholders.

There is one important exception to the earned surplus limitation. As we have previously explained, private corporations are sometimes initially capitalized on a "thin" basis; that is, part of the original investment is made in return for common stock, and the balance is loaned to the corporation by the principals (who can receive this amount later as a tax-free return of capital). On the balance sheet such investments are reflected as "officers' (or principals') advances to the corporation." These are *obligations* of the corporation (even though they constituted part of the original investment), therefore they can be repaid with cash any time the money is available.

Now look at the balance sheet we have used as an illustration for analyzing the acquisition financing possibilities. You will recall the following:

1. The seller requires $500,000 cash down payment.

2. The buyer is coming up with $100,000 cash of his own.

3. There is $440,000 available on the corporation's own assets for acquisition purposes.

Referring to the balance sheet, you will notice that there is $300,000 earned surplus—this is therefore the limit beyond which a dividend cannot be paid. But you will also notice that there is a corporate obligation of $100,000 to the officers, who are the selling shareholders. And finally, our buyer has $100,000 cash which he is free to use as he pleases. Even if the buyer is a corporation (which is usually the case) its own cash may be used for any purchase for which value is received.

Therefore, follow the steps which make this acquisition legally possible:

1. Selling shareholders and buyer execute the purchase agreement. This agreement creates a liability on the books of the buying corporation to pay $500,000 cash to the sellers. The agreement is joined into by the financing source (lender) to create a *turn-around*.

2. The "turn-around" calls for the sellers to deliver their corporate stock to the buyers who simultaneously pledge the stock to the lender as the lender's funds are advanced to the corporation being acquired.

3. The buyers have agreed to vote the stock of the corporation to authorize the pledge of the various assets to the lender which are required as security for the acquisition financing. As soon as the stock is delivered by the buyers, they do so, and the lender substitutes liens on the assets for the pledge of stock—thereby completing the turn-around.

4. The buyers have paid their own cash contribution of $100,000 *directly* to the sellers. In other words, this payment was not made through the corporation being purchased, but *outside* of it. This leaves $400,000 still owing on the cash down payment requirement.

5. The lenders have advanced $440,000 into the selling corporation on its assets. One hundred thousand dollars is used to liquidate the advances from shareholders. Since this is a corporate obligation, this may legally be done. This now leaves $300,000 cash owing on the down payment.

6. All of the stock of the selling corporation is now owned by the acquiring corporation which, through its appointed directors, declares an "upstream" dividend from the new subsidiary to the parent (the buyer). This dividend of $300,000, which is the total earned surplus, is paid in cash to the parent corporation (the buyer) on a virtually tax-free basis because the acquisition is reported on a consolidated tax-return basis. (Your accountant can give you more information about these matters, whose details need not concern us here.)

7. The parent corporation (the buyer) has already incurred a liability for payment to the sellers of the purchase price for the acquisition. It is therefore legally empowered to use the $300,000 cash dividend it has just received to pay off this corporate obligation—thereby completing the $500,000 cash payment required by the sellers. To recapitulate, the sellers received their cash down payment from the following:

Paid by the buyer outside the selling corporation	$100,000
Repayment of the selling corporation's indebtedness to its shareholders	100,000
Payment of the buyer's obligation to the sellers for their stock-using funds received as dividend from the acquired corporation	300,000
Total cash payment	$500,000

The parent corporation, which has been the buyer in this acquisition, will be responsible for payment to the sellers of $20,000 every year as the agreed liquidation of the $200,000 deferred payment. This can easily be accomplished with funds received as subsequent dividends from the profitable subsidiary which has been acquired.

From the foregoing description it is obvious that there will occasionally be acquisitions which cannot be accomplished as a purchase of corporate stock. This is true where the total cash down payment required exceeds the total of (1) earned surplus of the corporation to be acquired; (2) the cash the buyer has available to pay to the selling shareholders outside the corporation; (3) the amount owed by the selling corporation to its principals. In such cases an asset purchase is usually resorted to. As explained earlier, this is merely an acquisition of the individual assets of a corporation, free of all liabilities, and having no claim on the stock of the corporation. Even a complete going corporate business can be sold this way, with good will paid as part of the purchase, leaving the seller with an empty corporate shell which he may collapse or retain on an inactive status until he finds another use for it.

Of course the acquisition of a partnership or proprietorship does not become involved in corporate route problems because the buyer is then not confronted with a corporation in the first place. Such acquisitions are, by their very nature, asset purchases. Where a corporation does exist which cannot legally be used to meet the cash payment desires of the sellers, and an asset purchase is not desired—either by the buyer or the seller, for various reasons—the whole problem may be resolved by resorting to a statutory merger.

Under the merger route, the surviving corporation will represent a pooling of the assets and liabilities of both of the original corporations. Therefore, funds borrowed on the assets of the total complex should be available to liquidate the purchase obligation of the acquirer as it, becomes an indebtedness of the surviving entity. In some cases this may be the only solution, but it does present hurdles of its own. As explained previously, the statutory merger requires greater stipulated approvals from the stockholders on both sides of the transaction. Further, the merger must usually be completed before payouts can be made to the sellers, and there are many sellers who will not go along with this type of arrangement. As you will recall, in a straight corporate acquisition the sellers can be paid simultaneously with the release of their stock which they have delivered into the purchase escrow. This usually cannot be done if substantial outside financing is required for a consolidation accomplished through the statutory merger process.

COMBINING ACQUISITION FINANCING TECHNIQUES

While many acquisitions simply follow one of the various procedures previously described, there are also numerous cases where all the available techniques must be sifted in an effort to find a combination satisfactory to the buyer and the seller. Regardless of the legal route followed, it may still be necessary to mix cash with various types of securities—stock and corporate obligations. Most of the usual tools have already been discussed which, because of their variety, cannot be shown in all their possible combinations. However, a few examples should illustrate how these tools can be mixed to achieve the desired result:

Case #1. A very simple example of asset purchase. Seller has a small profitable business, distributing material handling equipment, and he wishes to retire. He sets a price of $75,000 on all his assets, including the good will of the going business. The buyer agrees to assume current trade obligations of $16,000 (which, although he will pay off when due, will be replaced by other newly incurred accounts payable. Remember, as we have pointed out, that accounts payable provide an increment of working capital). Buyer agrees to pay off a bank loan of $20,000 secured by a chattel mortgage. The seller already has receivables financing, so no extra funds are picked up from this asset. However, a combination of inventory lien and a new chattel provide $50,000. The buyer has only $5,000 of his own cash, but he owns an apartment on which he persuades the package lender to advance him $15,000 (the lender is secured by a *third* mortgage which, although in this case the owner's equity is good, would not ordinarily be financeable except as part of an acquisition package loan). There is sufficient working capital in the business residual in the small cash bank balance and receivables financing. Therefore, the transaction initially shapes up like this:

Cash from buyer	$ 5,000	
Chattel and inventory lien	50,000	
Apartment equity loan	15,000	
Total borrowing availability		$70,000
Less: Payoff existing bank chattel		(20,000)
Available to pay seller		$50,000

Actually, for tax reasons the seller wishes 29% down ($21,750) the first calendar year. Since the sale takes place in November, the buyer has to provide immediately for the second year. The buyer gives a note for payoff of the balance of the purchase price in three subsequent equal yearly installments of $17,750 each. As you can see from the above table, the down payment and first subsequent installment payment are easily covered by the $50,000 availability. The later installments will be provided for as the result of the ensuing three years' profits.

Case #2. A more advanced asset purchase. The seller owns a machine tool manufacturing company with excellent profits over $140,000 per year, but he has taken accelerated depreciation to such a great extent that he has backed himself into a tax corner. He is using receivables financing because he has withdrawn $200,000 cash from the company bank account to make an outside investment. An agreement is made to sell the company assets for $700,000, for which the buyer will receive all machinery and equipment, inventories, and the going business. The seller is to keep the cash which is in the company bank account at the time of sale. A purchase escrow is to be opened by buyer and seller on May 1 with a deposit of $150,000, the total cash outlay by the buyer in making this acquisition. On June 1 the sale will be completed and all accounts payable and accounts receivable created in the normal course of the business from May 1 will be assumed by the buyer. (Since the business is doing a sales volume of $100,000 per month, and material purchases represent 60% of sales, it is assumed that the receivable asset will be $40,000 higher than the accounts payable liability the buyer will have to assume.) The generation of new receivables will therefore provide some of the going-forward working capital. The heavily depreciated equipment is found to have an auction appraisal of $375,000 and, with an equipment chattel and inventory lien, $400,000 is committed by a lender who also agrees to finance the receivables of the new owners. The assets mentioned above are acquired by the buyer and placed in a new corporation. The stock of the new corporation is to be 100% owned by the buyer's presently existing corporation, which, therefore, becomes the *parent* of the newly formed subsidiary. The subsidiary is set up to reflect a $500,000 liability to the seller for the cash down payment increment of the $700,-000 total purchase price for the assets; this liability is

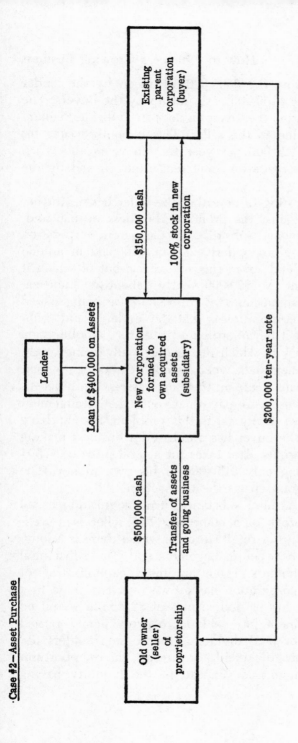

Case #2—Asset Purchase

paid off by using the $400,000 advanced by the lender plus part of the $150,000 cash put up by the buyers. The *parent* corporation then issues a debenture for the remaining $200,000 due to the seller. This debenture calls for repayment of $20,000 per year for ten years and is secured by a mortgage on some real estate owned by the parent.

It is interesting to note that the seller has no further direct claim against the profitable business he has sold; it is a wholly owned subsidiary of the parent corporation which will be able to derive about $100,000 in annual upstream dividends from this subsidiary, out of which it will easily meet the $20,000 yearly debenture amortization. Another significance of the debenture being issued by the parent corporation is that the lender would probably insist that it be subordinated if it were an obligation of the subsidiary to which the lender is advancing funds. Since many sellers balk when asked to subordinate their securities to loans made on their own assets, the proceeds of which are used to pay them out, the arrangement described above nicely skirts this problem. Summarizing this example, the buyer has purchased a business making $100,000 net profits after taxes for a total price of $700,- 000, while using only $150,000 of his own money. The following diagram charts the transaction.

Case #3. A more substantial true acquisition of all the common stock of a company. The seller is a well-established chain of retail stores in which there is a long-standing feud between management and some substantial inactive stockholders. From an initial capitalization of $100,000, the corporation has grown over the years to a point where it has earned surplus of $2.2 million and no debt. Management has held on to every penny earned and has neither paid dividends to the stockholders nor made any effort to expand. As a result, many opportunities have been missed. Instead of the liquidity having been used for sound growth, it has become merely a ripe fruit ready for an acquisition harvest.

Certain pressures are brought to bear on management by the inactive stockholders so that management finally agrees to sell its shares for $1.7 million cash. Meanwhile the inactive stockholders have been approached by a small outside company in the same industry who are willing to take over the management responsibilities after acquisition and to offer $250,000 cash; in return they ask for 50% of the common stock of the acquisition. These outside buyers are joined by some of the dissident inactive investors in the purchase of the company. These former shareholders of the selling company agree to surrender their stock in the old company in return for 50% of a new parent corporation to be formed. Their old stock represents one-third of the sellers' stock. Since management's two-thirds was evaluated at $1.7 million, the investors one-third which they will surrender to the buyer is worth $850,000. They are therefore making a much larger contribution to the buyer's equity than the outsiders who are putting up $250,000 in cash. However, the investors are anxious to terminate their position of having been locked in for years without receiving any dividends, and—they do not have the cash which any lender would insist be put up by new buyers.

The above disparity is easily corrected. The new parent corporation is formed, its capital reflecting that 50% of the common stock is given to the outsiders, who are coming in as new management, in return for $250,000 cash. The other 50% of the common stock—plus a corporate note for $600,000 from the new parent corporation to make up for the disparity in contributions ($850,000 value of one-third selling stock minus $250,000 equals $600,000)—is given to the former inactive investors in return for their selling to the new parent corporation their one-third stock in the old company being acquired.

The new parent corporation then incurs a liability to pay
to the selling management $1.7 million cash for its two-
thirds stock in the old company. In this way it has contracted to purchase 100% of the old company.

The old corporation, as we have mentioned before,
has no debt and is very easy to finance. On its real estate
alone, $950,000 is borrowed on a first mortgage. The
consumer accounts receivable qualify for a bulk commitment of $250,000 more; and a chattel mortgage on the
store fixtures creates $450,000 more availability. The total
acquisition financing potential shapes up as follows:

Cash from outside new management	$250,000
Real estate mortgages	950,000
Store fixture chattel mortgage	450,000
Bulk receivables financing	250,000
Total potential financing	$1,900,000

Obviously the purchase price is available. The corporation has over $200,000 cash in the bank when
purchased, which provides good working capital. In
addition there is a small building which is not mortgaged
and, since it is no longer essential to the operation, it is
sold for an additional $125,000 working capital.

In broad strokes, this case describes an actual acquisition in which I was involved and it illustrates how
new management, with a relatively small investment, obtained a dominant position in a substantial established
company. The "turnaround" method, described earlier
was used, with a commercial finance company advancing
$1.7 million into the purchase escrow in return for a
pledge of the stock of the corporation being acquired.
This money was paid to the old management for their
two-thirds stock holding. Using the voting powers of this
stock, the new owners voted to create the real estate
mortgages, chattel and receivable liens. Against these
liens the finance company advanced $1.7 million in a se-
cured financing transaction. In an exchange of checks,

259

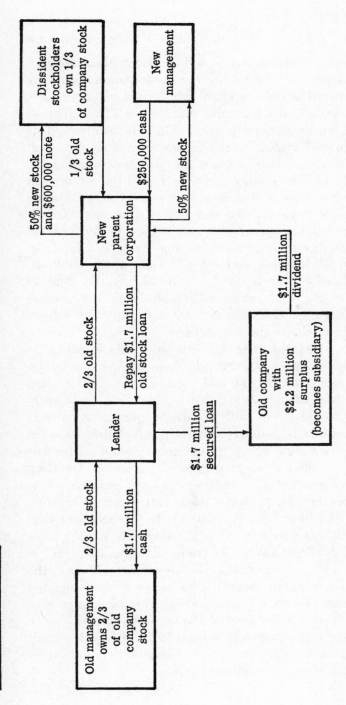

the acquired subsidiary accepted the loans, then declared a $1.7 million dividend to the new parent company (remember, the old company which was acquired as a subsidiary had earned surplus reflected as $2.2 million so this dividend was quite proper) which in turn issued its check for $1.7 million to the finance company to pay off its loan in that amount against the pledge of stock of the old company. The finance company ended the turnaround by having a single $1.7 million loan secured by real estate mortgage, receivables lien and store fixture chattel. This loan was quickly reduced to $1.3 million because of the extra cash in the corporation coming from the sale of the nonessential building and from the corporate bank account. Further, the lender gave its clients the right to substitute the real estate mortgages with longer-term lower-cost institutional loans after one year. The following diagram charts the transaction.

The foregoing case histories have dealt primarily with acquisitions where outside financing from a lender was required because the major part of the consideration paid to the seller had to be in cash. These same techniques can be mixed with securities, particularly where it is desirable to remove an overhanging obligation for making unusually heavy installment payouts after the purchase. When a seller originally insists on receiving only cash plus notes for subsequent cash payments, it is sometimes helpful to make these notes convertible into some of the buyer's stock, particularly in public corporations. The conversion price is set above the market price of the buyer's stock at the time of acquisition. If, as a result of the acquisition, the buyer's stock rises, the seller will have an incentive to convert his remaining unpaid notes to stock, particularly if its market price goes above the conversion level of the notes. In this way, even though the seller originally refuses to accept stock as part payment for his company, he may eventually wind up by taking the stock through conversion.

CHAPTER 10

International Finance

The jet age and the post-World War II global economic recovery set the scene for unprecedented growth in international trade. Manufacturers and distributors seeking larger markets found many opportunities in foreign lands. Other firms in numerous fields—retailing, electronics, plywood, metals, etc.—realized that, in order to be competitive in their costs, it was necessary to consider imported raw materials or finished goods. But this recognition presented a unique problem: how to meet the specialized financing requirements of international transactions. Few business professionals possessed experience in either importing or exporting. Information, previously very limited, had to be expanded and disseminated. As a result of the demands of quickly expanding international commerce, however, knowledge of import and export finance is becoming available—and, with it the fact has become obvious that almost every business expecting to compete successfully must be aware of the potential of global trade.

IMPORTING

A large segment of import trade is handled by specialized importers or *import brokers*. These firms, which have made a business of importing merchandise for re-sale, are usually well versed in the special methods in-volved as a result of stratified experience. To the business community as a whole, however, the procedural require-ments and financing techniques connected with importing seem so esoteric that only the daring will exercise the initiative required for beginning their own importing activities. Stranger still, this fear of the unknown extends even to a reticence on the part of many financial institu-tions whose executives, even though engaged in many diverse types of finance, will turn the other way as soon as an international transaction is broached. Yet the im-port side of the picture, with its ultimate credit risk localized in the U.S.A., truly does not present such a difficult or complicated proposition.

Import financing can be obtained from banks and from a very small percentage of the major commercial finance companies, a few of which, like A. J. Armstrong Co., Inc., maintain special international departments. By far the greatest sources of importing credit are banks. Specialized commercial finance companies can offer cer-tain advantages in larger importing programs—particu-larly where standard commodities are involved—but early aspirations in import financing can probably be much more readily accommodated by commercial banks.

It is not our purpose to go into detail relative to the broad field of importing; rather, we are primarily con-cerned with arranging for the specialized financing re-quirements which importing can create. There are certain foreign suppliers, primarily in western Europe, who will ship to their regular customers in the U.S.A. on an open-account basis. Obviously, no specialized financing is required when you are fortunate enough to be able to make import purchases on such a basis. However, this is the exception rather than the rule. By far the greatest majority of import purchases must be made on a cash basis. To satisfy this requirement, yet still protect the buyer who must pay cash for his purchase in a foreign country, sometimes before he receives his goods, the *letter of credit* provides the best solution.

LETTERS OF CREDIT

In international trade, when an "L/C" (letter of credit) is mentioned, it generally refers to an *irrevocable bank letter of credit.* Conforming to international banking conventions, a letter of credit is a standardized document which guarantees payment by the issuing bank of the amount of money stipulated. Once issued, it cannot be canceled prior to its stated *expiration date.* When funds are called for against a letter of credit by the payee, or within the banking chain involved in the processing, this is known as *drafting* against the letter of credit. The right to draft is subject to a group of limitations, normally referred to as "specifications," spelled out in the letter of credit itself, which can be either quite simple or very complex. As an elementary example, you might obtain a letter of credit from your local bank in St. Louis, Missouri, to use on a pleasure trip in western Europe. Since it is centrally located in your itinerary, you have the credit forwarded to the Bayrischer Vereins-Bank in Munich. The only requirements for drafting are that you appear at the bank in Munich, identify yourself, and request the money, up to the maximum of the letter of credit. By so doing—and if the expiration date you yourself set has not passed—you will immediately be handed the cash.

Letters of credit for commercial transactions are more complex—but there is one common attribute of all L/Cs. If the specifications are fulfilled prior to the expiration date, the payee can expect immediate cash payment. For this reason, irrevocable bank letters of credit, issued by banks of the leading nations, are recognized all over the world. For the American importer a letter of credit is the gilt-edged calling card which can expedite purchase orders placed with foreign suppliers. The foreign shipper knows that, as soon as he has complied with the L/C requirements, he can immediately draft his cash payment, usually at his own bank. In fact, there are even further advantages intrinsic to the use of letters of credit. Take, for example, the case of a manufacturer in Japan (where the use of L/Cs is practically mandatory for purchase orders from foreign buyers), who receives a $10,000 letter of credit payable upon shipment of fifty special photographic lenses. The manufacturer requires some operating capital to produce the lenses for this order. He therefore applies to his bank in Japan, which, with firsthand knowledge of the manufacturer's ability to produce, and with an irrevocable bank letter of credit in its possession, may lend up to 75% or more of the face value of the L/C prior to shipment. In this way, letters of credit become also a potent source of ready working capital.

LETTER OF CREDIT SPECIFICATIONS

Because the financing source of import financing—the bank or institution which opens the letter of credit—shares many of the risks to which the importer is exposed, the importer must know how to structure his L/Cs properly in order to obtain financing. The important structural elements are as follows:

1. *Maximum Amount.* A letter of credit is not necessarily limited to providing payment for one order or for one shipment. For this reason the maximum amount may be set up for several months' future requirements. This is particularly true where there is competition for

scarce merchandise or in cases where a seasonal output of a supplier is contracted for on an advantageous basis. For example, a credit which is opened for $100,000 maximum limit might cover payment for shipments of $25,000 per month for four months. If the total maximum limit is not used prior to the expiration date, the balance is canceled.

2. *Expiration Date.* The expiration date is a very important control because the cancellation privilege inherent in most undelivered purchase orders is denied in the irrevocable letter of credit. Since a letter of credit is a contingent liability, the expiration date serves as an escape valve should the supplier be unable to fill the orders in a reasonable time. Normally, therefore, most letters of credit carry an expiration date 60 to 120 days after the opening date.

3. *Purchase Description.* The purchase description is, of course, the definitive part of the L/C. As in any purchase order, it is important to specify exactly what is being bought. The quantities and descriptions should be described in detail. If there is insufficient space on the face of the L/C, a detailed purchase order may be attached.

4. *Base Terms.* The base terms in a letter of credit transaction describe general standard arrangements. These arrangements are identified by abbreviations recognized throughout the world of commerce. There are several components which vary within the basic terms: namely, freight, insurance, customs and duty. The base terms describe who pays for the cost of these components —buyer or seller. Let us take the case of a United States importer, located in Los Angeles, who purchases radios from a Japanese manufacturer in Tokyo who will ship from the port of Nagoya. If the base term is "f.o.b. Nagoya," or "ex dock Japan," the shipper will be responsible only for seeing that the shipment is loaded aboard a ship

at Nagoya; the American importer must pay for ocean freight, insurance, duty, and customs broker charges. In the opposite condition, when the Japanese manufacturer pays for most of the costs involved, the base terms would be f.o.b. Los Angeles, duty paid. Of course the individual elements are subject to bargaining between importer and exporter, so there are many varied combinations; however, there are two basic arrangements for which there is common terminology. Generally, "f.o.b." indicates that the foreign manufacturer is responsible only for the cost of getting his goods aboard a ship at a port in his country. The other frequently used term is "CIF" (which stands for customs, insurance and freight), indicating that all costs are borne by the exporter, except for the import duty. Unless the base terms state "duty paid," the importer is responsible for payment of import duties.

5. *Documentation.* The documentation stipulations are fairly standard, calling for papers necessary to insure smooth processing of the shipment to its ultimate destination. Most documents are called for in triplicate or quadruplicate and primarily include on-board ocean bills of lading, consular invoices, and commercial invoices and packing lists.

6. *Insurance,* Insurance may be paid for by the shipper or by the importer, although the importer more frequently bears this cost. Regardless of which party bears the cost, it is important to the importer that he have proof of the existence of such insurance. Normally the importer obtains a *blanket marine policy* which requires little or no advance deposit. These policies can be obtained from your customs broker, which presents the added advantage of convenience because the reporting and charges required under the policy can be handled— transaction by transaction—by the customs broker while performing his other duties of clearing the port and processing through customs. For the protection of the

importer, and to satisfy most financial institutions, marine policies are written to *exceed* the invoice value, usually stated as 110% to 120% of value, because of varying duties and other costs which may be intrinsic in the import. In fact, in recognition of this circumstance, marine policies are the only types of insurance which can be written for more than 100% of specifically known value.

7. *Inspections.* Many imports require inspections for protection of the buyer as well as his source of funds. Since letters of credit can be funded to the shipper merely on presentation of documents, the importer must either have confidence in his source, or appoint an inspector in the country of origin to check quality and quantity. Overseas purchasing agents can frequently perform this function, and some countries, like Japan, also provide official inspection agencies if requested. Further, there are certain categories of imports requiring specialized inspections before they will be admitted into the United States. Meat, flower bulbs and plants require U.S. Department of Agriculture inspection and approval; canned goods must have been processed in canneries which meet the requirements of the U.S. Department of Health, Education, and Welfare.

8. *Shipping Variations.* One of the controls written into letters of credit is stipulation of how shipments may be made. The standard L/C form asks if transshipments will or will not be allowed, or if partial shipments may be made against the total order. The latter clause must be considered carefully under certain circumstances. Usually, if major items, such as trucks or automobiles—or standard commodities such as grain, lumber or metals—are involved, partial shipments present no problem. On the other hand, if items are ordered as a total of balanced assortments, serious trouble in the financing can develop. For example, an importer of chinaware from Bavaria might order 100,000 assorted pieces of dinnerware, the

totals of each piece being determined by the usual assortment which the importer sells to his domestic customers. Under a partial shipment permission, the Bavarian factory could ship 10,000 coffee cups and back-order the saucers, which would probably hold up all the importer's orders from his customers, thus preventing creation of accounts receivable meant to provide liquidation of the letter of credit financing. Of course, partial shipments could still be allowed—provided—a stipulated assortment were contained in each partial shipment.

9. *Payment Terms*. While drafting against a letter of credit always produces full cash payment, there can be various payment dates relative to the completion of a transaction. The payee actually completes the transaction by conforming to the stipulations of the letter of credit. Thereafter, the letter may be drafted according to various cash payment terms, of which the following are some examples:

a. Cash upon presentation of documents—this form of immediate cash payment upon conforming to L/C stipulations is quite prevalent.

b. Cash ex dock at destination—the payee can draft when his goods are taken off the ship at destination and hence come under control of the importer's customs broker. Automobiles are frequently handled in this manner.

c. Ninety-day drafts—here the time lapse begins immediately upon conformance to the L/C by the payee. The seller presents his documents to the foreign bank, ninety days after which he is guaranteed to receive cash payment. Because there is banking responsibility for this payment, the seller has a gilt-edged receivable against which he can always arrange financing. Meanwhile, the importer can benefit by having a lower cost for his own financing and also by having three months' leeway in coming up with the full payment of the draft.

OBTAINING LETTERS OF CREDIT

Most letters of credit, even those obtained through other types of financial institutions, are physically opened by banks. The major commercial banks have international departments for this purpose; banks without such specialized departments can still provide letters of credit by working through their major correspondent banks. As mentioned previously, a few of the leading commercial finance companies will open letters of credit for their clients and, although they will use banking channels for this function, the client does not have to concern himself with this detailed aspect of the transaction.

There are, in fact, several important differences in the approach of the specialized finance companies as compared to that followed by commercial banks. Knowledge of these differences will help you to determine which financing source is best for you. Banks usually open credits where the role of the bank is restricted to the payment of the amount stipulated in the L/C—the purchase price to be paid to the foreign supplier—and do not cover the other costs which, including duty, can be quite substantial. An L/C covering $10,000 in purchases of Japanese woodenware from the manufacturer can require $4,000 additional for freight, insurance and duty. When the bank calls on the importer to pay the letter of credit draft, he is also faced with the problem of paying the customs fees and duties for the goods imminently arriving at his port. The commercial finance company, on the other hand, will compute *all* the costs, including duties, and arrange a financing program which will cover them. In fact, most commercially financed international credits will be combined into a complete package including domestic financing of the inventories and receivables. On the other hand, banks are prepared to begin with a modest program, yet are fully capable of handling the largest requirements.

Banks treat smaller letter of credit requests in a manner similar to their handling of unsecured borrowings. If an L/C is for $5,000, the banker will primarily count on his client's ability to pay it when the credit has been drafted. However—and this is important—banks will extend themselves further with letters of credit than with ordinary unsecured credits. There are several reasons for this attitude. Letters of credit relate to specific transactions with finite short-term liquidations (usually at the time of draft) so they are easier to control. Even though the approval may be made partially on the lines of unsecured credit criteria, each letter of credit creates a secured transaction with underlying commodities as collateral (see below). Also, letter of credit business occupies a favored position in the eyes of most sophisticated bankers. The fees earned are not handsome (ranging from ¼ of 1% to 1% of the face value of the credit) but there are side benefits. Banks handling large volumes of letters of credit may frequently enjoy deposits of foreign banks involving funds which have been drafted. Moreover, as there are always other banks involved in the process (the bank which opens the credit plus the bank to which it is forwarded) new interbank relationships are created with foreign banks which can reciprocate when their own customers enter into transactions requiring the services of an American bank.

For the foregoing reasons, you will probably find a receptive atmosphere when you apply for bank financing of a letter of credit program. Companies which have reached their maximum limits of unsecured bank borrowing will find they can still obtain an additional *letter of credit line*. For example, a firm selling wholesale meat to restaurants and markets purchases Australian lobster tails and boned beef from a specialized importer. The firm perceives a larger market for boned beef which can be combined with the suet and waste from its restaurant cuts to produce an acceptable grade of ground beef. A survey reveals that the resulting larger requirements can be obtained at a definite cost saving by dealing directly with the Australian shippers on an L/C basis. Even though the meat wholesaler is at his maximum line of $50,000 unsecured credit with his bank, he is agreeably surprised to learn that the bank will grant him an additional $40,000 letter of credit line. With his fast turnover, the meat wholesaler picks up an additional $400,000 volume per year at a good level of profit. The same situation of credit availability will prevail should an application be made to a bank by a business which does not already have an unsecured line but intends to use its line solely for importing on a letter of credit basis.

LENDER CRITERIA

In establishing a letter of credit line the lender will be influenced by several criteria. As we have mentioned, small applications will be granted simply on the basis of the qualification of the borrower for unsecured borrowings in the same amounts. Beyond this level the lender will base his decisions on the following:

1. *The foreign source of the goods being purchased.* It is a matter of great concern that the foreign supplier have a reputation for dependability. Inspections can, at best, be spotty, and the importer must be assured not only of proper counts inside master packing cases, which cannot all be opened for checking, but also as to consistent quality. The source should be checked with any trade references supplied, through international D & B reports, and with foreign banks in the local area. Branches

of foreign banks in the United States are very coopera-
tive in supplying this information. If sufficient information
cannot be obtained about a source whose products are in
demand, the importer should use the services of a
reputable foreign buying office. These offices charge about
5% of the purchase for their services, including inspection,
and can sometimes save their entire cost by negotiating
a better price with the supplier.

2. *The ready market for the goods.* When products
are first introduced into this country, their salability may
be questionable, but a bank will usually open up a modest
letter of credit if the project is feasible. When moving
into more substantial credit levels, however, the lender
will want to see more positive evidence that the goods
will have ready utilization. Purchase orders from customers are, of course, the best indication; the lender
prefers to open credits for goods *against customer orders,*
rather than for products to be placed into inventory for
future resale. Of course, if a manufacturer begins to import a material to use in his fabricating process, to replace
a domestic material already being used, the indication
of utilization is definitely present, subject to the quality
of the import being demonstrated in actual production.

3. *The commodity rating.* Letters of credit create,
as we have mentioned, a secured lending transaction.
Therefore, the underlying collateral is of definite importance. This becomes increasingly significant as large levels
of credit are utilized. The risk rating of underlying collateral is more closely related to broad commodity classi-
fications when letters of credit are involved because true
commodities have almost world-wide standards of value.
Coffee, wheat, soybean oil, tin, etc., are true commodities.
Not only can they be sold, under forced liquidation conditions, by making a few telephone calls, but they will
bring prices listed daily in the newspapers. True commodities, therefore, can be viewed as having a collateral

value of close to 100% of the purchase cost. Other commodities such as plywood, skein wool, steel strip or hardboard also have an immediate disposal market, but, because they respond to local supply and demand situations, can have a collateral value of 70% to 85% of the purchase cost. Other standard items of merchandise, such as transistor radios, skis, tulip bulbs, cameras or cutlery, respond even more to local disposal pressures and their collateral ratings vary from 50% to 70% of purchase cost. To all these rating levels must be applied a further factor to reflect the usual range of price fluctuations. Most commodities have a historical pattern of price fluctuations over particular time periods.

The time which must elapse from the opening of a letter of credit to the date the lender is repaid is the time swing to be considered. If, for example, a letter of credit were opened for the purchase of skein wool, over a sixty-day time swing, and wool has historically demonstrated a two-month price fluctuation never in excess of 5%, the basic collateral value determined for this commodity need only be hedged 5% against possible price changes. The resultant net collateral evaluation will determine the *margin requirement* for the letter of credit financing program.

MARGIN REQUIREMENTS

When modest letter of credit financing is initiated, a bank will rely primarily on its client's ability to repay. Therefore the credit is opened as a 100% contingent liability of the bank, backed by its client's creditworthiness. This principle cannot be extended beyond the limits of good banking judgment. Import financing can develop into substantial leverages—where the contingent liability of the lender to make good the letters of credit as drafted may be many times the worth of the client-borrower. Somewhere along the line, therefore, the lender must seek a buffer against loss; namely, a margin requirement. Stated simply, the margin is the buffer (or safety difference) between the lender's commitment on a letter of credit and the collateral evaluation—the amount the lender feels he can recoup if he is required to make a forced liquidation of the underlying collateral.

When a margin requirement is established, it must be deposited before opening the letter of credit. For example, if a credit line is arranged which calls for 20% margin, a letter of credit for $100,000 will require a $20,-000 cash margin. As you can readily see, the lender still provides a five-to-one leverage in the credit. Basically, all letter of credit transactions are created because of a requirement for virtual cash in advance payment by a foreign supplier. If, in the example cited above, the importer had to come up with the entire $100,000 out of his own funds—then had to have this money tied up for two or three months while awaiting shipment—a far greater financial hardship would be created, as compared to having only $20,000 tied up during this period.

The amount of margin required will depend on several different considerations. Once again, we encounter different treatments at various levels of size of credits. When credit requirements exceed the modest level where no margin is required, the borrower is apt to find that banks will first tend to apply a standard margin, rather than one specifically allocable to the underlying collateral. These standard margin requirements usually vary from 15% to 25%. As the credit levels move into a more substantial range, however, a definite margin arrangement must be set.

In the foregoing section we have discussed collateral evaluations of various types of commodities, and it is easy to see that the difference between this evaluation and the total letter of credit liability must be made up by the margin. For example, if the collateral evaluation is 75%, a 25% margin is required. However, these evaluations— and their complementary margin requirements—are always mitigated by the resale status of the goods being purchased. This status can be divided into three categories:

1. Back-to-back resale
2. Purchase order resale
3. Inventory purchase

In the field of importing, particularly where the importer is a wholesale distributor of standard commodities which he does not process—but merely resells—the *back-to-back* letter of credit arrangement is frequently encountered. In this arrangement, the importer's customer actually opens a domestic bank letter of credit in favor of the importer who, in turn, puts this up with the bank which opens the foreign letter of credit for him. Although the total value of the two credits will differ (the one opened by the customer will be higher because the purchase will include the importer's markup) the basic stipulations of both L/Cs must coincide. It should therefore be obvious that back-to-back letter of credit applications will require no margin whatever, regardless of the underlying collateral.

Margin requirements are also minimized, to a lesser extent, by the availability of firm purchase orders from creditworthy customers. Let us take, for example, sheet plywood in standard sizes, on which the commodity evaluation might be set at 75%. If the lender is presented with firm purchase orders from creditworthy customers covering the entire letter of credit risk, he will probably ask for only 10% margin. On the other hand, if the plywood falls into the third category of resale status—that is, ordered for inventory and future anticipated resale— the margin would certainly be 25%.

The margin may also be affected by the landing cost requirements. If the plywood has freight and duty cost of 15%, then a bank opening the credit would have to feel confident that the importer could come up promptly with these landing costs before opening a 10% margin letter of credit, even with the existence of bona fide customer purchase orders.

Here is where the handling of letters of credit by specialized commercial finance companies may differ from the procedures followed by banks. Remember, first, that these differences apply primarily to the larger, continuing programs. The commercial finance company, which may come into the picture as volume increases, will set its margin requirements *taking all costs* into consideration. Banks generally tend to consider only the total L/C value in setting margins.

An importer of electronic items, for example, has a landed cost of 30%, consisting of 17% duty, 1% customs and drayage, and 12% freight and insurance. He opens a letter of credit for $100,000 at his bank which, because the client is substantial and well known to them, requires only 10% margin. However, the transaction is limited to the L/C financing only; therefore, the cash margin is $10,000. When the goods arrive at the U.S. port of entry, the importer is drafted by his bank for $90,000 ($100,000 L/C minus $10,000 margin already paid) and must also immediately pay out $30,000 in landing costs.

If handled by a commercial finance company specializing in international transactions, the purchase would be viewed in its entirety and the landed cost would be computed at $130,000. Ten percent margin would be $13,000, but the finance company would assume the responsibility for paying the customs, duty, freight and other landing costs. Usually, a letter of credit arrangement with a finance company is combined with an accounts receivable financing program plus the occasional further addition of an inventory financing line. Therefore, if the borrower is able to provide the basic margin deposit, all other costs will be assumed by the lender and ultimate liquidation will come from receipt of payments from the importer's customers.

MARGIN PROVIDED BY EXISTING INVENTORY

The package financing arrangements mentioned above make it possible for a going business to enter into direct importing without seriously dislocating its working capital to meet margin requirements. Take, for example, a wholesale housewares distributor who decides to add a line of Solingen cutlery imported from West Germany. In order to obtain exclusive distribution of the line, the wholesaler must open a letter of credit for $100,000 on which his landing costs are another $35,000. A lender is approached who agrees to handle the arrangement on a 25% margin of landed cost, or about $34,000. Although he does not have this cash available, the wholesaler presently has a $70,000 inventory of domestic merchandise on which the lender agrees to make a 75% loan secured by an inventory lien. The wholesaler does not require all of this money but the liening of the inventory creates a fund availability of $52,500 (75% of $70,000 existing domestic inventory). The lender sets up this availability, then *freezes* $34,000 of this total to serve as margin. In other words, the wholesaler cannot draw these funds which have been made available through the liening of his inventory. However, he does *not* have to pay interest for the use of this margin, as the lender has not advanced it in cash but has merely blocked it off in a bookkeeping transaction to serve as margin.

Pursuing this example, the letter of credit is opened for $100,000. Other than a small opening fee, the importer has no further cost until shipment is made from Germany and the shipper drafts payment. At that point, since the lender must advance cash, interest charges begin. When the goods arrive at the U.S. port of entry, the lender advances the various landing costs, and the entire international transaction is paid off by a 75% loan on the new imported goods as same are placed into inventory, ultimately to be resold and liquidated from the proceeds of accounts receivable financing.

ACCEPTANCES

Differing from the package financing arrangement described above, banks handle liquidation of some international financing transactions by use of *acceptances*. The basic method of drafting payment of letters of credit is *at sight*—when shipment has been made and all stipulated documents are furnished to the foreign bank, cash is immediately disbursed to the exporter. However, in continuing trade relationships it is recognized that the customer may be able to function better—and to order even more goods—if he is not limited to the amount of cash he can offer at time of draft. There is also recognition that a customer frequently cannot turn over his purchases into immediate sales. To accommodate such conditions, acceptances are created.

An acceptance documents the fact that the payment of a letter of credit is being deferred for a reasonably short period of time. Most acceptances run for 90 or 120 days. Here is how it usually works. On prearrangement, the shipper and importer have agreed on 90-day terms and this fact is reflected in the letter of credit. Let us use the example of a shipper in Japan who sells to an importer in California. When the shipper presents his documents and proof of shipment to the Japanese bank, the Japanese bank forwards a draft to the California bank. The bank in California stamps "accepted" on the face of the draft, makes a notation of the maturity date, for example, 90 days after the date shipment was made, then returns this "acceptance" to the Japanese bank. The shipper can then borrow against this acceptance from the bank in Japan. Since this *banker's acceptance* is actually an irrevocable promise to pay on the part of the California bank, the shipper has no problem borrowing up to 100%, and at low interest rates.

Acceptances are also created in another way, involving only the importer and his bank. Taking the same example used above, the same basic letter of credit is opened, this time, however, calling for sight payment. The shipper presents his documents to the Japanese bank which immediately advances full cash payment. The Japanese bank calls for payment, and receives it, from the California bank. The bank in California forwards a draft to its customer, the importer, who accepts it on a 120-day maturity and returns it to the bank. The bank is secured under the letter of credit by a trust receipt, which remains the lien instrument for the acceptance. The importer may sell much of the goods prior to the maturity date of the acceptance and, being trustee under the trust receipt, must immediately pay the bank for the goods released from trust. These payments go into a *prepaid acceptance account* at the bank, to be disbursed for liquidation of the acceptance at maturity date. Interest is charged the importer for the term of the acceptance. Since banks sell these acceptances on the open market to raise funds, the interest is usually lower than normal bank interest.

HOW A LETTER OF CREDIT WORKS

When the terms have been agreed upon between importer and lender, several preparatory steps are taken.

The importer signs an intention to engage in trust receipt financing, which is recorded with the designated state office. Frequently, individual specific trust receipts in connection with each letter of credit transaction are also prepared in advance.

Prior to the opening of credits a customs broker must be designated. The selection of the proper broker is important. Not only should he be capable of handling the types of commodities in which the importer is dealing, but also—because he functions in a fiduciary position for the lender—he must be acceptable to the financing source. The use of a customs broker is practically a must. Because of his specialized knowledge, his location at the port, and his friendly contacts in the international commerce fraternity (including the customs inspectors) the customs broker does an amazing job of facilitating port clearance, insurance, payment of freight charges and duties—all at a remarkably low cost.

With the above preparation behind him, and having designated a customs broker, who has probably also arranged for marine insurance, the importer requests his first credit. To insure proper structuring, a special application form should be obtained from a bank which has an international department. These forms, if properly laid out, can be very helpful—a sample of a good form is shown on the opposite page, filled out for illustration of our purposes.

The application form is given to the lender, along with the margin deposit, if required. Very soon thereafter, a bank letter of credit will be issued, copy of which will be supplied to the importer. The original will be sent to the foreign bank designated by the foreign supplier. If the supplier does not designate a bank, then the bank which opens the credit will forward it to a correspondent bank located in a city nearest to the shipper. Normally the credits are sent abroad via airmail; however, if there

APPLICATION FOR COMMERCIAL LETTER OF CREDIT

Bank of America
NATIONAL TRUST & SAVINGS ASSOCIATION

Los Angeles, California   November 11.   19 64
(Place)   (Date)

Dear Sirs:

We request you to establish by ☐ Cable ☒ Airmail an irrevocable Documentary Letter of Credit on the following terms and conditions:

In favor of___Imperial Plywood Company, Nagoya, Japan___
(Name and Address)

For Account of___California Wood Importers, Los Angeles, California___
(Name and Address)

Amount___$100,000___ Available by drafts at___sight, Nagoya Bank___on___Bank of America___

covering___100% of invoice value___Invoice value of merchandise to be described in invoice as:
(Full invoice value unless otherwise specified)

___per purchase order #1408 attached - CIF___
(Omit unnecessary details but specify price basis, i.e., CIF, FOB, etc.)

Documents required: (Please indicate by placing "X" in applicable box)

☐ Invoice in duplicate
☐ Special U.S. Customs Invoice
☐ Consular Invoice in triplicate
☐ Marine and War Insurance Policy or Certificate in duplicate - 110% of invoice value, payable in U.S. Dollars
☐ Full set of clean ☒ On Board Ocean
              ☐ Railroad   Bills of Lading, to order of shipper, blank endorsed, marked:

"Notify___J. W. Smith Custom Brokers, San Pedro, California___

Other Documents___Inspection certificates from Honshu Trading Company___

Shipment from___Kobe, Japan___to___San Pedro, California___

Shipment latest___January 31, 1965___

Partial Shipments   ☒ Permitted   Transhipment   ☐ Permitted
                    ☐ Not Permitted   ☒ Not Permited

Drafts to be drawn and negotiated on or before___February 15, 1965___

Insurance to be effected by___Seller___

All documents to be forwarded in one cover, by airmail, unless otherwise stated under Special Instructions.

Special Instructions:___Partial shipments are to be proportional assortments in the same___

proportions as the total purchase order #1408. These assortments apply to various sizes ordered.

THE OPENING OF THIS CREDIT IS SUBJECT TO THE TERMS AND CONDITIONS AS SET FORTH IN THE COMMERCIAL LETTER OF CREDIT AGREEMENT APPEARING ON THE REVERSE HEREOF TO WHICH WE AGREE.

pg 21 Ch X

California Wood Importers
(Name of Applicant)

_____
(Title)

FX-130 4-62

is need for rush, they may be transmitted by special cable codes, for which there is a slight additional charge.

The foreign supplier delivers his goods to the port, obtains on-board ocean bills of lading, and takes these, along with all other required documentation, to the foreign bank to which the L/C was forwarded. At this time, under most circumstances, he is paid cash in full. The foreign bank drafts against the U.S. bank which opened the credit, and which in turn calls for payment from its customer. This is usually the first notice the importer receives that the shipment will arrive imminently.

Shortly thereafter, the customs broker will advise of arrival and request instructions for drayage and delivery. If the importer has paid off the drafted L/C to the bank, the customs broker will be solely responsible to him. If the lender remains in the picture, the customs broker will also notify the lender, and call for landing and clearance costs to be advanced.

The customs broker is instructed by the lender to clear customs in the name of the importer (to protect against the possibility of the lender being called upon to pay for a later assessment by the customs office), but subject to receipt of a *delivery order* from the lender. The lender has probably given this delivery order to the customs broker in advance, so there is little delay, although such an order may require a telephonic release from the lender after clearance through customs. At this point the goods are delivered to the importer, or transshipped according to his requests.

The role of the customs broker in a financed transaction is quite significant. As mentioned previously, a trust receipt relationship is established with most letter of credit purchases. The trust receipt validity arises from a true "three-cornered" transaction, involving the foreign supplier, the importer, and the lender, all of whom come together (transaction-wise) at the time the goods first enter the borrower's (importer's) ownership. The letter of credit will usually specify the customs broker as the agent "to notify" and he will be entrusted with the physical handling of the goods, protecting the lender's interest until the importer becomes trustee by virtue of the goods arriving at his premises as inventory.

EXPORTING

While import financing is relatively well developed and accepted in the United States, export financing has, until fairly recently, lagged behind. It is a sad fact that our country was a very slow starter in recognition of the financing needs intrinsic to competition for world markets. Even today, although some encouraging breakthroughs have been made, export financing availability in the United States is far from what it should be.

Yet this is a problem with which we certainly must reckon. To balance our imports we must build up our exports, otherwise we will have a continuation of balance of payments deficits, which the last several administrations in Washington have recognized and deplored. But, in order to make the biggest export showing, we must compete strongly with other countries that, in the past, have effectively used a very important tool against us. That tool has been better export financing.

Most of the countries to whom United States businesses sell their products were short of dollars and other hard currency. They had to rely on credit to make purchases which, in turn, abetted the growth of their internal economies so that they could become even better customers in the future. To the American businessman, this situation was not only a national concern; it related also to the broadening of markets essential to individual business success.

Both our business community and financial community were guilty in the past of not accepting the chal-

lenge of the problems—and there are indeed problems
of risk—connected with export credit. Europeans countries, particularly West Germany, stepped out briskly to
beat us in selling competitive items to foreign customers
by extending better terms. England, dependent on exporting to save its domestic economy, launched several
well-publicized programs. The B.E.E.O.C.—a consortium
of banks and private financial institutions—opened purchase credits with many foreign purchasers on extended
open-account terms. Lagging behind, the United States
has finally taken remedial steps, the most notable being
the formation of the Foreign Credit Insurance Administration (see below).

Prior to our realization that the problem deserved
national recognition, the American businessman had certain alternative terms to use in exporting which limited
his sales potential. In earlier days, when competition was
not serious, the exporter could insist on a bank letter of
credit from his foreign customers, guaranteeing payment
in dollars. As a method of financing, of course, this is
still most preferable. As an exporter you can draft against
a good foreign letter of credit as soon as you have made
shipment and presented the necesary documents to your
bank. If you need some production money, and the bank
has faith in your ability to perform, you can probably
borrow against the letter of credit prior to making shipment. Unfortunately, although the letter of credit backed
purchase is still widely used, it is becoming an increasingly smaller part of the financing and terms required
for our total export volume. Customers in some of the
weaker countries are not in position to provide letters
of credit. Customers in stronger countries take the position that they are stable enough not to have to put up
letters of credit and that, if you insist, your competition
will agree to dispense with such a requirement.

Faced with such a problem, many United States

firms began to ship on the basis of *Cash Against Documents* (C.A.D.). This is a widely used procedure, particularly with manufacturers of repeat items, staples such as chemicals and canned goods. In selling such items to their overseas distributors who maintain a continual buying relationship, sales on terms of cash against documents were found to be quite satisfactory. The goods are shipped to the foreign port, where they are held until released by an order from a bank in the same locality. The documents, including an *order bill of lading* which arranges the release of the goods, are forwarded to the foreign bank which calls upon its customer (the purchaser of the goods) to make the cash payment required. When this money is paid to the bank it releases the documents (which release the goods) and forwards the money through banking channels to the exporter. When this arrangement is used, it is obvious that the foreign customer cannot obtain possession of the goods until he has paid for them. Many European banks established C.A.D. lines of credit for their clients, advancing the funds on a loan basis to release the documents and goods. However, these lines have limits and therefore it is occasionally possible that the customer will be unable to pick up his order after it arrives. While the United States exporter has not surrendered possession in such cases, he is still faced with the problem of disposal in a distant location.

Once again, we see also that competition is creating a reluctance to use certain terms, as pressure to get away from C.A.D. begins to increase. For one thing, the procedure is fairly cumbersome; it can frequently involve much running back and forth between the purchaser's piece of business, his bank, and the port. Papers get lost in banking channels more frequently than you would expect; they sometimes arrive after the goods reach the port of entry, and the purchaser must then bear the cost of demurrage.

The next easing step is the use of drafts—*sight drafts* (payable upon presentation) or *maturity drafts* (payable in a specific number of days). In using drafts, the shipment is made without any restriction; it does not require a release and merely has to be brought through customs by the foreign purchaser and into his inventory. The draft is a legal form which the customer signs, agreeing to make payment on the due date stipulated. This draft is forwarded by your United States bank to a foreign bank (agreed upon between you and your customer) for collection. Most drafts used in international trade are *protest drafts* which call for a protest report if collection is not accomplished by maturity date. Although it is not always significant, protesting a draft can cause the purchaser concern for his local reputation as well as for his ability to obtain future international credit.

When a protest sight draft is forwarded to a foreign bank for collection, this draft is handled in a very specific way if not honored. Actually, the collecting bank has no obligation for payment and in all countries, as well as in our own, it is possible that the customer will not pay for a draft against him on the due date. This is known as failure to *honor the draft*. When protest drafts are not honored, the draft is stamped with the protest and returned to the shipper (creditor). In some countries all protested drafts are published in the daily commercial papers—a definite deterrent to the customer who values his reputation. If, despite this, the customer does not pay on time, the stamped protest draft is usually the legal requirement for initiating a lawsuit for collection in a foreign country.

It is important that the draft be drawn in the language of the buyer's country, to facilitate collection or legal action. A consulate or your own bank can help you to obtain the proper form.

Drafts should bear interest, at least after maturity

date. Not only does this provide an incentive to pay quickly, but it also provides a more readily financeable instrument. One of the tricks which seems helpful is the inclusion of any foreign broker's or agent's commissions in the draft. These individuals who are on the scene will take strong steps to facilitate collection of a draft which includes their remuneration.

EXPORT CREDIT CRITERIA

The ability to finance exports is dependent upon proper credit screening. Export drafts may be financed on a 100% non-recourse basis by some commercial finance companies, or may be financed simply by loans from banks or other institutions. In either case, the credit-worthiness of the customer is vital. In the field of exporting, this is no easy problem to solve. Not only are the credit sources unorganized, but also the volatile character of the buyer's country can add another risk dimension. In fact, it is this latter factor which demands that most foreign credit extensions be relatively short term.

The credit information should be obtained from as many sources as possible. Occasionally international Dun and Bradstreet reports may cover an application, but this is frequently not the case, and the report may not be sufficiently definitive in approving a credit or setting a limit. A balance sheet should always be requested. The form of reporting may not be completely reconcilable to our own format, but it will help establish the credit limit which may run from 10% to 25% of the true net worth. Bank references should always be obtained—and they will usually be readily given. Many European firms actually print their bank references on their stationery (including their account number). Most European bank references are dependable, which is not always the case with information obtained from banks in Latin America or other parts of the world. But, at least, these reports do contribute a part of the credit jigsaw you are trying to assemble from as many sources as possible.

If your prospective buyer also purchases from other United States firms, this can lead you to information couched in a familiar form, and you should always check for the existence of such an established relationship. Finally, one of the most important checks comes from reports of reputable people who are on the scene in the buyer's country. A bank with an international department will usually have a representative or agent whose information can be trusted. Certain commercial finance companies have foreign agents, and also send their American executives on frequent trips into foreign areas to gather information. Such companies can provide not only information preventing possible credit loss, but they may also be able to handle the financing and collection.

Finally, it is important to ascertain whether the buyer's country requires an *import license*. Not all countries require these, and they may be needed only for certain categories of items. However, the lack of an import license where one is legally stipulated can cause serious problems of collection and financing. Therefore, not only should its possibility be checked, but, if a license is needed, the exporter should be sure to have it sent to him prior to shipment.

EXPORT GUARANTEES

One of the best ways to facilitate the financing of export drafts is by obtaining a good guarantee. Most United States businessmen, unaccustomed to this possibility at home, are surprised to learn that it is common practice in many foreign countries to obtain bank, or even government agency, guarantees of purchases. In Latin

America, many substantial import orders are guaranteed by banks. Naturally this enhances the United States exporter's financing ability. However, also to the surprise of many of our businessmen, not all Latin American banks are sufficiently strong for their guarantees to be meaningful. The bank stability may be a combination of its own resources and of the volatility of the country it is in. Information relative to the true stature of these banks is available from international departments of United States banks or, sometimes even more realistically, from some of the specialized commercial finance companies who are in the day-to-day business of taking some non-recourse risks against foreign bank guarantees.

There are also government agency guarantees which can be quite good. For example, there is "CORFU" in Chile, and Nacional Financiera in Mexico. These agencies are somewhat similar to our own Reconstruction Finance Corporation which helped so many industries in the United States get back on their feet during the depression of the 1930's. A guarantee from Nacional Financiera, for example. is fairly widely acceptable in financial circles, at least up to two-year credits. Incidentally, rates of interest in Latin America are higher than our prime rates. The prime first mortgage rate in Mexico is 12% per annum. Mexican government purchase orders may stipulate 6% interest limitations, but, through the guaranteeing mechanisms, levels of 12% or more are achieved, and this is certainly helpful in arranging financing as the cost of discounting export drafts may easily run that high.

FOREIGN CREDIT INSURANCE

What should eventually be the greatest boon to financing United States exports was the creation of the Foreign Credit Insurance Administration in October 1961. This agency has only recently begun to show its practical potential, having started with only fourteen insurance industry members, whereas now there are over seventy-five.

Prior to the creation of the FCIA, our major governmental agency for insuring export credits, or for financing them, was the *Export-Import Bank* (EXIMBANK). While EXIMBANK serves important purposes in granting substantial credits to foreign countries to use in the purchase of United States goods, it is not suitable for routine automatic functioning at the transaction level of normal commercial export sales in general commerce.

Therefore, EXIMBANK was empowered by law to join in a fifty-fifty participation with a group of private insurance companies for the underwriting of political and credit risks arising from export sales. This participation —FCIA—is the agency designed to encourage exports by insuring these risks. Since the presence of such insurance can be very helpful in obtaining export financing, it is important that we understand how this tool can be used.

FCIA writes several different types of policies, some "comprehensive" and others "political" (which includes credit risk as well as political risk). From a financing viewpoint the most significant differences are to be found in the varying terms which can be insured; therefore our discussion will treat the comprehensive and political categories as one and the same.

The *Short-term Policy* covers exporters selling on credit terms up to 180 days. The policy insures up to 85% of the credit risk and 95% of the political risk, leaving the exporter with a very nominal coinsurance obligation. Except for certain excluded buyers or countries, the exporter is expected to insure all of his exports in order to obtain equitable distribution of the insurance risk. However, cash transactions and shipments to Canada may be excluded.

The policy may be written in any amount from

$1,000 to $15,000 and this is applicable to all buyers. In order to qualify the buyer, the exporter must obtain and *keep in his own possession* two credit reports, one of which should be a bank reference, or be able to show that he has had at least three years' favorable credit experience with this buyer. Under the short-term policy, it is also possible to qualify buyers for amounts in excess of $15,000. In order to obtain such coverage—up to $100,-000—it is necessary to send to the FCIA the previously mentioned credit reports for their review so that they may decide whether the line of credit is justified. Where credit is desired in excess of $100,000, the same credit reports must be made available together with a current balance sheet.

Under the short-term policy, a blanket arrangement covering all buyers within the limits described above can be arranged by submitting to the FCIA a simple application form describing the nature of the business, the countries to which exports are being made, and the terms which are to be granted. On the basis of this information, the FCIA rates the policy (see below) and, after the rate is agreed upon, a 10% deposit premium is required. Thereafter, premiums are paid monthly on the basis of the monthly shipments as reported.

The *Medium-term Policy* covers terms in excess of 180 days up to five years. The policy is designed to provide coverage for capital goods, machinery and equipment. The length of the credit terms will be influenced by the nature of the product and its estimated life in relation to the period of credit. A product with a life expectancy of three years will not be insured for payment terms of five years. When long-term payments are involved, a down payment should be obtained, preferably as much as 20%. Payments may be made monthly, quarterly or semi-annually. In addition, the exporter can charge interest on the sales contract, 6% per annum of which will be covered by the insurance policy. The exporter is required to coinsure 15% of long-term sales. Unlike the short-term policy, medium-term coverage is arranged on a sale-by-sale basis by submitting individual transactions to the FCIA. Rates are again based on the country of the buyer and the credit terms.

RATING AND COST OF EXPORT INSURANCE

The insurance policies written by FCIA are rated on the basis of several criteria. The most important differential is established by the country in which the buyer is located. These countries are rated from "A" to "D." A country rated "D," such as Egypt, requires an insurance rate over four times that of "A" countries like England and France. Of course, ratings can change, depending on political conditions.

Length of payment terms also offsets the rate. A class "B" country like Mexico may call for a rate of $0.69 per $100 for one year, $0.54 per $100 for six months, $1.61 per $100 for three years, and $2.52 per $100 for five years.

The rate, determined by country and by length of terms, is also affected by the *type* of transaction. The above examples were based on open account or sight draft. On a Cash Against Document basis, the rate drops about 50%; where there is a letter of credit involved, the drop is even greater, even if 90-day payment is allowed.

Without even considering the fact that the cost of the insurance could be loaded onto the price to the buyer, who is accustomed to paying far more for long-term payments, the insurance cost is very low, ranging from less than ½ of 1% to 2% or 3% on most of the five-year open-account transactions. Also—most important to our subject —the proceeds of FCIA policies are, by federal law, assignable to banks and institutions to facilitate export financing.

CHAPTER 11

Private Placements

Earlier in this book the fact was mentioned that there were certain forms of borrowing which, because of their special characteristics, served many of the practical requirements of equity capital. *Private placements* occasionally do just this. Either through original design, later conversion, or practical effect, the obtaining of financing through private placement can frequently be equated against equity benefits.

A private placement is a financing which consists of the securing of funds—in a relatively substantial amount as far as the recipient is concerned—from a *single* source (as opposed to a public issue which involves many investors and underwriters). Certain types of institutions, to be described later in this chapter, provide private placement funds. The arrangements are longer-term than those provided by most growth and working capital programs. Therefore, there is somewhat the same sustained usage of funds which only equity can otherwise provide. In addition, the drain of cash flow resulting from modest amortization and interest requirements can be less than the participation (through salaries, expenses, or sharing of profit) which an individual equity investor might demand.

Private placements almost always provide additional

financing leverage because, to a current lender such as a bank, they constitute equities which are subordinate to short-term loans. Many private placements actually contain specific subordinations to banks and other financial institutions. Even if such subordinations are lacking, the stretched-out term of amortization of the private placement will have the same practical effect of retaining funds in the company far beyond the maturity dates of any short-term financing.

TYPES OF PLACEMENTS

Although private placements of common stock are occasionally made, the greatest majority of such transactions involve some form of senior security. This is because the recipient is usually in a middle stage of growth where it is desirable to use borrowed money before diluting owner equities. Also, because the borrower is in an intermediate growth stage, the fund source will want to have liquidation preference on assets which a senior security enjoys. The types of senior securities most commonly used are *mortgage bonds, debentures, convertibles, and notes.*

MORTGAGE BONDS

Although the most venerable, this form of security has in recent years given way in popularity to other forms of placement securities, particularly where young growing firms are involved. Yet, stemming from this classic form are most of the standard provisions which are otherwise stated in varying arrangements.

Early bonds—or those widely distributed to public investors—were *coupon bonds* payable to the bearer upon presentation of coupons which matured on specified dates. In modern private placements, the coupon bond has been largely discarded in favor of a *registered* bond. The registered bonds are identified by number, and records of these numbers and the names of the legal owners are kept by trustees, transfer agents, and corporate treasurers. The institutions which buy bonds in exchange for private placement funds find it much easier to keep track of bonds under the registration arrangement. Registered bonds issued to a number of holders were frequently arranged and numbered according to maturity date, being known as *serial bonds*. All bonds of "series 1960" were, therefore, due and payable in 1960. In private placements the final date for payment in full is often referred to on the financial statement of the recipient as "series." Therefore, the total indebtedness of a bond amortized in equal semi-annual installments, but which is not due to be fully repaid until 1982, would appear on a corporate balance sheet as "mortgage bonds, series 1982."

Mortgage bonds usually involve first liens on property, real or personal, as security. They pay interest on the unpaid balance in a range of 4% to 9% per annum, and, depending on the quality of the issuer, sometimes even higher. Corporate mortgage bonds are geared to the useful life of the collateral and may extend in term from 10 to 40 years. Because of their long terms, certain standard protective provisions have been developed. A list of restrictive provisions is agreed upon and this list is formally set forth in what is known as the *indenture*. Simply stated, the bond itself is the security that is issued, and the indenture gives the terms of the issue. Most of the indenture, which can be quite lengthy, is devoted to a standard recitation of legal "boilerplate" to give the arm's-length long-term lender the legal protection he deserves against the myriad of future pitfalls which could develop. These are interwoven with much more specific provisions, relating to the particular transaction, which do the following:

1. Establish the basic security and collateral, describe it in detail, evaluate it, restrict its disposal without

permission, and provide for maintaining its value.

2. Stipulate certain standards of financial "health" on the part of the borrower, such as limiting maximum current borrowings, purchases of new equipment or investments in fixed assets. Working capital may be required to be kept above a certain minimum; debt-to-worth ratio, below a certain maximum. Cash dividends may only be allowed upon achievement of stipulated profits.

3. Provide for acquisitions, mergers or future stock issues.

4. Establish remedies or courses of action in event of default or failure to meet with other indenture provisions.

The term, interest, and repayment of principal are stated on the bond, but are usually repeated in the indenture. Since the indenture contains many provisions to be "policed," the services of a *trustee* are frequently used. This is particularly true where bonds are held by many individuals or entities, in whose interest the trustee is charged to act. Such trustees are usually corporations whose qualifications and procedures are regulated by the *Trust Indenture Act of 1939* under the administration of the S.E.C.

Remember, also, that there will be mortgages involved with bonds as we have discussed them, and that there may be significant limiting factors regarding them, in the indentures. Some indentures will prevent mortgaging additional fixed assets which are purchased in subsequent years, others extend the lien of the bond holders to all *after-acquired* assets. Inclusion of such restrictions must be weighed carefully in light of future growth financing aspirations.

SINKING FUND

After the type of amortization is agreed upon for a private placement, certain requirements are set up in connection with these repayment provisions. Once again, the making of a private placement with a single institution has brought about simplification. As originally established, the *sinking fund* was created by a stipulated schedule of repurchases (or retirements) of bonds over the total term. Each year the borrower was required to purchase a roughly proportionate amount of the total indebtedness, usually so that at least 80% of the bonds were retired by the last year before maturity. For example, if $1 million in bonds were originally sold with a ten-year maturity, the borrower might be required to repurchase $80,000 worth of bonds each year. These repurchases would constitute the sinking fund.

In the place of a sinking fund, *serial repayments* are sometimes used. Under this arrangement, the borrower repurchases bonds bearing certain specified serial numbers each year. This repurchase is at a fixed price, and will be the method usually favored in placements of bonds with a single fund source. Whereas, under the sinking fund arrangement, the borrower, faced with a spread-out holding of bonds, might be able to buy some of his own bonds at a discount in a depressed market, no such possibility exists with a serial repayment to a single institution. However, with the present custom of fixed amortization schedules well established, you may hear discussions of private placements with institutions which refer to the repayment scheduling as "sinking fund provisions."

DEBENTURES

A *debenture* is a general claim on the assets of a business. Therefore, individual assets are not specifically pledged to the debenture holder. He is senior in position —as to claim on assets—to the stockholders of a corporation. This position is established by law in the very definition of the word "debenture." Because a debenture is not directly geared to the value of specific underlying collateral—or to its expected useful life—the criteria on which debentures are placed with an institution rest heavily on the general financial soundness and future profit potential of the borrower. Of course, the indenture to a debenture may preserve a first position on specific assets by denying the right of the borrower to mortgage those assets. Therefore, even though there are no mortgages connected with a debenture issue, the debenture holders can prevent another secured lender from sliding in under them with regard to collateral.

Actually, the denial of future hypothecation of physical assets is frequently not rigidly set; once again because it might inhibit the healthy growth of the company on which the debenture placement has been postulated. It is true that, because the claim is general, and there are fewer standard legal protections to debentures than to mortgage bonds, the indenture to a debenture issue will tend to be even more lengthy and restrictive. On the other hand, these restrictions, which are applicable more to over-all financial condition than to control of assets, may be much less limiting of the flexibility required for mergers and consolidations.

Unquestionably debentures are becoming more popular and widely acceptable to the financial community. As credit analysis has improved and the writing of indentures has become refined, the use of *subordinated debentures* has become more common. The institutional lender will in many cases *insist* on the presence of unsecured bank lines, to which his debenture will be subordinated. The theory here is that the debenture lender makes a long-term loan and is in no position to monitor the borrower frequently. Unsecured bank lines, however, are traditionally renewable every 90 days; the debenture holder hopes that, as some of these renewals are made, the bank will be reviewing the trend of the borrower and will alert the debenture holder to any adverse changes.

Most bond and debenture private placements are made *at par;* that is, the lender pays the full face value of the debentures. Occasionally, for various reasons, a debenture will be placed at a *discount,* particularly if low interest is to be charged. For example, most debentures are issued in $1,000 multiples. One thousand of these debentures (total face value of $1 million) might be sold for $998.75 each in order to obtain a 4¾% interest rate instead of a slightly higher cost which would hamper cash flow in the early years of the term.

It is also true that, in private placements, the face value of the bond or debenture represents the total amount to be repaid. However, this amount—called the *redemption price*—must be clearly specified as, particularly where there are widespread or public placements by underwriters, the redemption price can be higher than the face amount.

KICKERS

Many private placements create tremendous growth opportunities for a progressive business, yet because they are *funded debt* (long-term repayable financing) the lenders receive only interest return and do not ordinarily share in the profit potential they help to create. For this reason, a modest added incentive—a side bonus usually called a "kicker"—is sometimes made part of the deal with an institutional lender. The kicker can be in the form of *warrants,* which give the holder the right to buy a modest amount of common stock at an advantageous price within a certain period of time. Warrants should not be confused with rights. Rights are offered to existing stockholders, granting them a purchase advantage on new stock to be issued. Warrants are actually an option to make a purchase, with a time limit established within which the option must be exercised or dropped. For example, the common stock of a company might be evaluated at $20 per share at the time a private placement is made. The lender, who is purchasing $1 million in debentures, is given warrants to buy 2,000 shares at $25 per share within a five-year period. If the company prospers and its stock rises above $25, the lender will undoubtedly exercise his option and pick up some extra return.

CONVERTIBLES

As with the public market, convertible debentures have become increasingly popular with certain sources of private placement funds. Here again there is an option to make an advantageous stock purchase as a kicker to the lender; however, under the conversion arrangement no additional money is required for the common stock purchase. The lender originally purchases debentures which carry a conversion feature whereby the debentures can be exchanged for common stock. The conversion option can be for a fixed price throughout the possible conversion period, or it can be scaled upward through several price levels over a period of years. The escalation of the stock purchase price tends to serve as an incentive for conversion if the borrowing corporation is demonstrating the kind of progress showing a good possibility for future appreciation.

The convertible debenture presents an example of a financing which begins as a loan but can culminate as equity capital. If the lender elects to exercise his conversion option, his money becomes a part of the permanent corporate capital represented by common stock. While this arrangement is frequently advantageous to a privately held corporation, it can present a unique problem when a public stock issue is contemplated. This is because an *overhanging convertibility* can affect the market price of a firm's common stock; the analysts will tend to compute per share earnings as if the conversion had already been made—penalizing the stock for potential dilution at the same time the corporation's earnings are being reduced by the payment of debenture interest. The solution of this problem can be anticipated by the establishment of a realistic *call price* for the debentures. If the call price is below the per share value of the shares of common stock to which a debenture can be converted, the debenture holder can be *forced to convert* because he can sell the common shares for more than the value of his debenture. If there were no call privilege on the part of the borrower, the forced conversion would have no teeth in it because the lender could delay in converting. However, when the borrower can call debentures, the lender must either convert quickly (10 to 21 days is normal) or be paid off and lose his profitable conversion opportunity.

PRIVATE PLACEMENT SOURCES

Private placements are made with the following sources:

1. Private investment companies
2. State-chartered investment companies
3. The Small Business Administration (SBA)
4. Small Business Investment Companies (SBIC) chartered by the SBA
5. Insurance companies and pension funds

Private investment companies vary from small loosely knit private syndicates to large organizations which function on a continuous integrated program of making loan and investment combinations. Financial consultants will usually be in contact with these sources in a particular local area. Some are quite well known nationally, such as American Research and Development Corporation of Boston, Industrial Capital Corporation of San Franciso, and Rockefeller Brothers, Inc., of New York.

Whereas such companies as these are strictly private enterprises which come under no special licensing arrangements, other types of investment companies are specifically chartered by special legislation.

Many states chartered state investment or development companies, particularly prior to the launching of the SBIC program (see below) on a national scale. The development companies were frequently designed to have the primary purpose of enticing new industry into the state; the industrial foundations went further, viewing their financing activities as leading to the creation of more jobs by industries already established in the local area. These entities are particularly helpful in providing funds for developing new plants and other physical business facilities. If the local chamber of commerce, corporation commissioner's office, or office of the Secretary of State cannot provide leads to industrial foundations, this information may be obtained from the United States Chamber of Commerce, 1615 "H" Street N.W., Washington, D.C.

THE SMALL BUSINESS ADMINISTRATION

Many government agencies have been designed to assist small business, but, by directly attacking the financial problems of young growth companies, the Small Business Administration (SBA) has probably been the most effective. After World War II, when growth of big companies became evident, the legislators in Washington perceived a growing popularity of the idea of giving small business a boost. Therefore, the SBA was set up in 1953 by Congress to succeed the Small Defense Plants Association which had been organized at the beginning of the Korean War. Prior to the formation of the SBA, lending functions of this type had been handled by the depression-born Reconstruction Finance Corporation; however, while RFC loans were initially emergency or restorative measures, SBA loans were designed to be constructive and forward-going.

Although many professionals in the financial field originally disputed the fact, there is now almost universal acceptance of the premise on which the SBA was founded: the inability of small businesses to obtain funded debt. Both with public issues and institutional private placements there is a prerequisite of relative bigness. A small business may be able to borrow short term—if at all, but has very few avenues of appeal for loans of a few years' duration.

Some of the early objections to the SBA were founded on the suspicion that this agency would put the government into direct competition with the banks and other financing institutions. The act contains provisions which practically make such a claim invalid; moreover, after the first few years of its existence, the SBA showed that it was designed to reinforce, rather than compete with the financial industry.

Before examining the particular lending gap which SBA fills, the definition of a "small" business should be understood. According to the SBA, in stating what business will qualify under its lending programs, small business is defined as follows:

1. *Manufacturing* concerns which employ under 250 persons—although a firm which employs not more than 1,000 persons can still be considered eligible depending on a set of employment size standards which SBA has developed for particular industries.

2. *Wholesale* concerns are considered small if their annual sales volumes are $5 million or less.

3. *Retail* businesses are qualified for SBA assistance if their annual sales do not exceed $1 million.

Obviously, when you have outgrown the above SBA limitations, you should be well qualified to satisfy your financing needs from one of the many other sources mentioned in this book. Realistic members of the financial fraternity had to admit, from the inception of the SBA program, that small businesses could not obtain loans which included stated terms of repayment that could reasonably be met. The solution supplied by the SBA was well tailored to fit the situation: while existing facilities provided short-term loans, primarily unsecured, or secured by *current* assets such as accounts receivable, the SBA provides loans up to ten years, secured primarily by *fixed* assets. Here the contention is that, given the breathing time afforded by reasonable repayment requirements, a small business has a much better chance of reaching successful maturity.

The SBA provides a number of advisory and management information services. In this book, however, we are concerned only with the financing services it offers. The SBA makes loans—very successful loans, if viewed by its historic records of loss. The SBA loss rate on loans reflects an amazing 0.8% average. Yet many of these loans could not have been obtained elsewhere. Either because of form, term, or other criteria, no conventional lenders would have extended the credit on most of the loans which have performed so admirably. In fact, one of the requirements of applying to the SBA for a loan is that it is *not available from other lending sources* on a reasonable basis.

The SBA loan application forms include a section titled "Recent Efforts to Obtain Credit." In this section the applicant declares that, within a period no longer than 60 days prior to the submission of the application, he has been unsuccessful in an attempt to obtain the loan he seeks from at least one bank. Actual letters must be obtained from a bank (or at least two banks if the applicant lives in a city of over 200,000 population) to support this declaration. Remember, a loan application to any institution consists not only of the amount of money desired, but also delineates the term required to assure ability to repay on the part of the borrower. It is possible, therefore, that you might obtain the amount of money you seek from a bank, but not for the length of time which seems most feasible. A rejection based on term could still qualify for SBA consideration.

However, it should here be pointed out that the SBA makes *two* kinds of loans. These are:

a. *Direct loans.* These are loans which are processed directly by the SBA and which involve solely the use of SBA funds. The application (SBA Form 4) must state that the financing sought is otherwise unavailable, and this declaration must be supported by letters from one or more banks.

b. *Participation loans.* The SBA will participate with banks, taking part of the loan on an equal risk basis. The SBA portion can be as high as 90% of the total participation, although the loan may be administered by the bank.

It can be assumed that, if any difference exists between the two above categories, the participation loan should provide a small edge to the aspiring borrower. The presence of a bank gives private business a part of the picture, always a desirable element in the eyes of the government. Also, as in many participations not even involving government agencies, the willingness of one lender to take a piece of the deal encourages acceptance from other participants. Further, since the bank participant is usually located close to the borrower, the SBA processors will feel that they have the benefit of this relative on-the-spot surveillance. Exploratory talks should be held with your bank, even if your previous relationship has been limited to a deposit, checking account, or small loan accommodation.

The first step to initiate the procedure would be to obtain from the SBA office nearest to you its regular application form. This form not only provides for a declaration of financing unavailability, as described above, but also contains a section in which a bank can indicate its desire to enter into a participation. Preparation of this form in proper and good order will provide a bank lending officer with the type of submission that deserves his respect, if not his credit approval. If the credit is borderline, you still may be able to obtain the bank's participation. The reason is simple.

Let us suppose you are applying for a $40,000 loan for five years, primarily secured by equipment you own plus some special pieces you wish to acquire to handle your business. Most banks will not be enthusiastic about a fixed asset loan in this amount over such a long (for them) term. However, when you point out that the SBA will take 90% of the loan, that the bank share will be a mere $4,000, the loan officer may see that, with this minor exposure, you may be able to use this more substantial financing to become a good future customer of the bank.

At this point, your application will be processed in one of the two directions described above. If the bank has agreed to take a small participation, the SBA Form 4 carries the declaration by the bank of its interest in the credit accommodation. Otherwise, the bank should be requested to supply the letter of rejection required before a *direct loan* from the SBA is granted. In either case, the application will be gone over in a personal interview between an SBA loan processor and the applicant. If the preliminary information appears satisfactory, within a few weeks an appointment will be set at the company premises so that an examination and audit of the operation, and of its books, may be made. After completion of the audit and a review period of about two weeks, the applicant, if successful, will receive from the SBA a *letter of authorization.*

The SBA letter of authorization, while not a bankable contract, gives assurance of the availability of the credit if the conditions of the letter are met. These conditions are usually a listing of the documents and filings required for creating the proper loan instruments and securities. In actual practice, the letter is given to an SBA attorney who acts as an escrow agent and, after all the required documents are executed properly and in his possession, can disburse the loan funds out of this escrow.

SBA LOAN CHARACTERISTICS

There is practically no minimum SBA loan; the maximum is $350,000 to a single borrower. This maximum is also applicable to participations in which the 90% maximum SBA portion cannot exceed $350,000.

The interest usually charged by the SBA is low, a statutory maximum of 5½% simple interest. In a participation the bank may go slightly higher on its share, which affects the total loan cost very little because the SBA usually has so much more of its funds invested. If the participant's rate is lower, the SBA can match this drop down to 5%. Lower interest rates are not available from the SBA except in distress areas designated by the Department of Labor or by the Area Redevelopment Administration.

SBA loans can be set up ranging from very short term up to a maximum of ten years. However, since the void which this agency attempted to fill was the lack of availability of funded debt to small business, the usual term is from five years to the maximum. In addition to the usual analysis of credit and ability to repay, the term will be determined by the anticipated useful life of the collateral. It is presently the agency's view that most standard equipment will have at least a ten-year useful life; therefore, loans secured by equipment generally have a maturity of six or seven years. Practically no loans are set up for the maximum ten-year term except those in which the underlying collateral is real property.

As compared to the fixed asset growth capital financing described in earlier chapters, the SBA takes a somewhat different approach to evaluation of collateral than that followed by institutional and commercial finance lenders. The SBA loan processors use *market value* appraisals in setting up loans secured by equipment; in fact, they are directed not even to refer to auction value in their processing. The usual range of advance against this value is 70% to 80% amortized over the life of the loan. Of course, other general credit criteria such as ability to repay, are considered by the processor.

While it is preferable that the cash flow needed for repayment of the loan be proven by past performance, the SBA recognizes that the funds it provides can make the sole difference in making changes in a business which will create future cash flow to repay the placement. Therefore, a well-prepared cash flow projection may satisfy the loan processor in this regard. In fact, a projection is required with each SBA loan application, whether or not adequate cash flow has been proven by past experience. On the following page is a simple example of such a projection.

SBA SMALL LOANS

The SBA has two programs which are intended to encourage more modest applications. Under the *small loan program* loans in amounts up to $15,000 are made up to maximum terms of six years at 5½% simple interest. The

PROJECTED STATEMENT OF INCOME AND CASH AVAILABLE
(cents omitted)

	July 1963 and prior	Aug. 1963	Sept. 1963	Oct. 1963	Nov. 1963	Dec. 1963	Jan. 1964	Total
SALES	$100,000	$200,000	$400,000	$500,000	$500,000	$200,000	$100,000	$2,000,000
COST OF GOODS SOLD								
Beginning inventory	$ 00	$190,000	$380,000	$475,000	$395,000	$207,500	$132,500	$ 00
Labor	56,876	66,252	61,252	26,876	00	00	00	211,256
Material and other	170,624	198,748	183,748	80,624	00	00	00	633,744
Total	$227,500	$455,000	$625,000	$582,500	$395,000	$207,500	$132,500	$845,000
Ending Inventory	190,000	380,000	475,000	395,000	207,500	132,500	95,000	95,000
COST OF GOODS SOLD	$37,500	$75,000	$150,000	$187,500	$187,500	$75,000	$37,500	$750,000
GROSS PROFIT	$62,500	$125,000	$250,000	$312,500	$312,500	$125,000	$62,500	$1,250,000
SELLING AND ADMINISTRATIVE EXPENSES	33,000	66,000	132,000	165,000	165,000	66,000	33,000	660,000
(before income taxes) NET INCOME	$29,500	$59,000	$118,000	$147,500	$147,500	$59,000	$29,500	$590,000
CASH ADJUSTMENTS								
Add: Accounts receivable at beginning of month	00	100,000	200,000	400,000	500,000	500,000	200,000	00
Accounts payable at end of month	170,624	198,748	183,748	80,624	00	00	00	00
Less: Accounts receivable at end of month	-100,000	-200,000	-400,000	-500,000	-500,000	-200,000	-100,000	-100,000
Accounts payable at beginning of month	—	-170,624	-198,748	-183,748	80,624	-200,000	-100,000	00
CASH AVAILABLE OR (SHORT)	$100,124	$(12,876)	$(97,000)	$(55,624)	$ 66,876	$359,000	$129,500	$490,000

Note 1: No provision has been made in this projection for federal income taxes.

Note 2: The operating cash requirements peak to $65,376.00 at the end of October, 1963.

processing is more streamlined on these loans, and, even
though the collateral may be borderline in value, an applicant may obtain approval if his future prospects appear
bright, and if his character and past history are good.

Recently the SBA has added still another type of
loan to its offerings, the *very small business* loan. Sometimes referred to as the six-for-six, this category covers
loans not in excess of $6,000 over a maximum term of
six years. Once again, the application procedure is very
streamlined, bare minimum documentation is required,
and even greater emphasis is placed on the individual
character and reputation for integrity of the applicant.

SMALL BUSINESS INVESTMENT COMPANIES

What may ultimately be one of the most important
sources of private placements and funded debt are the
Small Business Investment Companies (SBICs), which
were set up by an act of Congress in 1958, under the
jurisdiction of the Small Business Administration. By this
act, the government has encouraged the establishment of
privately owned investment companies, which run their
own businesses and make their own credit decisions, to
provide funded debt to American small businesses
("small" within the framework of the definitions given
earlier).

Once again, this offshoot of the SBA is attempting
to provide the type of needed business capital which is
not generally available to growth companies; namely,
long-term capital. SBIC funds may be provided on a
secured basis as a loan against collateral, as unsecured
general obligations partially convertible into stock, as
loan and stock combinations, or as straight stock equity
placements. To provide the profit needed in private enter-
prise, the SBICs are allowed to charge higher fees than
the SBA. Interest may be fairly low where warrants or
other kickers are present—such is the case with con-

vertible debentures—or it may be 10% per annum or higher (SBICs are limited to a maximum of 15% "cost of money," which must include all service or administrative fees as well as interest). However, the SBA officials connected with the SBIC program point out that *small business is not hurt by interest but by term.* I completely agree. The cost of money should always yield sufficient profit to make the acceptance of capital worthwhile; only the need of unrealistically accelerated loan repayments can hurt a business which is making profits as the result of a particular financing.

SBIC loans must be for at least five years, and the terms can extend as long as twenty. These funds therefore create growth and profit potentials which would otherwise be unattainable for many small businesses. To make this possible, the SBA helps to provide capital to the SBICs in a special way prescribed by the Act itself.

There are now over 700 SBICs located throughout the United States. They have already advanced more than $500 million to about 10,000 small businesses. An SBIC can invest up to $500,000—or not to exceed 20% of its capital, whichever is less—in the business of a single client. Although convertibles and various types of equity are purchased by the SBICs, they are prevented by law from acquiring more than 49% of a company. An SBIC, by this simple restriction, is obviously expected to be an investor, a lender, or both—but not to emerge as the owner and operator of a business by virtue of having achieved controlling interest.

As mentioned above, the SBA helps provide some of the funds which SBICs, in turn, place with their clients. This is done by the purchase of an SBIC debenture by the SBA. The SBA can purchase debentures equal to the entire capital of an SBIC, therefore matching the investment, up to a maximum of $700,000. In other words, if an SBIC has its own capital of $700,000, the SBIC can place another $700,000 debenture with the

SBA. This debenture is subordinated and therefore would provide a total of $1.4 million subordinated worth to another lender, such as a bank. In fact, the SBA can also lend up to 50% of the worth (including the subordinated SBA debenture) to an SBIC. Both the debentures and the loans can have maturities as long as twenty years, and bear interest of 5%.

With its fairly high capital cost, it is obvious that an SBIC would find it difficult to make much of a profit simply on the differential between loan cost and loan return. This is quite proper because the whole concept of an SBIC is to establish capital gains by investing in companies with good growth potential. Many members of the financial fraternity have felt that, because the really lucrative capital gain SBIC investments have been relatively few, the SBICs would move closer to routine loans and away from the semi-equity investments they were meant to provide. Actually this has not been the case. In 1960 a group of SBICs had placed outstanding loans of $22 million versus debt and equity securities of $30 million. In 1964 for this same group, the loans stood at $55 million as compared to debt and equity security placements of $98 million. Obviously, the semi-equity trend intended by the Act was being borne out.

The recipients of SBIC funds cover almost the entire spectrum of American industry. In June 1963 the following breakdown existed:

	No. of financings	Amount in millions
Mining and agriculture	223	$ 11
Building trades	910	36
Transportation and utilities	356	19
Retail trade	1,278	38
Wholesale trade	363	16
Other services	2,841	111
Manufacturing	2,230	170

It is interesting to note that, out of 6,241 non-manu-facturing financings in 1963, about 50% went to business firms whose annual sales were under $250,000. Less than 10% were made to firms whose volumes exceeded $1 million. In the manufacturing industries almost 25% of the placements were made to plants employing less than ten people; about 70% to firms which employed less than a hundred people.

A list of SBIC companies in any area can be obtained from the nearest SBA office. While coming under the licensing jurisdiction of the SBA, the SBICs have far greater latitude in their autonomous granting of credit. For this reason, the SBIC should be considered when flexibility and non-stereotype applications are desired. An SBIC can—and frequently does—subordinate its loan position; SBA loans may not be subordinated. All SBA loans can be prepaid without penalty. This is a matter of individual negotiations with the SBICs.

We have already mentioned that SBIC loans can have longer terms than those allowable to the SBA. However, the most important single difference—and that element which is most definitive about the uniqueness of the SBIC practices—is the fact that, either by use of an original security, or by later conversion into such a security, SBICs do take equity positions. The participation in equity—plus the over-all flexibility in providing various types of financing—has led to the hope that the nationwide network of SBICs will create "a fourth banking system."

At the beginning of the program, many false steps were taken by SBIC management. Investors who formed the early SBICs did not include seasoned finance executives and they were only indifferently successful. Over a period of time, however, good management has come into the picture and the "fourth banking system" has begun to demonstrate what it can really do. Properly developed,

SBICs offer the promise of entering more and more significantly into our national financing scene.

INSTITUTIONAL PLACEMENTS

Most of the modern private placements with institutions such as insurance companies and pension funds utilize debentures or senior notes. Almost invariably such financing can only be obtained if the applicant has—or will have as a result of the placement—an unsecured bank line of credit. As mentioned above, this introduces into the picture a current lender who will be watching the financial condition of the borrower on a 90-day basis, and this provides some protection to the long-term lender who provides the private placement funds. For this reason the institutional lender may sometimes provide a subordination of his funds to banks and financial institutions who extend short-term current financing programs.

While it is true that private placements vary in term very widely, there is a strong trend for institutions to make their growth capital available largely on terms of twelve to fifteen years. The notes or debentures which run such a term usually do not require a sinking fund in the classic sense. Instead, since the financing is based on the general soundness and growth potential of the borrower, it is assumed that future profits will provide the necessary cash flow to meet debt repayment schedules. To assure the generation of the cash flow required, the modern private placement will usually defer all principal repayments beyond the first two or three years of the total term. As the institutions view it, this deferment actually creates a sinking fund of sorts.

For example, take a private placement made by an insurance company in the amount of $1 million with a term of twelve years. During the first two years of the loan the recipient would pay interest only, making no principal reductions whatever. Beginning with the third year, however, he would be required to make payments of $100,000 plus interest on the unpaid balance. After making such payments for ten years—which would be twelve years from the time the loan had been first extended—the placement is paid off in full.

Typical institutional private placements as described above are limited in amount according to the *bottom line capital* of the applicant. The bottom line consists primarily of the common stock and surplus found in the capital section of the balance sheet. If there is preferred stock in the corporate picture, and if this is clearly subordinate to the placement, the paid-in value of the preferred stock will also be considered as part of bottom line equity (the institution can always place in its indenture a restriction against calling the preferred before the private placement is repaid).

Relatively young growth companies, particularly those applying for their first private placement, will find that they will be limited to a senior subordinated placement not in excess of 50% of their bottom line equities. Further, depending on their net current asset position, such companies will be able to obtain bank lines equal to, or somewhat greater than, the private placement amount. Therefore, a corporation with $2 million bottom line equity and net current asset position of $2.5 million might have a capital availability picture as follows:

Unsecured bank line	$1,250,000
Debenture placement	1,000,000
Capital and surplus	2,000,000
Total capital availability	$4,250,000

PRE-PLACEMENT PREPARATIONS

Before seeking a private placement you should be well prepared along specific lines. The preparation is

A.B.C. Company

FINANCIAL STATISTICS AND FIVE-YEAR FORECAST

(thousands omitted)

	Actual				Projected			
	Yr. End Dec. 60	Yr. End Dec. 61	Yr. End Dec. 62	Yr. End Dec. 63	Yr. End Dec. 64	Yr. End Dec. 65	Yr. End Dec. 66	Yr. End Dec. 67
Net sales	$ 146	$ 490	$ 906	$1,600	$2,500	$3,500	$5,000	$6,000
Cost of sales	106	345	824	1,137	1,750	2,450	3,500	4,200
Gross profit	40	144	82	462	750	1,050	1,500	1,800
Sales expense	24	99	200	223	325	455	650	780
General & administrative	21	38	50	111	175	245	350	420
Operating profit (loss)	[5]	7	[168]	128	250	350	500	600
Other expenses	[1]	6	4	22	32	45	50	50
NET PROFIT (LOSS)	[4]	1	172	106	218	305	450	550
Federal income taxes	0	0	0	0	72	152	230	280
ASSETS:								
Cash	$ 14	$ 40	$ 17	$ 10	$ 20	$ 30	$ 50	$ 70
Receivables	60	71	146	255	380	550	700	850
Inventories	56	124	151	200	500	700	900	1,200
Prepaids, etc.	8	19	19	12	20	30	50	80
Total current assets	138	254	333	477	920	1,310	1,700	2,200
Fixed Assets	37	93	162	260	400	550	800	1,000
Less Depreciation	[2]	[14]	[33]	[101]	[200]	[350]	[500]	[700]
Other	28	22	63	5	10	20	30	50
TOTAL ASSETS	$ 201	$ 355	$ 526	$ 641	$ 1,130	$1,530	$2,030	$2,550
LIABILITIES:								
Trade payables	55	31	118	103	150	200	250	300
Accruals	6	16	38	38	60	80	100	150
Total current commitments	61	47	156	141	210	280	350	450
Debt—Bank loan	0	0	140	160	300	440	560	680
Debt—Other	34	10	25	19	0	0	0	0
Capital—Stock	110	110	119	120	145	145	145	145
Capital—Surplus	0	192	261	270	270	270	270	270
Earned Surplus	[4]	[3]	[175]	[69]	77	230	450	720
Total stockholders' equity	$ 106	$ 299	$ 205	$ 321	$ 492	$ 645	$ 865	$1,135
Capital needed	0	0	0	0				

similar to that earlier described for term loans, but more refined. Once again, do not underestimate the importance of submitting a well-prepared proposal to the fund source. Depending on the size of the credit being sought, the financial information should be as full as possible.

The lender will want to analyze your picture in two directions—backward and forward. He will want to see your financial statements, both balance sheet and profit and loss, for the previous three to five years. He will also want to see a projection of your future operations with emphasis on two factors: (1) your *cash-need* projection, which is the demonstration of your requirement for the funds being sought; and (2) your *cash-flow* projection, which illustrates how the funds will be created to repay the loan.

On the opposite page is an example of how one company tackled this problem. The illustration is unique in that the applicant included some of his historic figures alongside his projection. Actually, he had also provided regulation financial statement for his three years' operations prior to the forecast. However, he repeated these in a summarized form to illustrate the continuity of the trend into the forecast portion. You will also note that the illustration includes both profit and loss—and balance sheet information. All this is correlated to create the cash need requirement developed along the bottom line of the report. Properly done, the illustration should have been carried out for several years more, to show how the cash-flow profits at the $6 million sales figure postulated to stabilize at the end of 1967 would create the funds required to repay the $285,000 capital being sought to satisfy the capital need.

While cash-need and cash-flow projections can be prepared fairly simply for smaller placement applications, the firm's accountants should be given this task where more substantial financings are being sought. Also, if the amount of capital sought is in the range of institutional placements (from $250,000 up) it is advisable to use a financial consultant or investment banker for this purpose. As is mentioned in connection with several other types of financing covered in this book, these professionals are experienced and well qualified in the eyes of the lenders who give serious consideration to their recommendations. The businessman who is not familiar with these channels can make a few false starts and, when this is done, the word somehow drifts through the financial community that the deal is being "shopped around"—a phrase which almost always leads to a complete dashing of the hope for a private placement. In one case I know of, the president of a privately owned steel company, whose statement and earnings history undoubtedly deserved a private placement from any first-rate institutional lender in the country, made up twenty presentation packages for a million-dollar debenture and mailed them to an equal number of investment bankers and life insurance companies. Not realizing this, one of the investment bankers called upon an insurance company that had received one of the presentation packages and was dismayed when the insurance company loan officer said he had already heard of the deal. As a result, both the loan officer and the investment banker decided the deal was being shopped around, the word spread through the financial community, and the steel company lost all chance for the placement it sought. The cost of professional handling is only a small percent of the total placement but, once mishandled as in this case, no professional will accept the assignment regardless of the fee. The brokerage charges for a $1 million placement, for example, will range from 1½% to 2½%, with the percentage varying in proportion to larger or smaller fund requests.

CHAPTER 12

Public Stock Issues

Companies that have progressed through various stages of financial growth achieve the ultimate by "going public." Almost every discussion about public stock issues goes into a standard line-up of pros and cons. Yet here I will disagree with many of my colleagues in the financial fraternity; it is my opinion that all discussion on this subject is academic. Putting it very simply and positively, I feel that, once a business has reached the stage where it qualifies for a *properly designed* public stock issue, no other form of financing can provide as much benefit.

The advantages of a public stock issue are as follows:

1. *Capitalization of earnings.* As you will see below, the evaluation of a corporation going public is based on its earnings. So long as a company remains privately held, any value based on what its earnings might impart is only a vague guess as to what a potentail sell-out would bring. The establishment of a public market for the stock firmly establishes the going business value of the company.

2. *Estate benefits.* As mentioned immediately above, the estate of a principal owner of a business is fairly and accurately evaluated. This can benefit such a principal even while he is living. In the event of a buy-out of other principals a firm valuation is established which functions

even better than the standard "buy and sell" agreements between principals which are invoked when there are irreconcilable differences, or when one principal wishes to retire and the remaining active principals do not wish to see a large block of control stock get out of their hands. In case of death of a principal, there are benefits both to the surviving principals and to the heirs of the deceased. The heirs are not subject to an arbitrary evaluation of the going business made by Treasury Department agents to determine inheritance taxes. Valuable equities in going firms have had to be sold to meet such taxes. On the other hand, the government agents can rarely argue the value of stock whose worth is set by the price at which it is traded over a wide public market. Further, the existence of an active public market makes possible the disposal without undue sacrifice of a portion of the stock in an estate to take care of the taxes needed to retain the balance. Not long ago I was consulted by the owners of a small chain of supermarkets who, several years before, had had to dispose of their most successful single retail unit when a partner died and they had to raise money to buy his stock. Had this been a public company, the lucrative store could have been retained.

3. *Financial leverage.* Most public financing is either in the form of stock which becomes a *permanent* part of capital, or senior securities which have long amortizations or conversions. They do not represent debt in the usual sense as do other forms of financing. Therefore, in addition to the funds received from the public financing itself, a public issue also provides for far more capital leverage. For example, a private company with $1 million net worth might be able to borrow $600,000 on a reasonable basis. After a public issue which creates an additional $1 million in stock equity, a long-term debenture could be obtained for another $1 million plus another $1.5 million unsecured bank borrowings. As compared to the original $600,000

availability, the $1 million stock issue actually creates a total availability of $3.5 million in fiancing.

4. *Acquisition potential.* The use of the stock of a public corporation is most helpful in making payments for acquisitions. Any corporation is allowed to use treasury stock—or—to issue more stock—for value received. Acquisition of another company represents such value. Moreover, purchase advantages can result from use of stock to acquire a privately owned company. The stock of public companies is usually priced by the market on a multiplier higher than is accorded to private companies. For example, a private company earning $100,000 after taxes would do well to be evaluated at $700,000 in an acquisition. A public company can easily have a multiplier of ten to twenty times earnings placed on its stock by the public after it has been out on the market. Assuming the lowest multiplier of ten times earnings for the public company, obviously the public company would be using "70-cent dollars" to purchase the private company.

5. *Personal gain for principals.* The capitalization of earnings mentioned previously accrues benefits to the principals of a company that goes public. Not only is stock sold to provide additional corporate capital but it is also sold for the account of principals. The sale of principals' stock (see "secondary selling" below) produces capital gains income which can, at one fell swoop, put more cash dollars in the pocket of a principal than many years' ordinary drawings could produce. A correct basis of comparison would involve a principal whose corporate salary places him in a 50% tax bracket. Additional drawings—or dividends—will raise the tax bracket even higher. Such a principal who sells only sufficient stock to yield him $450,000 would realize net cash of $300,000 after 33% capital gains taxes. In the form of higher drawings or dividends, the same principal could take ten or more years to develop as much after-tax cash.

Against such an array of advantages most objections are easy to discount. Control is not lost, as some detractors will claim; usually first issues do not even involve a majority of a corporation's stock. Moreover, as corporations grow and issue more stock, 10% or less can constitute working control. This is because well-managed issues spread the stock widely and the individual public stockholders hold infinitesimal percentages (on which they invariably vote the proxies for existing management). As the pros say, if an outsider tries to buy up enough stock to seize control he will drive the price of your own stock so high that you may be delighted to take your fortune and depart.

TYPES OF REGISTRATIONS

Public issues of stock require *registration* with government agencies. Although there are a number of different types of registration, commercial businesses seeking financing via this route generally use only the following three variations:

1. *Intrastate registrations.* Not all stock issues require registration with the S.E.C. The exceptions are those issues involving sales of stocks to bona fide residents of only one particular state. These are not found nearly as often as are the other two major forms of registration described below, and the services of investment bankers are not usually employed. Special purposes are served by these limited registrations, particularly when the funds are to be used entirely for corporate capital, where principals are not initially concerned about a national public market, and where the size of the issue varies from $50,-000 to three or four times that amount. With an effective registration of this type, local advertising and solicitation can be used to generate stock subscriptions. There is

usually a time limit for solicitations and, until the expiration of this limit, all funds received are usually impounded. Filing, accounting, and other registration requirements will vary depending on state regulations.

2. *Regulation A Issues.* This is the *short form* type of registration with the S.E.C. It is suitable for modest-size public financings which still come under the scope of a national registration. Under Regulation A, stock may be sold to the public in an issue whose total amount may not exceed $500,000. Although, as is true for any kind of registration, the services of an investment banker are not required, they are usually employed in short-form issues. Regulation A requires the printing of a prospectus which can be much simpler than is required in a full registration. Also, the financial statements do not have to go back as far in the past, nor do they have to be fully audited. The general theory behind the short-form registration is, of course, to save cost in a small issue. However, this saving can be less than anticipated. The usual cost will frequently be at least 25% of the gross amount of the issue. Despite this factor, there is still much to be said in favor of the short form for a small issue.

3. *Full Registration.* Beyond a gross offer to sell $500,000 of stock publicly, a full registration, or "S-1," is required to be filed with the S.E.C. In addition to a detailed printed prospectus, the filing requires fully audited financial reports plus written documentation of the facts stated in the prospectus. Investment bankers are almost always used for underwriting the issue, and legal counsel both for the corporation and for the underwriters must be retained in preparing the prospectus. All major issues, and those handled by the better underwriters, require full registrations. The dollar cost of preparation of the issue may be higher but, depending on the total size of the offering, the percentage cost will probably be less than that of a Regulation A issue.

TYPES OF SECURITIES TO BE SOLD

We have covered in considerable detail, in Chapter III, the many types of securities which can be sold by a corporation. All of these varieties can be offered in a public issue; however, the nature of the public market is such that the choice of securities to be sold is practically limited to just a few standard types. The older, well-established public companies may reflect wide varieties of securities on their statements, but a corporation that is going public for the first time would be ill-advised to attempt to market all but a few types of securities. Preferred stock, for example, has experienced diminishing popularity during the past twenty years. Investors in young corporations are likewise not much interested in taking senior securities. If they are seeking lower-risk investments, they can find such opportunities in stable, old established companies. Instead, the investor in a younger company, which is going public for the first time, prefers to have the growth and gain potential represented by common stock.

Therefore, if a new issue does not consist solely of common stock, it usually is designed to allow for ownership of at least some common stock, at the outset or in the future. One variation is the issuance of convertible debentures which provide a good interest income and senior position at the outset, but with the right to convert into common stock on a schedule of prices that increase over a five- or ten-year period. Debentures which may or may not be convertible are sometimes packaged in unitized combinations that give the investor the right to purchase common stock at a very reasonable price—but only in a certain ratio to the debentures he must also purchase (e.g., the investor who buys a $1,000 debenture bond is also allowed to buy 100 shares of common stock at $1.00 each). Returning to our earlier statement, however, the most desirable new issue is the straight common stock offering. The corporation commissioners of many states are becoming increasingly unenthusiastic about non-voting stock. There is, however, one acceptable variation; namely, the use of two classes of common stock for dividend purposes. Modest cash dividend features enhance new stock issues; however, the payment of cash dividends on all the common shares of a corporation may remove needed growth capital. The corporate principals who enjoy substantial salaries, and who still own the majority of corporate stock, would prefer to see the value of their shares enhanced through retention of surplus rather than to receive dividends on their own stock. Therefore, the stock issued to the public carries a dividend; the stock retained by the principals does not have a dividend feature. In subsequent years, management is allowed to exchange, say, 20% each year for the dividend bearing stock. In five years all outstanding stock is one-class dividend-paying common stock and will pose no problems in future issues of principals' stock.

CHOICE OF AN UNDERWRITER

Underwriters of public stock issues are found primarily in the stock brokerage field. Stockbrokers place this particular function into a group of activities which they perform and to which they refer as *investment banking*. Almost any brokerage firm holding valid security dealer licenses may handle an underwriting; however, there are some practical limitations. The great majority of securities firms are members of the National Association of Security Dealers. This organization, with offices in the principal financial communities, restricts its members from engaging in various types of transactions with non-member firms. Since most public stock offerings involve a syndicate of more than one underwriting firm, it is almost essential that you choose a member firm of the NASD (see Underwriting Syndicates below).

Security brokerage firms tend to concentrate in certain specialties. Some handle only the investment accounts of institutions, others concentrate in bonds, another category forms the group of well-known national retailers of stock in the open market, utilizing many branch offices scattered throughout the country and staffed with "customer men" (now officially referred to as *registered representatives*). While the head offices of such firms may have corporate departments equipped to handle underwritings, there is usually not an effective organizational link between these departments and the stock-retailing oriented representatives in the local branch offices. There is another group of very strong investment houses, primarily located in the Wall Street area in New York, which have no branch offices, but which have the power to sponsor substantial offerings. All along the scale are houses of various strength and scope, local or national, which can handle issues of varying magnitudes and qualitative levels.

A veritable hierarchy exists in the investment banking fraternity. At the theoretical top are a few firms handling only very substantial and important clients, and they are practically in the position of taking on no new clients. Other substantial houses are open to better quality new offerings—and so on down the line. The hierarchy extends to the underwriting syndicate where normally only firms of the same level are found in the management group. There is even an implied hierarchy in the placing of brokerage firm names on the prospectus. In a co-management, the left-hand position is supposed to carry more prestige than the right-hand position on the same line.

Without going into further detail, there are certain things a business should look for in a prospective underwriter. The underwriter should be able to handle his *takedown requirement* (see below) readily, should be capable of forming a representative syndicate, and above all, should have demonstrated a certain moral responsibility. As you will presently see, public issues can involve much work and expense before an actual binding contract is executed. It is significant, therefore, that the business whose stock will be offered have as much assurance as possible that informal understandings will be faithfully implemented.

THE FINDER'S ROLE

The role of a *finder* in an underwriting is a uniquely productive one, and its usage has been long established. For this reason the presence of a finder, particularly in first issues, is widespread. Generally a finder is an individual such as a financial consultant, or a professional in the financial community whose other activities do not include a direct involvement in actual stock underwriting firms. Not only should the finder be well grounded in the entire field of business finance, but in this instance he should be well acquainted with the roles and positions of many investment banking firms. As described above, the hierarchy and varying functions of brokerage firms are both diverse and esoteric; therefore, someone who can authoritatively recommend the right firm is of definite value. Further, the experience and contacts of a well-qualified finder gain him easy audiences with investment banking decision makers who respect his recommendations and know that he has used his own seasoned judgment in screening the application before presenting it. Also, as in many other types of presentations, an objective third party can frequently sound the praises of a business more effectively than its own principals can.

Acting as a consultant, the finder can advise when, and if, a company is ripe for a public stock issue. If it is, he can advise how to avoid certain future investment banker objections and problem areas, and how to initiate the preparatory stages, which can last a year or more. During the introduction to, and negotiation with, the underwriter the finder will primarily serve as protagonist for the corporation.

Finders' fees range from 1% to 4% of the gross amount of the issue. They are frequently paid by the underwriters, or partially or wholly by the corporation. All investment bankers recognize the role of the finder and will join with the corporation in working out a satisfactory compensation package. Normally, on the basis of having made a good underwriting possible, and also of having provided criteria from experience against which the deal can be evaluated properly, the cost of the finder is more than offset.

TYPES OF COMMITMENTS

There are three variations of underwriting commitments:

1. *Best Efforts.* The underwriter will commit to use his "best efforts" to sell a certain amount of stock at a specified price. There is no guarantee that all of the contemplated issue will be sold—or that any of it will be sold. However, an investment banking firm will not allow its name to appear on a prospectus, even on only a best-efforts basis, if it feels little chance of at least partial success. A certain time limit is established, during which the stock may continue to be sold. All proceeds from the sale are impounded until the selling period terminates.

Though it is not the best possible solution, the best-efforts commitment may be the only route available to an aspiring company. It is also frequently used when a company underwrites its own intrastate issue.

2. *All or Nothing.* In this type of commitment the proceeds from sale of stock are impounded as in the best efforts offerings; however, if the predetermined total issue is not sold, all sales are reversed and money is returned to the would-be purchasers. Some firm commitments (see below) are written on a contract which includes the phrase "all or none"; however, the actual condition is quite different.

3. *Firm Commitment.* By far the most desirable commitment is a *firm takedown.* In underwriter's parlance, a takedown is the amount of stock which the underwriter contractually agrees to buy, for resale to others. Under the conditions of a firm commitment the underwriter agrees to purchase the entire stock issue at a fixed price on a specified date. Because of the work and expense involved in many full registrations, plus the inevitable publicity and possible repercussions, most substantial issues should not be undertaken except in anticipation of a firm commitment. As you will see below, however, this type of commitment is not contractually established until well along in the public stock offering process.

PRICING OF THE STOCK

As I have described in the earlier chapters on equity capital and acquisitions, evaluating a company for the purposes of a public stock issue is almost always based on an *earnings multiplier.* The multiplier, which is applied only to after-tax corporate earnings, is usually set on the most recent fiscal year-end profits. Since most companies that go public are demonstrating a consistent growth curve, the use of the current earnings figure provides the most advantageous pricing base. S.E.C. requirements call for certified accounting figures as far back as five years, if available, and a company that hopes to sell stock publicly in the future should try to anticipate well in advance so that the CPA firm doing the audit will be able to provide the type of unqualified audit the S.E.C. insists on. It will be on the most recent unqualified audit after-tax profit that the multiplier will be set. Although it is permissible to show subsequent quarter profits in the prospectus, the underwriters normally set the price only on a full year's figures.

Prior to May 1962, a new issue boom occurred in stock offerings, during which earnings multipliers were set at ridiculously high levels. When the bubble burst, not only did the multipliers settle down to more realistic levels, but also high-priced issues sagged drastically and have never since returned even to their issue price. Both underwriters and corporate executives have learned a lesson from this sad history; as a result, the outlandish overpricing of a new issue may be a definite thing of the past.

It must be remembered that a first public stock issue for a previously private company comes into the market at a *negotiated price*. The price is set as the result of an agreement between the underwriters and the issuing corporation. Thereafter, once the stock is out on the market and is stabilized, it sets its own level, by the simple rule of supply and demand. It is true that certain stocks sell for as high as thirty or forty times earnings; however, these are stocks which have been out on the public market many years, and usually involve substantial companies with outstanding growth potential. (There are also public companies whose stock trades on the market at two or three times earnings, sometimes at a price less than book value; these are companies whose profit potentials are downgrading.)

Generally speaking, first public stock issues are priced on a multiplier of eight to twelve times per share earnings *before dilution.* "Dilution" results from the issuance of additional stock to the public. To understand how these figures are arrived at, let us follow the usual few steps taken in setting a stock offering price.

Assume that a corporation earns $150,000 net profit after taxes in its most recent fiscal year. If a ten times multiplier were placed on company earnings, 100% of the corporation would be evaluated at $1.5 million. The corporation has 100,000 shares of common stock outstanding—therefore, each share of stock has been priced at $15 ($1.5 million divided by 100,000 shares). Looking at it another way, each one of the 100,000 shares has earned $1.50 profit ($150,000 profit divided by 100,000 shares); therefore, a $15 price represents a ten times multiplier on per share earnings of $1.50. So far, this computation has been on a before-dilution basis.

Now, let us assume that an additional 50,000 shares are authorized to be issued by the corporation, to be sold to the public in an underwriting. When these shares are added to the original 100,000 shares held by the principals of the company, the new total of outstanding shares is 150,000. The per share earnings (obtained by dividing $150,000 profit by the new total of 150,000 shares) are now $1 per share. Obviously there has been a one-third dilution as the result of the public issue. The *after dilution* multiplier is therefore fifteen times earnings because the stock, as mentioned above, was sold at $15 per share.

While pre-dilution multipliers may normally range from eight to twelve times earnings on first issues, after-dilution multipliers vary from eleven to fourteen times earnings. In the case cited above, where the after-dilution multiplier came to fifteen times earnings, the underwriters might want to reduce the ten times pre-dilution multiplier to avoid the higher multiplier resulting from the dilution of such a large percentage of new stock being sold.

Of course, the range of multipliers I have quoted are only guidelines and are subject to many qualitative adjustments. In some industries, particularly in the financial and banking fields, book value may have some influence on the multiplier. More general with all industries, however, is the difference which can result from the presence of a long history of sustained earnings. Multipliers are justified by the expectation of a future continuation of higher evaluation premium. For example, a fifty-year-old company may be evaluated at a 50% to 100% higher multiplier than a company which, although it has the same earnings, has been in business less than ten years.

SIZE OF THE ISSUE

There are two categories of selling which can be included in a public issue, as follows:

1. *Primary selling*—the sale of stock which is issued by the corporation, in addition to its already existing stock, the proceeds of which go to the corporation.

2. *Secondary selling*—the sale of stock already owned by principals and other shareholders of the corporation. No new stock is created by the corporation for this purpose; therefore, secondary selling *creates no dilution*. The proceeds of such sales go to the selling shareholders and not to the corporation.

Either one—or both—types of selling can be found in a common stock issue. The first category to be considered is primary selling for the corporation. Every responsible underwriter wants to be sure that, as a result of the public issue, the corporation seems to be adequately financed for the immediate future. Therefore, a careful analysis is made of corporate financial needs to determine, in a gross dollar amount, what would constitute an adequate addition to permanent equity capital. In the example we have previously used, $750,000 additional capital was raised for the corporation. However, at the same time it is possible that some of the principal shareholders wished to obtain some capital gain and to put some cash in their own pockets. Therefore, another 25,000 shares—at $15 per share—were registered to be sold in the same issue for the benefit of the selling shareholders. This increment of secondary selling was acceptable to the underwriters. First, it caused no further dilution of the per share earnings. As explained above, the number of shares outstanding does not change as a result of secondary selling; only the names of the stockholders owning those shares change. In addition, the secondary selling added $375,000 to the issue to bring it to a total of $1,125,000, a respectable offering in the lower volume range. The additional 25,000 shares gave promise of providing a wider stockholder group, after the issue, than if only the shares for the corporation were sold.

There are several limitations on secondary selling. If the underwriters will only take down a certain maximum dollar amount—and this maximum is wholly required to satisfy the financing needs of the corporation—the would-be selling shareholders will have to wait for another day. Actually, this is very seldom the case. A more serious limitation imposed by the underwriter is to avoid the appearance of a *bailout*. If principals sell too large a percentage of their stock holdings in a first issue, the public (and their stockbrokers) can become suspicious that these insiders of management are not optimistic about the future of the business and wish to unload. As a general rule, any offerings (in a single issue) in excess of 35% to 40% of the holdings of management, prior to the issue, risk appearing to be bailouts.

On the other side of the coin, principals must sometimes be induced to sell more of their shares than they originally intended, in order to secure a wide enough public stock holding. If, for example, only 10% of a company is held by the public, small possibility exists of an active market made in the stock after the issue—the stock price can respond wildly and unnaturally to sales or buy orders for even small blocks of stock. Principals must be willing to provide some of their shares to round out a first offering if the corporate financing requirements have been met and there would still be insufficient shares in the hands of the public to provide a decent *after market.*

There is one more consideration in determining the size of the issue. If the corporation desires listing on one of the recognized exchanges, it is important that sufficient shares are issued—and sold to a sufficient number of stockholders—to satisfy the minimum requirements of the stock exchanges on these points. The exchanges also have other requirements, including earnings levels, as a prerequisite to becoming listed.

Beyond the satisfaction of minimum requirements for listing, or for obtaining a sufficiently widespread public holding in the after market, it is wise to limit the size of the first public issue. Here we come to what I consider among the most important attitudes to be adopted in connection with going public.

First, a basic fact: *whatever benefits the public stockholders will also benefit the insiders.* The principals of a public corporation will inevitably find themselves in the same boat as their public stockholders. A reasonably priced first issue presents the possibility of a price rise in the after market. When the stock goes up, the public is benefited—but so, also, are the insiders. In fact, the value of the unissued stock held by principals frequently appreciates far more significantly from after-market reaction than could have been achieved through attempts to negotiate a higher issue price with the underwriters. Therefore, it is wise to limit the first issue in size, in recognition of the fact that subsequent issues will yield the higher values set by the public in the after market. Shareholders who, for example, sell 20% of their holdings for $1 million in a first issue, may find they can obtain an additional million dollars from a second issue for the release of only 10% more of their stock.

COST OF GOING PUBLIC

The cost of small public issues can be expensive, frequently 25% or more of the gross amount of the stock sale. However, as the issue size increases, the cost becomes much more reasonable. The cost for a million-dollar issue would include the following:

Special CPA audit for prospectus	$18,000
Corporate counsel	14,000
Underwriters expenses and counsel	6,000
Prospectus and contract printing	7,000
Blue sky registration	2,000
	$47,000

The above expenses would obviously approach 5% of a $1 million issue. They would drop to 3% for a $2 million issue: 2% or less for issues over $3 million. In addition the underwriter receives his commission, referred to in investment banking circles as the *spread,* or *concession.* Underwriting commissions vary from about 15% to 6% on common stock first issues. The higher range applies to small issues, such as those filed under Regulation A. Issues of a few million dollars generally do not require commission over 10%; thereafter, depending on size, the percentage will drop lower. Combining the preparation costs, shown above, with the underwriter's commission, a·

new issue for $3 million might be expected to have a total cost of about 10%, or $300,000.

The underwriter's commission is not nearly so high as it appears. This is because the fee is broken up—and passed down along the line in the underwriting syndicate—in a series of *re-allowances*. The largest single portion of the fee will go to the individual registered representatives (stockbroker customer men) in the field who place the stock with their personal customers. Out of a 10% commission the registered representative may get 4%; the selling group stock brokerage firms, 3%; the underwriting group, 1½%; and the managing underwriter, or *originator*, 1½%.

LETTER OF INTENT

When the corporation and underwriter have established at least a tentative interest in exploring the possibility of a public stock issue, arrangements are made to provide the underwriter with sufficient information and audit material to make a decision about going forward. Not only will the underwriter be concerned with the corporation, but also with the entire industry in which it functions, plus reviewing every possible economic area which can conceivably bear on the company under study. When the review is completed on a satisfactory basis, representatives of the underwriter and of the corporation will meet informally to discuss details of a possible deal. If there seems to be general agreement, the underwriter will forward a *letter of intent* to the prospective client.

The letter of intent is frequently misunderstood by those not actively engaged in the investment banking field. First of all, it is *not* a binding contract. Yet it is as close to a contract as either party can come, prior to a few days before the actual issue date for the public stock. As you will see, the actual underwriting contract is only executed at almost the very end of the underwriting process. There is no alternative. Until that time either party can walk away, with no further obligation. Yet a great deal of reliance can be placed on a letter of intent from an ethical brokerage firm. The letter contains various contingencies and *market outs;* but it is a fact that an ethical investment banking house begins to feel a moral obligation once the letter is submitted and accepted. Only a serious break in the market, or a drastic change in the company itself during preparation and registration of the "S-1" (the form for full registration with the S.E.C.) will cause the letter of intent not to be fulfilled.

Here is an example of a theoretical letter of intent:

"April 30, 1974

"Mr. John Jones, President
Jones Distributing Company
Los Angeles, California
"Dear Mr. Jones:

"At the time of our visit on April 14, we agreed to submit to you in writing our general recommendations with respect to a public offering of Jones Distributing Company, Common Stock for the account of the Company and certain shareholders. Accordingly, in this letter we have outlined for you the thoughts which Williams Investment Bankers has regarding such a contemplated offering.

"First, let us compliment the management of Jones on its exceptional performance in developing the business so successfully over a very short period of time. We have been unusually impressed by our contacts with management and by the comments we have received from a variety of others whose views we have solicited in the normal course of investigating your fine organization. If we mutually agree on proceedings towards an eventual public offering, we will, of course, continue to investigate and analyze your business, but we have every expectation that this will result in a verification of what we have learned to date.

"In order to provide you with as specific a financing plan as possible, we have used a number of assumptions which we would like to set forth at this point:

1. The public offering would take place after the completion of fiscal 1974 which ends August 31. Based upon the present backlog of registrations being reviewed by The Securities and Exchange Commission, and the normal five-six week lag between the end of a fiscal year and the availability of audited figures, we would estimate that a Jones filing could be accomplished by mid-October. The actual public offering would, therefore, take place sometime around mid-November. A filing could be accomplished earlier this year based upon interim 1974 figures, but such timing would not be in the Company's or the selling shareholders' interest primarily because current earnings are in such a sharp uptrend that a significantly fuller realization in terms of market valuation can be achieved at year end as opposed to an earlier date.

2. Net sales according to your estimate for fiscal 1974 will approximate $18 million and net income after taxes will be in a range of $700,000 to $800,000.

3. The Company requires new capital of approximately $2.0 million to $2.5 million and the selling shareholders will sell up to $2.0 million of their holdings.

4. Present shareholders and management of Jones have no strong views as to whether or not a reasonable quarterly dividend rate is established on the Common Stock. If a dividend is necessary for

marketing purposes, or if shareholders require it, a dividend could be established consistent with the Company's financial position.

5. No material changes in the nature of Jones' business are contemplated by management, nor does it expect that the trend of growth as indicated by the record over the prior three years, will be significantly different.

6. General stock market conditions will remain strong, and the improving investor attitudes towards merchandising type stocks, on which valuations were quite modest throughout 1973 and early 1974, will continue to improve.

"We recommend a split of the shares presently outstanding to enable the establishment of the initial offering price at a level which reflects prestige yet indicates the youth and vigor of a growing company. It is also vital to have a public issue of sufficient size to obtain an American Stock Exchange listing (minimum 400,000 shares owned by the general public). We suggest a split involving the issuance of one new share for each two of the 476,000 shares presently outstanding resulting in a new share capitalization of 714,000 shares outstanding. Estimated earnings per share for the fiscal year ending August 31, 1964, would be $1.05 net income after taxes of $750,000.

"Based upon this new capitalization, we would suggest that the company sell 200,000 shares which would increase the number of shares outstanding after the completion of the offering to 914,000 shares, or a dilution by the addition of the new shares of approximately 27%. Estimated earnings per share for fiscal 1974 on the basis of 914,000 shares outstanding would be $0.92. We recommend that the selling shareholders make available up to 200,000 shares for inclusion in the offering. Therefore, the total offering would consist of a maximum 400,000 shares, which in our judgment would provide sufficient shares for good secondary market trading activity as well as exceeding the minimum American Stock Exchange listing requirements by a reasonable margin.

"The pricing of initial stock offerings is always difficult and frankly still remains an art which is not subject to highly definitive statements until the proposed offering is only a matter of days off. In the case of Jones, pricing projections are even more hazardous because we are looking ahead to November and the stock market, economic conditions, and world affairs can all have changed markedly during the interim.

"As we have attempted to indicate in the above paragraphs, if general market conditions, pricing of similar issues and the over-all business situation continue to improve, then we think an offering of Jones Common Stock could be accomplished late this fall in the 12 to 14 times earnings range. It is our opinion that the objectives of the Company and its shareholders, and the present financial condition of Jones are such that an offering which could only be accomplished at a lower price basis is neither necessary nor desirable. We would, therefore, advise that no offering take place until this kind of valuation could be achieved. Under different circumstances, however, our conclusions in this respect might well be different.

"The offering price per share would be $12 to $14 related to estimated earnings per share of $1.05. An offering price in the 12-14 earnings multiple range related to estimated 1974 net income of $750,000 would place a total valuation on Jones of $9.0 million to $10.5 million prior to the sale of shares for the account of the Company. Using a 13 times earnings multiple, a total offering of 400,000 shares would amount to $5,460,000 with $2,-730,000 being sold for the Company and $2,730,000 for the account of the selling shareholders. After the offering, the general public would own 43% and the present shareholders would account for 57% of the 914,000 then outstanding shares.

"We estimate that direct expenses of such an offering, other than underwriting commissions, such as legal, auditing, printing and other costs should not exceed $45,000 to $50,000. The greater portion of such costs can be paid by the Company although certain expenses are customarily assumed by the selling shareholders. Of course, auditing and certain other expenses would be incurred at fiscal year end regardless of the public offering and so are not really added expenses to the Company.

"If we were to proceed with a public offering as outlined above, it would be our intention to form an underwriting group of established investment banking and brokerage firms with offices in principal cities throughout the United States to distribute Jones Common Stock on a national basis. The gross commission charged by the underwriting syndicate would be approximately 8% of the public offering price, although the actual size of the offering would have a bearing on the final determination of this commission. Underwriters bear their own legal expenses, advertising costs and the other direct expenses involved in merchandising such an issue.

"The following sets forth in abbreviated form an approximate time schedule for a Jones offering along the lines discussed in this letter:

October 5—Audited Financial Statements for Fiscal
    Year Ending August 31, 1964, Available
October 9—Registration Statement Filed with S.E.C.
October 30—Receipt of Deficiency Letter from
    S.E.C.
November 10—A Public Offering of Jones
November 18—Closing with Company and Selling
    Shareholders

"This timing is based upon the present backlog and processing schedule of the S.E.C. and, of course, can be subjected to a variety of changes.

"The foregoing statements in this letter are preliminary recommendations and should not be construed as a binding contract of Jones Distributing Company, or yourself, or of Williams Investment Bankers, or any other proposed underwriter. We have stated to you our interest in this potential financing and our ideas as to how it might be successfully accomplished. All relevant terms, conditions and circumstances and legal matters relating to such proposed stock sale must be mutually satisfactory to us and to our counsel.

> Very truly yours,
> WILLIAMS INVESTMENT BANKERS, INC.
> Henry Brown
> Vice President"

You can see from the above example that a great deal of thought and careful preparation go into the letter of intent. Considering the costs of an abortive issue, both to the corporation and to the underwriter, the parties are careful not to go beyond this stage unless they feel they can deliver the performance stipulated in the letter. If the corporation figures and facts are borne out, only a serious break in the stock market will cause delay in the underwriting. Therefore, when an acceptable letter of intent is negotiated, the corporation is justified in committing for the expenses incurred prior to the actual stock issue.

RECAPITALIZATION

Almost all companies which go public for the first time face the necessity of taking special steps to provide the proper stock structure. If the company is a proprietorship or other form of noncorporate entity, it must first incorporate to create the stock which it will sell, as well as that increment which will be retained by the principals. Most companies which reach the public issue stage are, of course, already incorporated; yet they, too, usually require stock restructuring.

The usual problem is that there are too few shares to sell at a reasonable price. Most private corporations do not bother to issue additional stock, beyond the original authorized amount, as they grow. Therefore, you will find fairly large companies with only one hundred to several thousand shares of authorized stock. When a public issue is undertaken, more shares must be created to provide a sufficiently broad holding in the hands of the public.

We have previously described the method of evaluating an aspiring public corporation as the result of negotiation between management and the underwriter. After the evaluation, the size and shape of the issue is determined. In other words, there is agreement on the percentage of the company stock to be sold—and how much of the proceeds of the issue will go to the corporation or to the selling shareholders.

The total amount to be sold is computed in dollars. If, for example, a corporation earns $600,000 after taxes and is evaluated at $6 million, an issue which contemplates sale of 40% of the company stock would involve a gross underwriting of $2.4 million. Now the underwriters must resolve the problem of determining the number of shares among which this gross amount will be divided. There are several definite guidelines which influence this decision, as follows:

1. Will there be sufficient shares to assure a proper stockholding in the hands of the public?

2. Will the individual share price be correlated to the quality of the stock being offered?

Small issues, such as those governed by Regulation A, have involved stock which sold at $1 to $3 per share. Many Regulation A issues in the past followed the pattern of offering 100,000 shares at $3 per share. Full registrations in the modest range can be designed to offer stock at $4 to $6 per share. However, when an offering moves above the million-dollar range, and is handled by more substantial underwriters, the per share price requirement is elevated. A "respectable" price for a larger issue is $10 or more (which gives the stockbroker a minimum $1,000 sale for a "round lot" of 100 shares); most new issues range from this minimum up to slightly over $20 per share. Only very large, long-established firms, such as the renowned first issue of the Ford Motor Company at well over $50, are exceptions to this practice.

Returning to our example where $2.4 million worth of stock is to be sold, it is quite likely that the underwriters will decide to offer 200,000 shares at $12 per share. With this number of shares to market, an underwriting syndicate which does its job well by restricting large purchases will obtain a fairly wide public distribution. However, we find that our example has a total of only 100,000 shares authorized and outstanding stock, so a *recapitalization* is necessary.

Through the recapitalization process, additional stock is authorized, and new share values are set, usually by applying to the corporation commissioner of the state in which the corporation is domiciled. The total authorization might be increased to one million shares with a permit to issue 200,000 shares to the public in the first offering. However, the shares retained by the principals must also be adjusted in the recapitalization.

Before the issue and the recapitalization, principals held 100,000 shares which represented 100% of the stock in a company evaluated at $6 million. After the issue, principals will retain 60% (40% being sold to the public) worth $3.6 million. Now, remember that the price per share for the public issue—the *issue price*—has been set at $12 per share. On this basis, the principals would have to be the holders of 300,000 shares of new stock ($3.6 million divided by $12). To accomplish this, the corporation approves a 3-for-1 stock split—the principals receive 300,000 shares of new stock for their original 100,000 shares for which permission has been obtained from the state corporation commissioner. Therefore, after the public issue, there will be 500,000 shares of stock outstanding —200,000 shares in the hands of the public, 300,000 shares retained by principals.

PREPARATION OF FILING—TIMETABLE

The filing of a registration requires the teamwork of a group of qualified professionals. Probably the first category to go to work will be the accountants; in fact, since a well-advised corporation will anticipate far in advance the possibility of a public issue, the CPA firm may have been engaged—and told of the possibility— a year or more before the beginning of a filing. The choice of CPA for Regulation A and the smaller issues is fairly free on the part of the corporation. When tackling a larger issue, however, ($1 million up) the underwriter will have to be satisfied and this will probably limit the choice to one of the nationally known CPA firms. If one of such accounting firms has not previously been retained by the corporation, possibly an arrangement can be made for an affiliation of effort between the local CPA firm used and a national firm. It is important that the CPA firm engaged have experience in preparing the financial reports for a public issue.

The corporation must also have its own attorneys for the issue—*corporate counsel*—and, since this is one of the many specialties in the legal profession, a qualified law firm must be chosen. Upon this firm falls the major burden of prospectus writing, as well as working on the recapitalization and preparation of the voluminous supporting documents required by the S.E.C. In addition to doing this specialized job correctly and efficiently, it is the responsibility of corporate counsel to safeguard the corporation from any possibility of civil or criminal exposure which could arise from improper filing procedures. The underwriters have their own counsel—the *underwriter's counsel*—who will exercise similar protective functions on behalf of the investment bankers and will also handle the *blue sky* requirements. "Blue skying" is the term applied to the registration of a stock for sale in the individual states. This is simple in some states —merely the mailing of a prospectus to the corporation commissioner or Secretary of State—more involved in other states where special applications must be filed. Although the requirements for blue-skying may be complex in some states like California, they can be complied with easily by most sound offerings. A few states, like Texas, have such ridiculously unrealistic codes that most underwritings by-pass them. Many issues will blue-sky in the eight or ten major financial states, others will go for sales in twenty-five or more states. After the issue is out and the market has stabilized, the free trading of a stock throughout the country will make its sale unrestricted; blue-skying applies only to sales of the original issue.

When the letter of intent has been confirmed by both sides, a meeting is usually held to coordinate the schedule. Most underwritings are timed to incorporate the financial reports of the latest full year of operation, therefore the fiscal year-end date becomes significant. The schedule can be expected to look something like this:

1. Four months before the corporate fiscal year-end, letter of intent is confirmed, based on reliable year-end operating figures.

2. Applications for recapitalization of corporate stock are processed as quickly as possible after the decision to go ahead with the issue.

3. Accountants begin working on past year's figures for conformity and, at least two months before fiscal year end, begin making tests of inventories and receivables so that the entire procedure does not have to be accomplished at the last minute.

4. During the month prior to fiscal year end, corporate counsel begins to gather prospectus information and, within thirty days after the year-end, prepares first rough draft of prospectus and sends copies to underwriter's counsel. This is usually done before the financial information is received from the accountants.

5. Approximately six weeks to two months after the fiscal year-end, the accountants have their financial reports ready. Meanwhile, both of the counsels have been working on redrafting various parts of the filing, including the prospectus. The filing is then put together with the financials and the first S-1, including the prospectus, is actually printed. The prospectus printer does this within twenty-four hours, then keeps the type set awaiting corrections. At this point all parties, their counsel and accountants, get together for a hectic two or three days to polish the prospectus which, inevitably, is reprinted sometime between midnight and dawn, then flown to Washington by one of the counsel for filing with the S.E.C.

6. Three weeks after filing, a *deficiency letter* is received from the S.E.C., listing certain suggested corrections. About ten days to two weeks later the *effective date* is set (the actual issue date of the stock). Firm underwriting contracts are finally signed.

7. Seven to ten days after the effective date is the *settlement date,* on which the corporation and selling shareholders receive their money from the underwriting.

From the above, it is obvious that a minimum of three months after fiscal year end is required before reaching the effective date of the issue. Four months to settlement date is more normal. Considering the fact that certain things have to be accomplished prior to the fiscal year-end, including the early contact and negotiations with the underwriter, it is also obvious that a lead time of nine months or more can be required to transform the idea of a public financing into actuality.

THE UNDERWRITING SYNDICATE

When a filing, such as the S-1 registration, is made with the S.E.C., it includes a full printed copy of the prospectus. In connection with the underwriting, many more copies of the prospectus are printed and distributed under the control of the underwriter. However, these first prospectuses carry a unique designation, printed in bright red wording across the face of the front page, which states that they are *preliminary prospectuses,* or what are known among stockbrokers as *red herrings.* Although restricted from distribution to the public, red herrings are freely circulated in the investment banking fraternity for the purpose of forming a syndicate.

In all but the very small issues, the originating investment banker participates with other brokerage houses in making the offering. This joint effort is triggered by the circulation of red herrings to a great number of potential participants who are invited to join the underwriting syndicate. The investment banking firm which has negotiated with the corporation, and issued the letter of intent, is known as the *managing underwriter.* From the time the issue is first filed with the S.E.C., the managing and other underwriters will be checking with some of their regular customers for possible interest in buying shares of stock in the new issue. During the red-herring stage, no purchase orders can be accepted, but stockbrokers are allowed to accept *indications of interest.* While these indications are not binding, over 90% usually stick, so the *feedback* which they provide to the managing underwriter gives real assurance relative to proper share pricing and general acceptability. Other underwriters, who begin to see feedback from their own customers, request invitations to join the underwriting syndicate.

The managing underwriter will take the largest share of the offering; however, this increment will rarely exceed 25% of the total issue. Not only is it prudent for the managing underwriter to spread his risk by laying off parts of the total commitment to others, but also he hopes for reciprocity from other brokerage firms which will invite him into the syndicates of their own originations.

When the red herring is first circulated, there are several items which are left blank. Chief of these is the price per share and the space provided for the underwriting syndicate. Usually only the name of the managing underwriters appears. During the syndication, the other brokers are advised of the probable price range and the feedback information helps firm the issue price. Just before the effective date the syndicate is definitely formed and the precise price is set. The final prospectus shows this price, which is what the public will pay, and also lists the underwriting syndicate in detail. The managing underwriter receives about 1½% (or about 15% of the total brokerage commissions). The other members of the *underwriting group* may, along with the managing firm who is also in the group, receive another 15% of the gross commission. This means that between 60% and 70% of the gross commission remains for the *selling group* who normally pass on at least half of this to their individual registered representatives who are on the front line making the actual sales to the public. Recognition of this division makes it obvious that the managing underwriter, who has done so much work in negotiating and bringing the issue to the market, receives no inordinately high compensation for his work.

The members of the underwriting group assume responsibility for payment to the corporation of the full cash committed proceeds. This group comes under certain S.E.C. *takedown requirements* which vary depending on the type of issue (bonds vs. stocks, etc.). The requirement for the usual common stock financing issue, for example, is that the underwriter takes his takedown commitment into his books with a "haircut" of 30% and that he have, at the effective date and thereafter until settlement is made, sufficient liquid cash assets to meet all common creditor obligations (which includes the obligation to pay the corporation being underwritten for its stock which is to be resold to the public). Using an example, let us assume that one of the underwriters makes a takedown commitment for 25% of the 200,000 shares being sold, or 50,000 shares at $12. The gross value of these shares is $600,000 which, less an underwriting commission of $60,000, leaves $540,000 worth of public stock which can be counted as a liquid asset, less the 30% haircut, or $378,000. Therefore this underwriter must be able to show that he has sufficient liquid assets to pay all his common creditors plus $162,000 for the takedown.

The takedown requirements are frequently academic, although they are always complied with. Normally the issue is "presold" on the basis of indications of interest received prior to the effective date. After the effective date, customer confirmations are sent out and, since payment is required four days after confirmation in new issues, funds flow in to provide the cash required seven to ten days later on the settlement date. On that day the underwriters hand their check to the corporation— and the long process has been completed.

THE AFTER MARKET

When the final settlement has been paid by the underwriters to the corporation, the financing role of a particular public stock issue has been completed. However, management must then consider the behavior of the stock which has been sold to the public. The principals who still retain some of the corporate stock (although they might have sold a portion of their holdings in the public issue) realize that, as the market price of the publicly held stock rises or falls, the values of their own holdings do likewise. Also, growth companies, during their histories, will probably have many additional public issues subsequent to the first offering. Stock sold in the first issue is evaluated as the result of a *negotiated price* with the underwriters. Subsequent issues will go out based on the market price of the issue at the effective date; therefore, a stock which does well in the market will yield more money to the issuing corporation in ratio to dilution.

The performance of the stock of a corporation after its first public issue is known as the *after market*. There are several categories of after market, as follows:

1. Major stock exchanges
2. Over-the-counter market
3. Regional exchanges

The major exchanges, which are national in scope, are the New York Stock Exchange (NYSE) and the American Stock Exchange (AMEX). The activities of these exchanges are well recognized and the quotations of the stocks traded on them are reported daily in the newspapers. These daily newspaper transaction reports cover the stocks of every corporation listed by the exchanges and it is therefore common to refer to such stocks as *listed securities.*

A corporation which desires to be listed on one of the exchanges must meet with certain qualifications and must also agree to abide by the rules of the exchange including the issuance of stipulated financial statements. There are a number of qualitative admission requirements which any good company should be able to meet. Most significant, however, are certain size requirements as to the following:

    a. Profits
    b. Net worth
    c. Number of stockholders
    d. Number of shares held by the public

The requirements of the New York Stock Exchange in the above categories are higher than those of the American Stock Exchange, as shown in the following table:

	NYSE	AMEX
Pre-tax Profit	$2.5 million	$750,000
Net worth, tangible	$16 million	$4 million
Number of stockholders	2,000	1,200
Shares of public stock	1 million	400,000
Market value of public shares	$16 million	$3 million

There is a particular significance to the last three categories as the number of stockholders—and the number of shares which they hold—actually constitute the *trading market* of the stock. If too few shares are held by too few people there will be very little activity in the stock. The shares held by the public are known as *free-trading stock*, the sales of which are reported in the newspapers. The last price at which these shares are bought and sold daily (the "closing price") constitutes the quotation. If there are few transactions, the stock price may remain dormant even if a company is progressing. Conversely, where there is a very limited stockholding, the sale of even a small block of stock by someone who must liquidate his holdings can cause an unnatural drop in the stock prices. Therefore, these minimums are sensibly set, and it is wise to consider them prior to completing the planning of a first public issue.

The major exchanges constitute what is known as an *auction market* because buy and sell orders are matched by price in open trading on the floors of the exchanges. Many excellent descriptions of the workings of a stock exchange have been written and we will forego this aspect as our concern is limited to the implications of the after market relative to corporate finance. There are many arguments pro and con about the relative validity of an auction market compared to the nature of the over-the-counter market, which is a *supply and demand market*. From a financing point of view, I think this difference is academic.

The *over-the-counter market* is made up by the trading activities of stock brokerage firms throughout the United States, each of whom has an OTC trading department. When a new stock is first issued, the managing underwriter *makes the market* immediately thereafter. By so doing, he stands ready to buy or sell reasonable amounts of the stock being traded. This is handled through nationwide trading wires so that, even if the broker making the market is located in San Francisco, a buy or sell order can be placed with a stockbroker, for example, in Atlanta, Georgia. The prices quoted in OTC trading consist of a *bid quotation* and an *ask quotation*. The bid quote is the price being offered on a particular day by prospective buyers; the ask quote is the price demanded by sellers. If you wish to sell some OTC stock you will be paid the bid price; if you wish to buy you will be charged the ask price. Normally the difference between the bid and ask prices—the *spread*—is about 5% (for example, bid 10, ask 10½). The spread compensates the broker-dealer for his commission, including the share of other brokers in the transaction, and his costs of maintaining an inventory of the stock.

Once a stock has been on the over-the-counter market for a short while, several broker-dealer firms may trade actively in it to make the market. This is done by a listing "in the sheets." These sheets are daily reports put out by general quotation bureaus reflecting the bid and ask prices and the names of the broker-dealers who have decided to join in making the market. Each broker so listed is announcing to all the security dealers in the country that he stands ready to buy or sell reasonable quantities of the stock.

There are no particular requirements for admission to the OTC market. The very fact of having a public issue places the stock of a company in the OTC market. Therefore most new issues find their aftermarket to be over the counter. However, there are no specific waiting periods required for a listing on one of the two major exchanges. For this reason some companies which qualify for the NYSE or AMEX will be listed on one of these exchanges a few weeks after their first public issue becomes effective. During the short interim period their stock will be traded over the counter.

The regional exchanges present few significant differences with regard to financing considerations. Some small stock issues may apply for regional listing because they have a limited local market at best. Many other regionally listed companies are also listed on one of the national exchanges or are very actively traded over the counter. Some specific categories of stock are traded on specialized exchanges, like the San Francisco Mining Exchange, to get more attention than they might otherwise command.

The big decision is between a major exchange listing and being traded over the counter. If a corporation can qualify for either, management must carefully weigh the choice, particularly that of a growth company which looks for stock price enhancement to abet future public financings.

It is not quite correct to assume that prestige companies are all listed on one of the major exchanges. Stocks of most important banks and insurance companies are traded solely over the counter. Such well-known companies as Avon Products, Cannon Mills, Time Magazine, Dictaphone, and First Boston Corporation have been on the roster of the OTC market. In the past, the OTC market did not impose some of the regulations and reporting requirements called for by the major exchanges. Also, proponents of the OTC market claim that, through the activities of the broker-dealers who regularly trade in an OTC stock, it gets more play and can benefit more from this sponsorship. This may be true, particularly immediately after a first issue when the managing underwriter will over-allot sales of the stock to *stabilize* the price. However, after the stock has been out and free-trading a while, this aspect decreases in importance. Present S.E.C. tendencies indicate that OTC reporting requirements will be brought closer to those of the major exchanges. As a result, both NYSE and AMEX listings are increasing appreciably. Even though the listings are growing longer, however, they are small in comparison with the OTC market which probably includes the stocks of over 40,000 public companies. While the sponsorship of a broker-dealer can make a significant difference in the OTC market, the lack of sponsorship can create a very stagnant effect. Even though there are advantages which can be recognized for either type of after market, it is my opinion that the major exchange listing, because of stricter regulations, provides more prestige plus the added benefit of the daily newspaper quotations for all the public to see. It is just good psychology that individuals will tend to trade in stock whose progress they can watch daily merely by turning to the financial pages of their newspapers.

CHAPTER 13

Evaluation of
Potential Acquisitions

In the period from 1960 to 1968 we witnessed in the American economy the greatest splurge of acquisition activity in our economic history. Growth by acquisition became an important analytical consideration for investment fund managers. Frequently, during sessions with investment analysts, corporate officers would be asked about the possibility of the potential acquisition market drying-up—in other words, would there be fewer and fewer candidates left in the field of activity of the acquirer, thereby reducing the present rate of corporate growth? It was at this point that the conglomerates came into high fashion because, by using the word *conglomerate,* management could acquire any type of business and throw it into its corporate pot—a veritable salad of diverse activities.

Conglomerates were very exciting to the stock market for several years until a few facts of life began to surface and, at first, the conglomerate managers came up with some satisfactory answers. They began to use the word "synergistic" to imply that, somehow, each of the diverse entities which was being acquired reinforced the other business activities in the total corporate bag. This fiction persisted for a period of time until the public began to realize that widely diverse activities required different types of management expertise—and it was almost impossible to find all of those types in one corporate entity. Moreover, this condition was aggravated by the fact that, after acquisition, many top executives of the acquired corporations were either terminated or left of their own volition. As a result, companies like Republic, Litton, and Whittaker Corporations—to name a few—were trying to run widely divergent activities from central committees comprised of generalists who could not completely provide the definitive expertise and individual attention needed in certain types of operations.

Finally, as a result of several swings of the pendulum, the picture clarified and acquisitions, properly concerned and evaluated, became an integral increment of corporate growth. But the science of evaluating acquisitions was still not completely definitized. It has been only recently that certain value approaches have been recognized as being valid, based on actual experience gained during the post-acquisition period of successful acquirers.

EFFECT OF POOLING AND PURCHASE
TREATMENT ON EVALUATION

The acquisition era of the sixties came upon the scene so suddenly, and to such a great extent, that the professionals in the field of investment and finance found themselves groping for realistic bench marks of evaluation. The New York Stock Exchange went through a period of maintaining almost the same total of listed companies for several years. The addition of newly listed companies was being regularly offset by the disappearance of old listed companies which had been acquired or merged. The Accounting Principles Board and the Securities Exchange Commission went into a flap which lasted approximately four years, during which the relative validity of *purchase* accounting and accounting by *pooling of interests* were contested. (We describe the differences between these accounting approaches in another section of this chapter.) At first, "pooling" was almost considered to be a dirty word, and it was thought that "purchase accounting" represented a more valid picture. During the long period over which this controversy stretched itself, an entirely different conclusion was reached by actual experience. It became obvious that many of the acquisition-oriented companies were obtaining "instant earnings" by using the purchase accounting method. "Pooling" was then retrieved from the doghouse and analysts began to talk about "dirty purchase accounting."

Pooling was redeemed by two sets of requirements. First, a strict set of pooling qualifications was formulated, calling for, among other things, the following:

1. A continuity of the same type of business activity by the acquired corporation.

2. A continuity of a substantial portion of the former management.

3. Acquisition of at least 90% of the acquired corporation.

4. Payment of the acquisition price initially; no "earn-outs" on future earnings are permitted.

5. Acquisition payment by the exclusive use of common stock of the buyer.

Another pooling requirement was a continuation of the practice of *restatement of prior years' earnings*. After a pooling acquisition it is necessary that all subsequent financial reports of the combined entities reflect *prior years' earnings as if the two corporations*—acquirer and acquired—*had been combined in the five years* prior to the acquisition. This, in part, eliminates the "instant earnings growth" of an accomplished acquisition. For example, Company "A" reflected $1.02 earnings per share for the year 1971 and, without an acquisition, would have shown $1.22 for the year 1972. However, during 1972 Company "A" acquired Company "B" on a pooling basis —and Company "B" 1972 earnings will add 12 cents a share to Company "A" earnings—or a total 1972 per share earning of $1.34 for the combined entity. On an "as-stated" basis, therefore, Company "A" would show an earnings increase of 32 cents per share ($1.02 for 1971 and $1.34 for 1972). However, Company "B" earned 10 cents a share in 1971, and pooling requires that this amount must also be added to the Company "A" 1971 earnings on a *restated* basis (as if the two companies were already combined in previous years). Company "A" 1971 earnings on a *restated* pooling basis would, therefore, be $1.12 per share (Company "A" $1.02 plus Company "B" 10 cents) as compared to $1.34 per share combined for 1972—or a *restated* earnings increase of 22 cents (instead of the 32 cents increase which would have been reflected on an *as-stated* basis). Analysts and accountants agree that the *restated* basis gives a more valid picture of true growth by comparing the earnings increase as if the two entities had already been combined—and they are correct.

In *purchase* accounting there is *no restatement* for previous years; therefore, the earnings of an acquired company contribute to total earnings from the day the acquisition is completed (in poolings the earnings are combined for the whole year, regardless of when, during that year, the acquisition is finalized). Using the same examples given above—Company "A" 1972 earnings of $1.22 per share would be increased by Company "B" earnings of 12 cents per share *proportional to the percentage of the 1972 year Company "B" is owned* (if "B" is acquired at midyear, then 50% of its earnings are added—or 6 cents per share—to Company "A's" total of $1.22, yielding a combined 1972 total of $1.28 per year). But—the combined total *is not restated* for the previous year; therefore, it would be compared to Company "A's" 1971 earnings ($1.02 per share), reflecting an earnings gain of 26 cents per share per year—a greater rate of earnings growth than can be shown on a pooling basis. Obviously, if Company "B" had greater earnings in comparison to the per share earnings of Company "A," which we have given in our example, the "instant earnings growth" effect of the purchase accounting would be even more pronounced. It is also more pronounced if the acquisition is made in the earlier part of Company "A's" fiscal year (as a larger percentage of "B's" earnings would be added to the combined 1972 total of the "A-B" entity after the acquisition)— and the inflation of the per share earnings growth rate would be more drastic. This artificially inflated effect may persist for two years, because purchases always compare to *non*-restated past years, but there is then a reverse effect; after a while the earnings growth will begin to drag, unless a steady stream of new purchase acquisition is maintained. Since poolings require restatement from the very outset, they do not have this future problem. Recently, however, there have been some accounting rule changes which somewhat mitigate the purchase accounting "instant earnings growth" advantages. Chief among these has been the requirement that *goodwill* be *amortized* in purchase acquisitions.

The goodwill depreciation factor can be quite serious. Many growth companies which are acquired for their earnings command prices far in excess of their book values. Such companies are acquired for their contribution to earnings growth and the purchase price is primarily based on an *earnings multiplier*. A typical example would involve a "purchase-treated" Company "K" whose earnings are $150,000 after taxes which, based on a 15× earnings multiple, can be purchased for $2.25 million;

however, the net worth book value of Company "K" is only $525,000—therefore, the goodwill would be $1.7 million. The maximum depreciation period allowed is 40 years (it must be less in certain areas) so the goodwill amortization is $42,500 per year which *must* be deducted from *after*-tax earnings. For the acquirer, therefore, the reportable earnings of Company "K" drops to $107,500— a serious hindrance, yet a sound accounting principle of protecting investors from possibilities of false growth reporting in the absence of sufficient net worth. There are, of course, cases where companies are purchased which have greatly depreciated assets on their books, primarily real property, such as plants, warehouses, hotels, retail stores, etc. In such cases, the CPA will accept qualified outside appraisals of the true higher value and some of the goodwill can be allocated to such physical assets. Any future depreciation of such assets will, at least, be an expense *before* taxes, and the balance sheet, by reflecting less goodwill, will exhibit stronger tangible worth to an investor.

Until the 1972 rules were clarified, there were many cases in which an acquisition could be treated either as a pooling or a purchase, but this optional possibility has now been eliminated. Under the new regulations, those acquisitions which meet pooling criteria *must* be pooled —and the converse goes for purchases. Since the evaluation of any acquisition can be seriously affected by its accounting treatment, it is necessary that—almost from the first exposure to a potential acquisition—an early look at the balance sheet be taken to determine *a priori*, whether a purchase or a pooling is involved.

ASSET VALUE EVALUATION

The most elementary form of evaluation of a going business takes into consideration only the true value of the assets, less the liabilities shown on the balance sheet. To this net worth is usually added a goodwill factor which will vary according to a set of criteria. In general, these criteria relate to the staying power of the business, the degree to which one can expect the business to continue at its present level of earnings—or better—because of some sort of franchise or exclusive location, established reputation, relative freedom from competition or from obsolescence through changing technology. Until some time after World War II, most evaluations took this simple approach. Transactions involving small businesses— particularly outside of the U.S.A.—may still use this evaluation.

In arriving at "true" asset value, the assets on the balance sheet are brought up to their present values, usually on the basis of an outside appraisal. If management has been understating its inventories for tax purposes, a new physical inventory is taken, costed and totaled. If reserves, such as for accounts receivable, are unnaturally high, the values are restated to conform to normal practice. Heavily depreciated real property (which may have actually appreciated far beyond its original cost) is appraised by outside professionals. From the total of all these restated values are subtracted the liabilities, to yield the present true value. Then, frequently, goodwill is added —which, historically, was the first step developed to recognize the difference between asset *liquidation value* and the potential of the same assets to create profits in a going business. Various industries developed their own differing goodwill factors to be added to true value. A service industry company might add a goodwill factor of three years after-tax profits. Heavily entrenched manufacturing companies might add five years after-tax profits, employment or advertising agencies with little book value would add goodwill equivalent to one year's billings (or more).

These factors evolved empirically and related gener-

ally to the return on investment which could be anticipated from those gross revenues. Some goodwill was even
based solely on unrealized potential, particularly in the
media field. It has been jokingly stated that, until fairly
recently, FM stations were evaluated on the basis of three
times losses—and this almost seemed proven by the increasing sale prices of FM & TV stations, many of which
had yet to show a profit. Of course, these stations represented valuable franchises in a tightly government-con-
trolled field, where it was recognized that wider use and
population growth could create future yield values.

In some countries which have not yet reached the
degree of evaluation sophistication found in the U.S.A.,
some systematic approaches have been developed. I encountered one such system recently during a negotiation
in France. With the balance sheet before us, the seller
presented a manual, apparently prepared by a national
accounting or appraisal group, which contained a set of
tables for determining appreciation to present value of
certain categories of assets. These tables ran for ten years
and were applicable to good, well-built properties in
"solid" areas of established and growing communities
(which was the case of the company involved in this
negotiation). The land had been purchased by the seller
five years earlier, and, since land appreciation had been
running 16% per annum, the table suggested the land be
increased by 206% (16% compounded for five years). The
building had been completed two years before and—
based on the combined consideration of twenty-five years
depreciation expense offset by increased current construction cost—was qualified for an increase factor of 18.6%.
To these increased values were added all the other tangible assets—minus all the liabilities—on the balance
sheet, to attain *current value*. Then, to the current value,
the seller claimed we should add one year's gross revenues
as goodwill. Incidentally, this was a high margin business

(10% net after-tax profit on gross revenues) and—by strange coincidence—the final price was not far off from the 14× multiple of after-tax earnings my board of directors had authorized. While there was indeed some professional basis for this coincidence, it only took place because of the high-margin aspect (to be explained later) and because certain other growth criteria were present. Using the same French approach, a business with lower margin and a slow growth prognosis might be valued fairly close to the same figure—which is the fallacy of such an approach. As we will see later in this chapter, only an earnings basis can provide true going-business evaluation.

DISCOUNTED CASH FLOW

Up to this point we have described evaluations of potential acquisitions on the basis of *static* criteria, primarily the elements reflected on the balance sheet, adjusted to true, or present realistic value. It was a major evolutionary step when, early in the 1950's, emphasis shifted to the *dynamic* aspects of a business: namely, the return expected to be gained annually on the assets or goodwill being purchased. Attention moved from the balance sheet and began to focus on the operating statement. Acquirers would make profit and loss forecasts, on a pro forma future basis for as much as ten years from the time of acquisition. On these forecasts cash flow figures would be developed (after-tax profits plus non-cash expenses, such as depreciation). Then—to explain the matter simply—a computation would be made to determine what amount of purchase price could be repaid out of the forecast cash flow over a limited number of years. In other words, how much money could be recaptured by the acquirer in five, seven, or ten years?

Of course the first step in such a process would be the somewhat arbitrary determination of the number of years the acquirer was willing to wait before having his purchase price paid back by the cash flow generated by the acquisition. This would depend on the assumed staying power or stability of the business being purchased. I would say that almost the maximum time found to be acceptable was ten years. Even stable industries were expected to "pay-out" in seven or eight years. And the pay-out had to include an added increment to replace the interest earnings on the money tied up by being used to pay for the acquisition. Since the buyer did not receive his pay-back from the cash flow soon after the acquisition (except in some cases of raids on cash-rich companies— see below) he had to postulate a value of the *future* pay-out *discounted to present value.*

Elementary economics speaks of "opportunity cost" of money—the cost attached to invested money which represents the amount of interest it might have earned if it were left on deposit in a bank, or invested in high-grade bonds. This cost varies, of course, with the money market, but—because money markets go through complete cycles in a few years, from high interest to low interest—it is usually valid to assume an average 6% per annum opportunity cost on a ten-year pay-out—equal payments each year over ten years. The present value of the pay-out must be discounted approximately 40%. In other words, $100,000 received in ten equal annual installments is really worth no more than $60,000 cash received immediately, today (and this makes no allowance for the additional loss from possible future currency inflation). Therefore, an acquisition must create at least 140% of its purchase price in cash flow, if the pay-out over ten years is deemed to be acceptable.

In the discounted cash flow approach, the purchase price is obviously determined by the pay-out period viewed as acceptable, and the cash flow is projected over that period. Assume that a potential acquisition earns $250,000 after taxes per year, after depreciation expense of $50,000. Beginning cash flow is $300,000 per year. It is a stable business and the buyer determines that a ten year pay-out is acceptable. During the ten years it is forecast that cash flow increases smoothly to $500,000 a year—or will average $400,000 during the pay-out. Therefore, total cash flow for the ten years will be $4 million, which—discounted 40%—will justify a purchase evaluation of $2.4 million cash to be paid now for the acquisition.

Although discounted cash flow has largely been supplanted by price-earnings ratio approaches, it still has a value when used in conjunction with newer price-setting methods, particularly in adjusting the evaluation for acquisitions involving unusually high or low asset values— or unusually tight or liquid balance sheets—in relationship to the after-tax earnings. Discounted cash flow is also sound in acquisitions where the acquirer is a private company—or—in particular—when a private or public company sets out to acquire a company with a large tax loss carry-forward, or a cash-rich company. In the case of the tax-loss company, it is obvious that these loss carry-forwards will, for a few years, shelter the earnings from taxes, and the cash flow will recapture the purchase price more quickly in the first few years.

In the case of the cash-rich company, you can have the same effect. The corporate "raider" looks for cash-rich companies, public or private. If the company is private, it has usually developed excess cash because its owners were in high personal income tax brackets and did not wish to pay out corporate earnings in the form of high taxable dividends. Public companies which have accumulated excessively large cash reserves may have an unprogressive self-perpetuating management without sufficient shareholdings to assure practical control in the face

of a tender offer. A corporate raider can offer a price
higher than the prevailing market based on the ability
to utilize the excess cash, declaring a massive dividend
to the acquiring corporation immediately after taking control, thereby reducing the payback discount, to justify
the original acquisition price.

EVALUATION BY EARNINGS MULTIPLE

The evaluation of a going busines by an earnings
multiplier has become much more recognized and, in fact,
prevalent in the U.S.A. The money used to acquire a
business is undeniably capital; therefore, where such
capital is invested should be determined by the return
which can be generated on that capital, compared to
other *equal-risk* investment opportunities. The return is
a function of the profit level of a business being bought.
A multiple of that per annum return is the converse of
yield on investment. For example, if a business is acquired
on the basis of 5× (five times) annual earnings, it means
the acquirer would earn a yield equal to his total investment in five years—or 20% per year, a typical return on
a high-risk investment. In the case of a price being set at
a 10× multiple, the return is equivalent to a 10% per
annum return on an investment—a lower risk rate of
return, but obviously higher than even more conservative
investments such as bank deposits or holdings in high
grade bonds, both of which yield considerably lower
returns.

The risk level and staying power of the acquired
business have much to do with the multiple, as is illustrated by Dewing's table which has been reproduced on
page 232 of our earlier Chapter 9 "Acquisition Financing." This table describes gradations of earnings multiples from 10× for "businesses with long existence and

established goodwill among many customers" to 1× for "businesses of a personal service character or businesses dependent on the skill of a single person like an author's agency or an animal hospital." However, there is one important element missing in using a static table for evaluations, at least in the more substantial situations. I am referring to the element of *potential future growth of earnings*. The earnings multiple is applied to the *current* earnings level (remember, this level is always *after-tax* earnings); therefore, if earnings increase, the effective earnings multiple over the period until payback is lowered. The importance of this factor—and means of quantifying it—are described in the last section of this chapter. It is the predictable growth element that sometimes justifies earnings multiples above 10 and as high as 20× or more.

EARNOUTS

There are some cases when a company being acquired is very obviously headed into a period of increasing profits. For example, the company may have been operating at full capacity and it is doubling its facilities with some assurance that revenues and profits will increase substantially as the additional facilities are constructed and come in line as more staff is trained. Perhaps this expansion program will take several years to complete, but the groundwork has been done. An earnings multiple of 10× *current* earnings is offered but the seller feels he is getting nothing for having set the scene and prepared the plans for the higher rate of earnings which seems inevitable. If no accommodation is made, the seller may say "come back in several years when I am earning much more, and then I will accept your 10× multiple offer on the higher profits." But, the buyer wants to make the deal now—it may reinforce other sectors of the buyer's operations—and he sees good continuing growth. The buyer also knows that he *cannot pay today* for future profit levels which are still several years off—otherwise his return on investment for the first two years will be too low (for a public company this can be a real interim depressant on the market price of its stock). This problem can sometimes be solved by using an *earnout* formula.

The earnout formula has two parts—an original purchase based on curent profits—and a second incremental payment based on additional earnings gained in the future. Good earnout formulas also provide a special earnout base to take into consideration the normal anticipated growth, beyond which the substantial profit growth is compensated for by the earnout formula. Let us say that Company "K" is presently earning $100,000 per year after taxes. However, its goods or services are very much in demand and an expansion program is planned which is anticipated to jump the profits to $300,000 in four years. Buyer and seller agree on 10× the current profits, or $1 million as the price for acquisition. It is further agreed that the seller will be compensated for the additional profits after four years. Usually, in a case such as this, the earnings for years three and four will be averaged. Therefore, the earnout period begins at the start of year three. Assuming *normal* profit growth to be 10% per annum (the earnout formula is devised to accommodate *unusually substantial* growth) the current earnings might be increased 20% to 30% to establish the *earnout base,* beyond which the earnout profits are to be computed. Since Company "K" currently earns $100,000 per annum, the earnout base might be $130,000. Then, the amount by which the average earnings of years three and four exceed the earnout base of $130,000, represent the figure used in making the final payment.

If Company "K" earns $200,000 in year three and

$300,000 in year four, the average earning is $250,000. That average exceeds the $130,000 earnout base by $120,-000, which is the *earnout overage*. Buyer and seller have previously agreed that the second payment will be 6× the earnout average; therefore, the seller receives an additional $720,000 at the end of the fourth year. The earnings multiple paid on the earnout is usually less than that paid in the original purchase because it is recognized that the *buyer* contributes time, effort and capital during the earnout period to help make it successful. Sometimes, if substantial capital contribution is required of the buyer to complete planned expansions during the earnout period, an agreed money cost is deducted from the earnout average.

If stock of a public company is used as consideration paid for the acquisition, there are two important factors to consider:

1. The value of the stock to be paid at the end of the earnout must be based on the *then*-market price of the shares, not the share price at the time of the original purchase; otherwise, if the stock price has risen considerably during the four year (as per example given above) earnout period, the buyer would have to book a far higher acquisition cost than would be indicated by total dollar value of the earnout (since the share price must be computed at market value at the time those shares are issued).

2. There should be an upper limit to the number of shares to be issued for the earnout, to protect against temporary downside market risk. Usually the limit is set at a number of shares equal to the number issued at the time of original purchase. In the example used, if the acquirer's shares had a market price of $20, then the original purchase for $1 million would have involved 50,000 shares; therefore, an additional 50,000 shares would be reserved for the earnout. If the earnout of $720,000

takes place when the acquirer's stock is selling at $40, only 18,000 shares would be used. However, if the acquirer's stock dropped to $10 in four years, 72,000 shares would theoretically be required, but only the maximum of 50,000 would be issued, thus illustrating the protection against excessive dilution, particularly were there a temporary market low at the time of the earnout settlement. There is a good argument to present to the seller in favor of a maximum: He can spoil his tax-free exchange if he receives more than 50% from an earnout.

Recently, the use of earnouts has been diminishing, particularly by listed public corporations. Pooling is no longer allowed where there are earnouts. If there is no goodwill problem, and the acquisition is not qualified for a pooling, the earnout arrangement might be used for purchase-treated acquisitions. Also, for purchases, the buyer can purchase a portion, say 75%, of a business, at the outset. Then, several years later, there can be put and call options between buyer and seller to purchase the remaining 25% on an earnout overage formula, in proportion to that part of the selling company retained by the seller.

PRICING INFLUENCE OF THE ACQUIRER'S BUSINESS

The evaluation criteria presented in this chapter relate to the value determination of the business to be acquired—and, since this is the element which is being sold, its value is the primary determinant of its price. There are, however, certain mitigating factors which arise from the position of the buyer. When the buyer has made his evaluation—and is going to pay the entire purchase price in cash—then the cash paid should coincide with the buyer's evaluation. If part of the purchase price is paid with notes, and the notes bear at least 6% interest, there may be no premium demanded by the seller if he has confidence in the buyer's ability to pay off the notes as agreed.

The use of stock presents the possibility—in some cases only (see below)—that the seller may demand, and receive, a higher price than if the consideration were to be paid in cash. It should be first realized that there are many sellers *who prefer to receive stock rather than cash, because only through the use of common stock can a seller receive a tax-free exchange.* Therefore, do not minimize the value of stock used as consideration for an acquisition. On the other hand, there are some elements which can tend to diminish the value of stock in the seller's mind.

If stock is offered by a private corporation, the seller must have faith in the package and in the fact that he will ultimately be able to liquidate his stock. For that reason, the buyer may demand more than the for-cash valuation of his business, and this premium may run up as high as 50% or more. However, if the stock received gives the seller a tax-free exchange and a dominant position in what he views as an attractive after-acquisition entity, he may ask little or no premium.

If "Restricted" stock is offered by a public corporation, the seller realizes his ability to liquidate is limited and subject to delay. Stock received in an acquisition is called "restricted stock" or "lettered stock" because the certificates bear a legend describing the restriction. This legend is removed when the shares are ultimately sold, but, in order to be sold, they must either be *registered* or must qualify for *exemption from registration.* To register a stock, the acquiring corporation must file a registration with the S.E.C. (and if it is a listed corporation, a *listing* application with the stock exchange). Therefore, if the seller plans on having his stock registered, sometime in the next year or two, for total sale of all his shares (at which time he will be liable for taxes on all of his capital gains, thus ending his tax-free exchange period) he will ask for registration guarantees. One such guarantee is a *mandatory registration* which commits the buyer's corporation to register at least once, within a stipulated period of time (usually two or three years) all of the stock received by the seller. Another approach is the *piggy-back* registration which commits the buyer to include the seller's shares in any (or the first) future registration which the corporation makes after the acquisition. If, for example, the acquiring corporation registers a public common stock issue for additional financing, the seller's shares must also be included in that registration and be sold by the underwriters, along with the company shares which are being offered.

If non-registered stock is exchanged by a public company to the shareholders of a private company, there are two possibilities. Where there are a number of private shareholders, not active in the business being sold, those shareholders come under S.E.C. Rule 144 which provides for exemption from registration with the passage of two or three years—at which time the stock can be freely sold by any stockbroker. In the case of a "control" selling shareholder, or one who continues in an executive or directorial position after the acquisition, his exemptions come under S.E.C. Rule 145, according to which he can sell his shares on a periodic basis, through regular stockbrokers, under certain restrictions, the most important of which is that he may only sell 1% of the total outstanding shares every six months. This may not be as much of a restriction as it initially appears. If a seller receives 50,000 shares from a company which has three million shares outstanding, the 1% limitations would still allow him to sell 30,000 shares (1% of 3 million) every six months. Therefore, if the sellers receive stock in a company in which they have confidence—and if there is sufficient normal daily trading in that company stock so that, when the sellers wish to dispose of their shares from time to time they will not depress the market price they will receive—then there should be little or no difference in the acquisition price, cash versus stock, particularly since there will be the advantages of tax-free exchange.

Finally, there is the case *where registered stock is offered by a public company.* Many public companies today have *shelf-registered* shares of stock for use in future acquisitions. Therefore, they can issue fully registered shares to all of the sellers who can immediately sell, if they wish, through their stock-brokers (subject to Rule 145 in the case of "contol" persons). Here the potential of tax-free exchange gives the seller the best of two worlds: (a) immediate liquidation or partial liquidation and; (b) holding some or all shares on a tax-free exchange basis for future appreciation. *Naturally there is no premium over the cash sales price given to the sellers when free-trading registered shares are exchanged as consideration in an acquisition.*

ACQUIRER'S MULTIPLE HAS NO BEARING ON VALUATION

I have many times been involved in negotiations on behalf of acquiring corporations who were fortunate enough to enjoy market prices on their shares which reflected high multiples on their earnings. The shares of one such company, listed on the New York Stock Exchange, regularly sold at a Price-Earnings ratio of 30 to 40 times earnings—a price well deserved because of consistent high per share earnings growth over a period of years. Frequently the sellers in acquisitions would have the fallacious idea that, because the acquirer had a high earnings multiple, a higher multiple should be paid to the sellers in an acquisition. It is true that the P/E multiple of the buyer does somewhat influence one of the *limitations* on the acquisition valuation—cost of capital (see below) but that factor is secondary.

Let us make one unequivocal statement: *The earnings multiple of the buyer has no influence on—or relationship to—determination of the proper multiple of earnings set as the evaluation of a business being acquired.* Would the seller accept a very low price from a buyer who suffers with a low price-earnings ratio on his stock? Of course not. *The earnings multiple valuation is intrinsic to the company being acquired*—its staying power, its future potential, its profit margin and profit growth.

Many executives of acquisition-active corporations make the mistake of thinking their high multiple companies can make successful acquisitions merely by buying companies at a lower earnings multiple than their own company enjoys. That is true—but only for the first year *unless* the acquired company also enjoys a high rate of earnings growth. If not, the acquirer will have an earnings growth millstone around his neck in the future. If you enjoy a 40× multiple—and buy a company for a 25× multiple—you will receive a one-shot benefit in per-share earnings the first year. But, if your 40× multiple is based on your corporation's consistent 20% per annum profit growth—and the company you acquire for 25× earnings has only 10% per annum profit growth—you will have a future drag on total earnings, *ad infinitum* after the first year following acquisition. I repeat: *The price-earnings ratio of the acquirer's stock has no bearing on the valid evaluation of the prospective acquisition.*

COST OF CAPITAL APPROACH TO EVALUATION

The determination of *cost of capital* is important in many aspects of financial planning. It is used in determining feasibility of expansion programs, and financial planning. The topic can be quite complex and an interested student can find much reference material on the subject. Wtihin the purposes of this book, however, we will touch only on an elementary explanation and then go directly to application of cost of capital principles to acquisition evaluation.

Cost of capital studies are determinations of the cost of all elements of capital structure found on the liability side of the balance sheet of a particular corporation. Normally, the capital shown thereon will consist, at least, of the following:

1. Bank borrowings.

2. Long term institutional or mortgage debt.

3. Equity, in the form of common stock and earned surplus.

Cost of capital is the weighted average cost of the above. If all capital were debt, the cost of capital computation would be rather simple, since debt costs are simply the interest rate plus concessions, if any, such as warrants, compensating balances, etc. Although it was previously held that bank debt, being relatively short term, should not be included in the cost of capital, I feel otherwise, particularly when considering acquisitions in the presence of bank credit agreements for two or more years (and they sometimes run up to five or seven years). Under such conditions the bank borrowing cost is as easy to determine as the interest cost on long-term institutional loans.

When we come to the cost of equity, the determination is not so simple. Basically, the cost of equity varies according to what the company will have to pay to attract such capital, and, of course, this is the same principle which applies to the debt market. Obviously the market price of the common shares at the time of any funding by a stock issue bears a direct relationship to the cost of

equity. The higher the price/earnings ratio—and therefore the higher the market price per share—the lower the
cost of equity. This is because the dilution of earnings,
resulting from the sale of such equity, is less. But, when
you are dealing with a high P/E ratio stock, it is short-
sighted—in fact, fallacious—to base your calculations
solely on present conditions.

The stock exchanges list many good stocks with mod-
erate earnings multiples, among which most of the companies on the Dow-Jones Index are included. These are
solid companies with long histories of stability and payment of good dividends. Normally, such companies average 3 to 6% growth per annum and therefore their shares
sell at nine to eighteen times earnings, with some notable
exceptions. At times of market peaks the DJI average
multiple may be 17×; during bear markets the DJI multiple has averaged as low as 10×. For such companies
the cost of debt will usually be lower than the cost of
equity, and many economists have concluded that the
equity cost of such corporations is 10 to 11% per annum.
Since they can borrow at lower rates—and since the interest on borrowings is tax deductible—debt is, for them,
cheaper than equity (provided they do not borrow too
heavily and drive up their own cost of borrowings by
lowering the quality of the balance sheet with too high
a debt/equity ratio).

The fast-growth, high-earnings multiple corporation
finds the opposite situation. At first glance it appears the
cost of equity is almost ridiculously low. To find *immediate* cost of equity in *today's market*, the following formula
is used:

$$100\% \div \frac{\text{Market Price}}{\text{Earnings}} = \text{Cost of Equity}$$

Therefore, a fast-growth stock which earns $2 per

share, and which has a market price of $100, would compute as follows:

$$100\% \div \frac{\$100.00}{\$2.00}$$

$$100\% \div 50 = 2\% \text{ Cost of Equity}$$

To this 2% cost must be added approximately 15% for cost of underwriting—prospectus printing, attorneys, accountants, underwriters commissions, etc. But this is *not the true equity cost*. One factor, which bears on the future of the company in the market-place, has been overlooked: namely, the attraction to the investor.

Obviously, when an investor buys this stock at 50× current earnings of $1 per share, he does not believe the earnings will increase 5 or 6% next year. This investor is buying a fast-growth stock—which is why he is willing to pay such a high multiple now—and he expects the stock to earn $3 next year, and $4.25 the following year. The analysis of the investor's rationale is consistent with the well known principle that people buy growth stocks *in anticipation* of substantial near-future earnings appreciation. From the company point of view, recognizing that it must continue to seek financing in the future, the *anticipated* multiple must be taken into consideration, particularly since equity shares stay with you forever—diluting future earnings growth—and common shares are normally not retired as is the case with debt amortization or pay-off.

It is therefore important that the growth company use its anticipated price/earnings ratios two or three years down the line. Let us take the case of a company which has a track record of 20% compounded per share earnings growth per year. This year it earns $1.33 per share and its shares sell in the market for $45 (approximately 35×

earnings). The investor expects $1.60 per share earnings next year—and nearly $2 per share the following year. His expectation assumes that the historical 20% compounded growth rate will continue. The investor is "buying" the earnings level two years down the line (a fairly common procedure in American investing) and the price he is willing to pay relates to that $2 per share earning he is looking for in the future. But—at $2 per share, the $45 price now represents a much more conventional 22½× earnings. Since that is the *price* the investor pays, it is also the *cost* to the growth company which recognizes it probably cannot forever sustain its high rate of growth. It is proper and conservative for the company to assume a 20 or 25× multiple two years down the line (still quite handsome a P/E ratio compared to the Dow-Jones Index average of 10 to 17 P/E) and should the multiple move downward to that level two or three years hence, the company by having postulated the lower future multiple will not have overpaid for an acquisition and will therefore still be able to have additional stock issue financing in the future.

Taking our second example, immediately above, the formula based on the earnings anticipated two years down the line would be:

$$100\% \div \frac{\$45.00}{\$2.00}$$

$$100\% \div 22.50 = 4.4\% \text{ Cost of Equity}$$

To the above cost is added 15% for underwriting expense, so the cost of equity would be approximately 5.1%.

Now let us compute a complete cost of capital. Assume that long term debt is 8% and constitutes 25% of total capital. There are some medium term bank lines at prime plus ½% plus 20% compensating balances, consisting of 25% of capital (assume 6% plus ½% × 20% equals 7.8%). Equity, computed at 5.1% above, constitutes the remaining 50% of capital. Since the interest on debt is tax deductible (assume 50% corporate bracket) the debt cost is reduced by the tax; however, the dilution caused by equity shares is after-tax, so its full cost must stand. The weighted average will be computed as follows:

Medium Term Debt 7.8%	After Tax 3.9%	× 25%	1.0% rounded
Long Term Debt 8%	After Tax 4.0%	× 25%	1.0%
Equity Cost 5.1%		× 50%	2.6% rounded
	Weighted Cost of Capital		4.6%

Theoretically any acquisition which does not yield at least 20% more per annum than the above cost of 4.6% (about 5.5%) would be too costly. Translating 5.5% into earnings multiplier (100% ÷ 5.5%) would indicate that a maximum of approximately 18× earnings should represent the limit to be used in an acquisition; but this approach has its drawbacks (see below).

A single broad-brush approach to find corporate cost of capital is as follows:

$$\frac{\text{After-Tax Profits} + \text{Interest Paid on Long-Term Debt}}{\text{Total Capitalization}}$$

From the investor's point of view, the above fraction computes the return which is presently being made on all capital. Theoretically, if the same return or better can be achieved from an acquisition, it is feasible to proceed. But the same flaw exists even with this method.

Most old established companies have high ratios of equity to debt—85% equity to 15% debt, up to 70% equity to 30% debt. Since their earnings growth is not rapid, the equity capital costs more than the debt, and therefore total cost of capital would appear to be 10 to 11%, and payment of more than 10 times earnings for an acquisition would seem improper if viewed strictly on a cost of capital basis. On the other hand, fast growth companies may have lower or higher profits in relationship to total capital, but their low costs of equity can imply feasibility for an acquisition which, in the future, will turn out to be too costly. Whereas cost of capital can be helpful as a guideline—as a partial limit—and as a tool for calculating the cost of an entity's need for additional capital after acquisition—one variable is not properly weighted. *I am here referring to the predictable earnings growth rate of the proposed acquisition.* The *static aspect of yield* is analyzed properly; but the *dynamic aspect of profit growth* is not.

EVALUATION BY REVERSE RISK-RATIO

We have come now to the value which is intrinsic to the acquisition itself—the predictable compounded growth rate. It is this factor which primarily influences the value of the company under consideration. If an established company has a cost of capital of 11%—and turns down an acquisition with compounded earnings *growth* of 20% per annum because the initial yield might be only 6% (admittedly less than their cost of capital) then the executives should surely be faulted. By the same token, a fast-growth company with a low 4% cost of capital has no justification for making an acquisition which, on the basis of the price demanded to acquire, will initially yield 12% (8½ times earnings is the purchase price) but which has indicated future *profit growth* of only 4% a year.

In both instances cited above, the intrinsic growth of the company being acquired has not been properly evaluated—and this error has negated a fine acquisition in the first case, and encouraged a poor acquisition in the second case.

What establishes a price/earnings multiple of a public company? A number of considerations, but by far the most important is the rate of profit growth. And the same principle applies to a potential acquisition candidate. By its own rate of growth it can contribute to—or cause to lag—the acquiring corporation's per-share earnings growth rate.

The setting of a P/E multiple is actually done by the investor who, based on expectancy of future earnings, assigns this value. The basis of all intelligent investment decisions between situations of equal risk is the determination of which company offers the best *future yield* possibilities. If, between two companies of equal risk quality, the first company's profits grow 7% per annum and the second company increases at the rate of 9% per annum, obviously the investor will opt for company number two. The more difficult part of the problem is the actual gauging of the yield.

The bench marks for yield are the blue-chip corporations, old-established-stable, usually with long dividend paying records. Historically, these companies have produced an average annual yield of about 9% to the investor. The total yield has normally been comprised of 3 to 4% dividends and 5 to 6% appreciation due to profit growth. Such companies will carry P/E multiples from 8 to 11 in bear markets and from 12 to 17 in bull markets. Let us use an 11 × P/E ratio as a base. In order to attract an investor to pay a higher multiple for a stock, it is obvious that there must be an anticipation of a return higher than 9% per annum. Therefore, a 15% compounded growth rate of earnings per share would command a higher P/E multiple, but how much higher?

The precise relationship between various rates of earnings growth and the applicable P/E ratios has been set forth in what are known as *Risk-Return Tables*. These tables give the proper value to growth, expressed in P/E ratios. The table will show, for example, that a stock growing 20% a year in profits is a better investment at a cost of 30× earnings than a 10% profit growth stock costing 14× earnings. It is simply a matter of higher yield—or a quicker return of the investment. Consider the following:

> 20% compound earnings growth will increase the investment 100% in four years.
>
> 10% compound earnings growth will increase the investment 50% in four years.
>
> 6% compound earnings growth will increase the investment 25% in four years.

The relationships are quite obvious. A stock with 20% annual profit growth should carry four times the multiple of a stock with 6% growth. If the 6% growth stock carries a 10× multiple, the 20% growth stock should carry a 40× multiple. Variations in rate of annual per-share profit increase will change the price of a company's shares in relation to its current earnings.

Although P/E ratios will change between good times and bad—in bull and bear markets—following is a general average of multiples by category of profit growth:

Rate of Annual Profit Growth Per Share	Average Price/Earnings Ratio For Share Market Price
3% to 5%	8× to 9×
6% to 8%	10× to 15×
9% to 11%	16× to 20×
12% to 15%	21× to 28×
16% to 19%	29× to 36×
20%	40×

These ratios would apply primarily to established public corporations. They would have respectable balance sheets; if lacking in liquidity or growth capital, it would be assumed that such companies might have to do more equity financing—diluting their earnings—so the multiple would be lower. In the lower growth ranges on the table above, there will usually be a 3% to 5% dividend paid. At the upper ranges the dividend might drop to 1% or even zero (high growth stocks are not expected to pay much in the way of dividends, in order to conserve capital for growth). It would also be expected that there are a large number of traded shares outstanding, creating a valid market, plus reasonable institutional holdings. Smaller public companies, without all these factors present, should be evaluated somewhat lower, although, if it is determined there is an honest market being made on the stock of a small growth company, premiums of 10% to 20% above market price can be paid in an acquisition, provided evaluation of the multiple stays below the above table.

When evaluating a *private company* for acquisition, the values in the above table should be *reduced 30% to 50%*, the higher discount being applied to the higher ranges of multiples. Of course, the financial position of the acquired company will have an influence, which can go either way:

1. If the acquisition candidate is cash-rich, the acquirer can figure on utilizing the excess cash as a reduction of the price being paid. Let us say a private company has 8% profit growth and is evaluated at 7× earnings. The earnings are $100,000 after-tax and the seller wants $1 million for his business. The buyer feels $700,000 is the proper price; however, he notes that—beyond all needs of the business, and beyond that which is required for a good balance sheet—the seller has $300,000 excess cash. The seller can mentally subtract this amount from the $1 million price tag (since the cash is not needed for the con-

tinued profit growth of the business), to arrive at his $700,000 purchase. He will actually pay the seller $1 million, but he will be paying him $300,000 of his own (the seller's) money.

2. More frequently the acquired company is short of the desired capital; lack of growth capital can be one reason for selling a business. In this case the buyer must postulate the effect of supplying the needed capital. Sometimes the figure needed is based on that required for expansion of facilities, or to finance the expected future growth. In other cases, theoretical supplementation of capital is made to meet the acquiring corporation's own financial profile discipline. For example, a company which has good financing capability might insist that each new acquisition create no more debt than equity. The capital structure would be 50% debt–50% equity. Let us imagine an acquisition which earns $200,000 after tax—evaluated at $2.4 million. Its capital consists of $500,000 equity and $800,000 debt. The buyer feels he must reduce the debt by $300,000, and, since his combined cost of capital is 7%, he will mentally reduce the $200,000 earnings by $21,-000 (7% of $300,000) to arrive at a pro forma earnings of $179,000. On the basis of the same 12× multiple, the evaluation would now be $2,148,000.

The above examples illustrate that there definitely can be differing evaluations placed on similar growth companies, to compensate for stronger or weaker balance sheets. With that weighting taken care of—and the lack of ability to make financial strength adjustments removed as an obstacle—there can be no further objection made to the heavy reliance placed on *earnings growth* as the prime criterion for evaluation.

We have initially taken the position of the investment fund manager, who uses his risk-return tables for evaluations. We have then moved to the opposite side of the table and used this same evaluation as pricing limitations on evaluations of the indicated profit growth of acquisition candidates. I have seen acquisition-prone companies boom—and then go flat. But, I have seen only continued progress in companies which adhered to the "Reverse Risk-Ratio" process, along with the other disciplines described in this chapter, in the evaluation of their successful acquisitions.

CHAPTER 14

Eurodollar Financing

WHAT IS A EURODOLLAR;
HOW DID EURODOLLARS ORIGINATE?

When I think of Eurodollars, I am sometimes reminded of Einstein's theory involving the interchangeability of matter and energy. Most of us have heard of the theory and are aware that it has been proved. A few of us may know how to make use of the theory, yet none of us really knows why it works. We find the same sort of limited knowledge in the financial community regarding Eurodollars. To a majority of laymen as well as bankers, Eurodollar financing is somewhat mysterious. Its origin is not clearly understood. But the pool of Eurodollars is now unmistakably with us, estimated at the beginning of 1973 to be as large as sixty billion dollars.

What is a Eurodollar? Even the definition is a subject of argument among financiers. There is no such piece of currency, no Eurodollar bill in any denomination. However, it is rather freely exchangeable into Euro*sterling*, Euro*francs*, Euro*guilders*, etc. To illustrate the exchange flexibility of these funds it might be more academically correct to refer to the entire subject as *Eurocurrency* financing. Even the prefix "Euro" is no longer correct, because we now see the strong entry of Japanese yen into the picture. An *Australian* corporation recently had a debenture issue underwritten by a syndicate headed by some *German* banks, the total issue being denominated in *yen.* What would one call that particular issue? Euroyen? Asiadollar? The tag we put on it is unimportant. We are talking about a new, fast-growing pool of available growth capital, and regardless of source or denomination, the present tendency is to leave all of the varieties under the same heading used when the pool first became recognized in its present form and usage—Eurodollars.

An over-simplified definition of Eurodollars is *dollars deposited with banks outside the United States.* Eurocurrencies are currencies deposited in banks outside the countries which originally issued such currency. Probably some of the earliest cases involved official reserves of foreign central banks and government treasuries which, possessing dollar reserves, kept them in banks outside the United States. Certain large international insurance companies which did business in the United States made a practice of keeping part of their policy reserves in dollars, but on deposit in European or London banks. Other European and Asian multinational companies, engaged in such global businesses as oil and shipping, did the same. One of the more amazing aspects of the Eurodollar pool development was the practice of Communist-controlled banks which attempted to camouflage their ownership of dollars by placing these funds on deposit with European banks. (How quickly political differences fade when money is involved!)

All of the foregoing may represent the early beginnings of the Eurodollar pool, but these practices could not alone have created the picture as we see it today. Something else happened. A number of European countries developed economic stability in the decade of the 1950's, and the demand for capital in these growing economies offered foreign holders of dollars more ad-

vantages than could be obtained by keeping the same
funds on deposit in the United States. With safety and
liquidity equal to that found in U.S.A. banks, the foreign
holder felt more secure about seeking a higher return on
his money in London or European financial centers. In this
way the holder still kept funds in dollars (in the beginning of the 1970's decade this changed, although we may
see that switch reversed in a few years), but enjoyed
multinational diversification and higher yields. Many for-
eigners remember that during World War II the U.S.A.
froze Swiss assets in the U.S.A. (on the assumption that
many were the camouflaged property of Axis governments
and corporations) and were concerned that any assets or
deposits belonging to a country which might experience
a Communist takeover could possibly suffer a similar
blocking by the U.S.A.

Against the background briefly outlined above, many
independent holders of dollar credits began to swell the
ranks which formerly consisted only of central banks,
official government reserves and holdings of the largest
multinational companies in the world. The amount of
dollars grew as foreign firms increased their sales to the
U.S.A.—and retained their dollar profits. Profits from
tourism, from costs of American occupation troops abroad,
from the development of world trade in general, increased
the Eurodollar fund. Swiss bankers say that the Eurodollar pool grew because of the fiscal irresponsibility of
the United States government in deficit spending and,
later, in balance of payments deficits. They are partially
correct—but that is not the whole picture. Even if the
U.S.A. does balance its budget, and does again achieve
a positive trade balance, I believe this new private world
currency pool will persist and it will continue to grow.
Having started, the trend will attract more and more
capital to the view of global investment.

The Eurodollar market has an interest rate situation
which is unique. It is one of the most classic examples of

cost (rate of interest) being determined by supply and demand. This is because interest rates of these external funds are virtually independent of any single government controls, such as those we can see exercised by the Federal Reserve activities in the U.S.A., or by control of bank discount rate or money supply by the Bank of England. Normally, Eurodollar interest rates are slightly higher than those in the U.S.A., both for long-term issues and for short-term bank lines, but the differences are not unrealistic for the borrower. When the world is in a tight money period, the spread between Eurodollar rates and U.S.A. domestic rates is greater, because the law of supply and demand is exerting more influence. When money is loose, the rate differentials are less.

During the peak of the tight money period of 1969-70 when U.S.A. prime bank rates reached a ceiling of 8½%, Eurodollar rates ranged from 12% to more than 15% per annum—for shorter term loans. (It must be realized that the comparison should be adjusted to the fact that U.S.A. banks look for an average of 20% compensating balances, whereas Eurodollar bank lending normally involves no balance requirements; therefore the differential is less marked than it would initially appear.) At that time, also, the big U.S.A. bank branches in London began actively to seek Eurodollar deposits—which they re-lent to customers in the U.S.A. This illustrates another point—that the acceptance of such deposits actually constitutes *borrowings* by such banks. Thus began a new era during which, if a customer would pay the cost, banks could, through the Eurodollar market, find more funds to lend, even in tight money times.

The reader should not jump to the conclusion that the Eurodollar market is a high-cost source of money. It is simply realistic, and realism creates broader differentials in times of stress. During 1972 there was only about 1% difference between the Eurodollar deposit rates and the negotiated certificate of deposit rates in the U.S.A., and the short-term borrowing rates were very close together. Also during 1972 the Eurodollar medium-term rates were slightly higher, but the long-term rates were almost identical, or even lower, depending on currency denomination. To illustrate the sensitive realism of the market, during the summer of 1972 Eurodollar deposit interest for 6-month deposits was approximately 6%. At the same time, however, when dollar speculators scrambled to cover short sales at the end of June, the rates for 3-day loans zoomed to over 20% per annum, while the 3-month and 6-month rates remained unchanged.

The example mentioned above highlights one of the major attributes of the Eurodollar market—that money is usually available for special purposes, perhaps at a high cost in some instances, if the end justifies the borrowing. During the tight money period of 1970 the American entrepreneur, Kirk Krekorian, borrowed more than 50 million Eurodollars to purchase a dominant block of Metro-Goldwyn-Mayer stock. It was publicly reported that part of this loan carried interest in excess of 13% per annum and another increment, in excess of 15%. The borrower obviously reckoned that the returns he sought justified the cost; also, his interest expense was tax deductible. It must not be assumed, however, that the rate of interest reflected a high risk to the lenders. The loan, arranged primarily with German banks by a London merchant bank, was amply secured by free-trading MGM stock and other securities.

I have given some extreme examples of Eurodollar interest rates; however, they are not representative of the broad picture. Normally, Eurodollar financing costs are attractive and realistic for the special purposes which are served so well. These purposes will be described below; however, as a summary to the general background, several points should be made.

The professional academicians in the field state that dollar assets do not become Eurodollars until they are deposited in banks outside the U.S.A.—and until those banks re-lend the funds. For the purposes of this book, I think that qualification is too academic. We are interested in potential sources of capital, and the fact that such capital is *potentially* available represents the reason attention should be paid to this new funding pool. The Eurodollar market functions between banks—but, of course, finally provides financing to the business borrower. By "banks" we mean to include more than the usual commercial banks we know in the U.S.A. The term also embraces private banks, merchant banks, foreign savings, investment banks, etc. The corporate borrower will still receive the funds, as described below, but the solicitation or syndication for Eurodollar financing will not include any direct approaches to individuals, as is the usual case in public stock issues in the U.S.A.

The Eurodollar market looks as if it is here to stay. It seems to have grown beyond a phenomenon to fill a temporary gap on the world financial front. It has accomplished international cooperation among financing sources yet, at the same time, has remained free from national controls and inflexibilities. The Eurodollar market is truly competitive and is capable of unusual speed, both of which are benefits to the seeker of capital.

PURPOSES AND TYPES OF EURODOLLAR FINANCING

Eurodollar financing is usually obtained for one or more of the following reasons:

1. To obtain offshore funds, free from U.S.A. government restraints, for investment in foreign operations.

2. To borrow growth capital offshore, to use in foreign subsidiaries.

3. To obtain competitively priced junior convertible securities, with relatively few restrictions by the investors, *for use in the U.S.A.* or offshore.

4. To obtain special situation spot financing, *for use in the U.S.A.* or abroad.

5. To obtain major financings much more quickly than the same amounts could be obtained by the route of filing a prospectus with the Securities and Exchange Commission for an underwritten security issue.

6. To obtain medium-term financing for a period not generally available in the U.S.A.

Before commenting in detail on the above purposes, it should be recognized that Eurodollar financings are generally accomplished in the following formats:

1. Short-term bank loans, secured or unsecured, for one year or less.

2. Medium-term bank loans, secured or unsecured, for terms from three to ten years.

3. Long-term unsecured senior debt, generally in the form of twenty-year debentures, with only interest required to be paid for the first ten years, principal and interest thereafter.

4. Long-term unsecured junior debt, broadly subordinated, generally in the form of convertible debentures, usually for twenty-year terms, interest only payable for the first ten years, principal and interest thereafter.

From the above we can see that financings involving a wide range of types and terms are available in the Eurodollar market. Let us now take an in-depth look at these variations.

OFFSHORE FUNDS FOR INVESTMENT IN FOREIGN OPERATIONS

For many years the U.S.A. imposed little or no restrictions on investments by persons or corporations in foreign operations. Among the major financial powers, few other countries with the exception of Switzerland, took such a *laissez-faire* attitude. In fact, after World War II few countries could afford to have their national capital resources dissipated, and strong currency controls were in effect in Great Britain, France, and many other world financial centers. Japan sustained the strictest policy for the longest period of time but, in so doing, rebuilt a strong producing economy, ultimately with enormous positive payments balances and foreign currency reserves. Only in 1972, when the Japanese balances continued to strengthen at the expense of other world financial powers, were these controls relaxed. By the end of 1972, Japanese merchant banks began aggressively to seek financing opportunities throughout the world, under their newly gained freedom to act as international lenders and investors.

In 1968, the United States government, recognizing increasing problems arising from uncontrolled external investments, imposed foreign investment controls. These were made the responsibility of the Office of Foreign Direct Investment (OFDI) in Washington. The controls consisted of two basic segments: (a) limitations on future foreign investments made by major multinational corporations, establishing a control related to a base of existing foreign investments at the time the controls were initiated; (b) an annual dollar limitation on new foreign investments, subject to change. Since this book is addressed to those interested in learning about the subject from scratch, we will consider only (b) above as it relates to future Eurodollar financings for those persons in corporations who have not yet gone into the Eurodollar pool for financing.

The maximum foreign investment allowed by an American citizen or corporation was initially only $100,-000 per annum, but increased gradually to $2 million per annum. This "allowable" is non-cumulative, so any year of zero investment is a lost allowable. President Nixon has expressed the desire to increase the per annum allowable to $4 million and, based on the theory that returns on such investments should ultimately accrue to the payments benefit of the United States, indicated he might like to go further, but there has been strong resistance by some members of Congress, with complaints of the exportation of U.S. jobs and reduction of needed capital at home, the validity of which is questionable. However, it is not within the purpose of this book to debate those questions; rather it should be pointed out that the controls are subject to Congressional and Presidential whim, and the situation provides little confidence to a financial planner who wants to expand abroad. On the other hand, all Eurodollar financings are, under the controls, permitted to be *added* to the allowables; therefore, you can count on any foreign investment aspirations being limited only by the amount you can raise in the Eurodollar or foreign national currency markets. To summarize, the reasons for seeking Eurodollar financings for *interests in foreign operations* are as follows:

1. Freedom from OFDI limitations set by the U.S. government.

2. Assurance of being able to expand internationally to the extent of the Eurodollar financing you can obtain.

3. The ability to *add* to your domestic U.S.A. financing arrangements. Usually, U.S.A. bank line and long-term debt agreements will permit foreign borrowings for foreign operations.

4. The readiness of Eurodollar sources to finance operations in their own areas—as compared to reluctance by many U.S.A. banks and insurance companies to lend out of their areas (surprisingly!).

TO BORROW GROWTH CAPITAL OFFSHORE
FOR USE IN FOREIGN SUBSIDIARIES

After making initial investments in a foreign operation, such operations, if successful, should grow and require more capital. The reasons for using Eurodollar capital for these purposes are generally the same as those stated in the immediately foregoing paragraphs. It might be added that, once you have been able to consummate a Eurodollar financing successfully (and we will describe this procedure fully in a later section of this chapter), many of the participating banks will ask for the opportunity of bidding on future growth financings in their local areas. Once you become a "member of the club," the welcome mat is out, provided your operation suffers no materially adverse changes.

TO OBTAIN COMPETITIVELY PRICED JUNIOR CONVERTIBLE DEBENTURES WITH RELATIVELY FEW RESTRICTIONS BY THE INVESTORS FOR USE IN THE U.S.A. OR OFFSHORE

Here we come to the aspect that is surprising to many corporate executives and bankers—*that the proceeds of this type of Eurodollar financing can largely be brought back to the U.S.A. for domestic financing needs.* The money *need not* be used exclusively for foreign investments, although where such foreign investments are contemplated, it is indeed the ideal funding to use offshore as well.

The practice of underwriting Eurodollar convertible debentures for U.S.A. corporations developed quickly in the latter 1960's. It reached almost hectic proportions by 1968-1969. Then, with the recession and tight money period of 1969-1970 in the U.S.A., this activity diminished. There were several notable cases of issues for companies which went sour, such as the Four Seasons Nursing Home chain. Not all of the European merchant or investment banks participated in these debacles, but they had the effect of refining analysis and diligence, and today the marketability of convertible issues is once again strong.

Convertible debentures are very appealing to the Eurodollar investing community, and the reasons are quite understandable. They are traditionally long-term investors, usually committed to the idea of making a first review of the investment after five years. Unlike American or Japanese investors, who switch a great deal over shorter periods, the Eurodollar investors look at the bond coupon (the debenture interest rate) as downside risk protection for a number of years. The expectation of capital gain as a sweetener, arising from conversion of the debenture to underlying common stock which has appreciated, is anticipated much later. For this reason the earlier Eurodollar debentures contained prohibitions against *calling for conversion* (see chapter 11) for the first five years. In 1969, while negotiating a convertible issue, I suggested that we might introduce a sliding scale of conversion provisions for the first five years, as follows:

1. During the first year the debentures could be called if the underlying common share price rose to 200% of the conversion price.

2. During the second year the debentures could be called if the underlying common share price rose to 175% of the conversion price.

3. During the third year the debentures could be called if the underlying common share price rose to 150% of the conversion price.

4. During the fourth year the debentures could be called if the underlying common share price rose to 125% of the conversion price.

Initially there was resistance, but after the underwriting bankers polled their syndicate, they came back with a flat requirement that the common share price must be 175% of the conversion price (see below) any time during the first five years, in order to qualify the corporation to make a call of the debentures for conversion into common stock. This provision is now widely available.

Following are the normal terms of Eurodollar convertible debentures:

1. Term—20 years.
2. Interest payable semi-annually or annually.
3. Only interest is payable the first 10 years.
4. Principal is repayable in 10 equal installments during the last 10 years (in many cases this repayment may be eliminated by conversion to common stock.)
5. Principal amounts of issues have usually ranged from $6 million to $50 million, with a few large exceptions.
6. Interest rates will depend on the international money market. However, smaller convertible issues ($10 million or so) for less well known companies coming to the market for the first time have ranged between 6 and 7%. Larger issues for better known companies, or for those coming to the Eurodollar market for a second time have ranged from 4½% to 6%, depending on the world money market.
7. Conversion premium—The debentures are usually convertible into the common stock at a price 5% to 15% above the market price of the common stock at the time of the debenture issue.
8. The debentures constitute junior debt and are very much subordinated to other types of financings; therefore, they represent an excellent building block for a large financial structure.

The appeal of the classically structured Eurodollar convertible includes the fact that there is no withholding tax required by the U.S.A. on the debenture interest payments and—depending on the status of the ultimate investor—may be relatively tax-free to him. This facet of the convertible is accomplished through compliance with certain international tax conventions. One of those most popularly used involves the tax conventions between the U.S.A. and the Netherlands, under which *non*-U.S.A. persons may invest in obligations of a Netherlands company which lends money to a U.S.A. corporation, the interest payments on which are not subject to U.S.A. withholding tax. The Netherlands government and economy has long had a reputation for stability, which instills confidence in the investor. However, since the Netherlands Antilles, possessions of the Netherlands in the Caribbean, have lower local taxes, the corporate vehicle required is usually incorporated in the Antilles, for example in Curacao. Following are the steps which are usually taken:

1. The borrowing corporation (let us call it American Widget Corporation) forms a Netherlands Antilles "financing subsidiary" (which we will call Widget International N.V.). The capital of Widget N.V. must be an amount equal to 20% of the intended Eurodollar financing total.

2. A Eurodollar prospectus is prepared by the European managing banker or underwriter. This prospectus will state, among other things, that:

a. The debts of Widget N.V. to the Eurodollar investors are guaranteed by the parent U.S.A. corporation.

b. The convertible debentures will be sold only to *non*-U.S.A. persons.

3. Based on the above facts—particularly the exclusion of U.S.A. persons from the investor group—a ruling will be obtained from the U.S.A. Internal Revenue Service that interest payments are not subject to U.S.A. withholding taxes.

4. The parent corporation guarantees the Eurodollar investors against U.S.A. withholding tax liability.

5. The managing bankers complete a trust indenture for the bonds (or a "Fiscal Agency Agreement") and alert their possible syndicate to the offering.

6. Top corporate executives travel with the managing bankers to visit the leading prospective bank members

of the syndicate and to answer any questions regarding the prospectus.

7. Within 8 to 10 days, all investment commitments are received and totaled, allocations are made if the issue is over-subscribed (it normally is), and a settlement date is set, usually 15 days later.

8. On the settlement date, money for the entire issue is received in collected funds.

9. If desired, *all* of these funds can be lent to the parent company immediately by the Netherlands Antilles subsidiary. The 20% original capital of the N.V. subsidiary can be invested in a foreign operation or placed in an interest-bearing deposit with London banks. The funds are free to travel anywhere in the world, or to be repaid and re-borrowed at any time by the parent U.S.A. corporation.

The above procedure can take place very quickly (see below). It is interesting to note that the entire placement is among foreign banks, who make these investments for their customers' accounts. The debentures are denominated in $1,000 bonds, and these are *bearer* bonds with detachable interest coupons. The issuing corporation has no contact with the ultimate investor as the debentures are not registered. Interest payments are made by the corporation in a lump sum to the trustee, or fiscal agent, in London, who in turn remits payments to the bankers who send in the coupons which their customers clip and remit.

TO OBTAIN SPECIAL SITUATION SPOT FINANCING FOR USE IN THE U.S.A. OR ABROAD

As mentioned earlier, the Eurodollar market is a true supply-demand type of money source. Money is usually available for any credit purpose, provided the cost demands can be met. Commercial banks in the U.S.A. normally attach to their lending arrangements the requirement that the borrower be, or show a possibility of becoming in the future, a regular bank customer with demand deposit accounts, payroll or trust accounts, etc. Balances maintained are part of the compensation sought. Therefore a large "spot" borrowing for a special or non-recurring purpose is not warmly greeted by U.S.A. commercial bankers. Not so with Eurodollar bankers—they represent funds frankly seeking straight revenue returns with safety. For this reason the Eurodollar market is a good source for special borrowings for terms of less than one year, or for two to three years. These loans can be arranged by London merchant bankers or branches of U.S.A. or other banks foreign to the United Kingdom, located in "the city" (the E.C.2. district of old London, around the Bank of England). The rate is based on the *"interbank"* rate (the interest charged by one bank to another) plus an amount known as the "spread." The spread can be less than 1% for highly regarded loans, or up to more than 2 to 3%. As mentioned earlier in this chapter, the Krekorian loans to buy MGM stock bore 12 to 15% interest, but that was when the world money market was at its tightest, the interbank rate was high, and the spread was high. In the fall of 1972, the interbank rate had fallen to approximately 6%.

TO OBTAIN MAJOR FINANCINGS QUICKLY

One of the most definitive characteristics of the Eurodollar market is its speed. Private placements with banks can be made in a matter of weeks after the first application, provided credit information is complete. However, there is an even more dramatic time differential between domestic U.S.A. and Eurodollar convertible debenture issues. In the U.S.A., even a well-documented corporation usually requires at least four months from the date of the original financing decision to the finalizing of the underwriting, primarily because of delays within the S.E.C. and various other regulatory bodies. Eurodollar issues are *completely outside* the scope of the S.E.C. or any other national securities regulatory body, as the Eurodollar managers have done a fine job of self-regulation. For this reason I have seen Eurodollar debenture issues take only five or six weeks from the date of decision to proceed with the issue to receipt of funds. Moreover, the timing of Eurodollar issues is less subject to artificial cut-off dates relative to accounting or to other technical requirements encountered in the U.S.A.

TO OBTAIN MEDIUM-TERM FINANCING

It has long been a complaint in U.S. financial circles that we have one big gap in our financial spectrum—the medium-term loan. Banks prefer short-term loans, rested once a year, but they will usually also extend two- and three-year revolving lines, or amortizing lines up to five years. Our institutional lenders, like insurance companies, feel their preparation and monitoring make it mandatory that their loans be a minimum of 12 years—preferably 15 years—and sometimes 20 years. The gap between these two extremes remained unfilled, until fairly recently, when the Eurodollar banks stepped in. Probably these sources realized that, lending being their prime activity, they could capitalize on the medium-term void in the U.S.A.

There is now available in the Eurodollar market secured and unsecured financing with terms of from four to eight years, or up to 10 years in special cases. This medium-term financing is being pushed by the new group of "consortium banks." The consortium banks function in many ways along the classic merchant banking lines; however, they have been formed by groups of U.S.A. commercial banks in combination with private or London merchant banks, plus many of the largest French, Belgian, Dutch and West German banks. Almost all of the consortiums have head or major offices in the "city" in London. Their interest charges will be negotiated on a spread over the interbank interest rate. The rate may be fixed for the full term of the loan, or it may fluctuate with the interbank rate.

CHOICE OF CURRENCY DENOMINATIONS

As mentioned earlier in the chapter, the bulk of Eurocurrency financing was for many years denominated in dollars. Following the dollar devaluation at the end of 1971, and again during the time of uncertainty created by the float of the pound sterling during June, 1972, investors began to favor issues which were denominated in other currencies such as Deutsche Marks, Guilders, Yen, etc. In other words, in the case of notes or convertible debentures, the corporate borrower can commit to repay the debt when it is finally due in a currency other than dollars. During 1972 when the Deutsche Mark and the Yen were viewed as having relatively stronger value than the dollar or the pound sterling, the investor showed willingness to accept a lower interest rate if repayment were guaranteed in those currencies. Therefore, if the corporate borrower wished to enjoy a lower interest rate he could arrange for a Deutsche Mark or Yen denominated obligation. At the same time it should be recognized that the corporate borrower is underwriting the possibility of a further upward revaluation of those currencies against the dollar. On the other hand, it is a two-way gamble because, over the maturity of a long-term obligation it is quite possible that the dollar would again gain strength against other currencies. It is the nature of money markets that relative currency values are established on the basis of today's foreign exchange markets. For this reason, in late 1972, French Franc, Guilder, Swiss Franc and Deutsche Mark denominated debt or convertible debt issues all carried lower interest rates than did the same types of obligations issued by similarly rated U.S.A. companies in domestic U.S.A. underwritings.

Regardless of the currency denomination, the proceeds can immediately be switched into another currency, such as dollars, at the going rate of exchange. In fact, Swiss Franc denominated obligations for foreign issuers are required to be switched—and the switch must be at least 60% into U.S. dollars. Such switches would always be the case when the proceeds are to be used largely in the U.S.A. On the other hand, if you are borrowing for the expansion of a foreign subsidiary in a country in whose currency the obligation is denominated, the switch may not be necessary—and—the cost will definitely be less. For example, Swiss Francs borrowed internally for development of an entity in Switzerland on a medium-long-term basis at the end of 1972 enjoyed an interest rate nearly 2% less per annum than the same borrower would have to pay for a similar type of debt borrowed in the U.S.A.

WHO QUALIFIES FOR EURODOLLAR FINANCING?

Generally the qualifications for Eurodollar financing are the same as those in the U.S.A., Eurodollar financing being chosen for the special reasons enumerated in this chapter. Obviously, the minimum size of the financing will depend on the type of funding selected. Local Eurocurrency loans for local growth of a foreign subsidiary can be quite modest. Short- and medium-term loans can go from several million dollars to over $50 million; debenture issues from $6 to $50 million. If you qualify creditwise for these ranges in the U.S.A., you should also qualify in Europe.

Obviously, convertible debentures require the existence of underlying common stock whose price is readily determined. Therefore, the issuing company preferably should be listed on the American or New York Stock Exchange.

HOW IS AN APPROACH MADE TO THE EURODOLLAR MARKET?

The worldwide Eurocurrency pool functions in some ways like a private club and the avenues of approach are not well known. If you can make contact with anyone who has been active in this market, he can probably assess your chances and assist you if you qualify.

There are also a number of institutional avenues to which you can turn for assistance. These consist of certain commercial banks in the U.S.A., domestic investment banking firms, and specialized financial consultants. However, among these categories, you will probably find Eurodollar expertise only in the largest financial centers, such as New York and Los Angeles, and even there it is necessary to be selective about the individual whom you approach, and persistent about your objective. In the case of investment banking firms and commercial banks in the U.S.A., it only makes sense to approach those who have international connections. A number of our leading investment banking firms maintain offices in the city of London and in such other world financial capitals as Paris, Amsterdam, Geneva, and Zurich. A few of the largest commercial banks in the U.S.A. are members of consortiums with offices in the same world financial capitals. Your inquiries will have to be limited to such categories of international operations. Moreover, only a few individuals in those qualified investment banking firms and commercial banks have had actual exposure to the Eurodollar market, so an inquiry must be directed to such individuals and should not be diverted to alternative plans of domestic financing if—based on the reasons given earlier in this chapter—a Eurodollar financing is the preferred method of funding.

Finally—Eurocurrency financing represents an exciting new development in international cooperation. Chauvinistic attitudes are being broken down; a single standard of financing for all nations may be developing. In a rapidly shrinking world, this viable pool of capital may be the financial community's major contribution to global unity and equal economic opportunity for all people on the planet earth.

Index